Penguin Books
A Russian Beauty

Vladimir Nabokov was born in St Petersburg (now
Leningrad) in 1899. His father was a well-known
Liberal statesman. When the Revolution came he
began a long series of wanderings, during which he
studied Romance and Slavic languages at
Cambridge, where he graduated in 1922. He then
lived on the Continent, largely in Berlin, and
established himself as one of the most outstanding
Russian émigré writers.

In 1940 he and his family moved to America, where
he began to teach at Wellesley College, while at the
same time holding a Harvard Research Fellowship
in entomology. Later he was Professor of Russian
Literature at Cornell University for eleven years.

His other works include *Ada*, *Laughter in the Dark*,
Nabokov's Dozen, a collection of stories, *The Real
Life of Sebastian Knight*, *Mary*, *Bend Sinister*, *Glory*,
Transparent Things and *Pale Fire*. These are all
available in Penguins. His best-known novel is *Lolita*,
which brought him world-wide fame and was
filmed. He has also published translations of
Pushkin and Lermontov and a study of Gogol.

Vladimir Nabokov, who now lives in Switzerland, is
married and has one son.

D1337713

Vladimir Nabokov

A Russian Beauty
and Other Stories

Penguin Books

Penguin Books Ltd,
Harmondsworth, Middlesex, England
Penguin Books Australia Ltd,
Ringwood, Victoria, Australia
Penguin Books (N.Z.) Ltd,
182–190 Wairau Road, Auckland 10, New Zealand

First published in the U.S.A. 1973
First published in Great Britain by Weidenfeld & Nicolson 1973
Published in Penguin Books 1975

Copyright © McGraw–Hill International, Inc., 1973

Made and printed in Great Britain by
Richard Clay (The Chaucer Press) Ltd,
Bungay, Suffolk
Set in Monotype Times

This book is sold subject to the condition that
it shall not, by way of trade or otherwise, be lent,
re-sold, hired out, or otherwise circulated without
the publisher's prior consent in any form of
binding or cover other than that in which it is
published and without a similar condition
including this condition being imposed on the
subsequent purchaser

To Véra

Contents

Foreword

The Russian originals of the thirteen Englished stories selected for the present collection were composed in western Europe between 1924 and 1940, and appeared one by one in various émigré periodicals and editions (the last being the collection *Vesna v Fialte*, Chekhov Publishing House, New York, 1956). Most of these thirteen pieces were translated by Dmitri Nabokov in collaboration with the author. All are given here in a final English form, for which I alone am responsible. Professor Simon Karlinsky is the translator of the first story.

A Russian Beauty

'A Russian Beauty' ('Krasavitsa') is an amusing miniature, with an unexpected solution. The original text appeared in the émigré daily *Posledniya Novosti*, Paris, 18 August 1934, and was included in *Soglyadatay*, the collection of the author's stories published by *Russkiya Zapiski*, Paris, 1938.

Olga, of whom we are about to speak, was born in the year 1900, in a wealthy, carefree family of nobles. A pale little girl in a white sailor suit, with a side parting in her chestnut hair and such merry eyes that everyone kissed her there, she was deemed a beauty since childhood. The purity of her profile, the expression of her closed lips, the silkiness of her tresses that reached to the small of her back – all this was enchanting indeed.

Her childhood passed festively, securely and gaily, as was the custom in our country since the days of old. A sunbeam falling on the cover of a *Bibliothèque Rose* volume at the family estate, the classical hoar-frost of the Saint Petersburg public gardens ... A supply of memories, such as these, comprised her sole dowry when she left Russia in the spring of 1919. Everything happened in full accord with the style of the period. Her mother died of typhus, her brother was executed by the firing squad. All these are ready-made formulae, of course, the usual dreary small talk, but it all did happen, there is no other way of saying it, and it's no use turning up your nose.

Well, then, in 1919 we have a grown-up young lady, with a pale, broad face that overdid things in terms of the regularity of its features, but just the same very lovely. Tall, with soft breasts, she always wears a black jumper and a scarf around her white neck and holds an English cigarette in her slender-fingered hand with a prominent little bone just above the wrist.

Yet there was a time in her life, at the end of 1916 or so, when at a summer resort near the family estate there was no schoolboy who did not plan to shoot himself because of her, there was no university student who would not ... In a word, there had been a special magic about her, which, had it lasted, would have caused ... would have wrecked ... But somehow, nothing came of it. Things failed to develop, or else happened to no purpose. There were flowers that she was too lazy to put in a vase, there were strolls in the twilight now with this one, now with another, followed by the blind alley of a kiss.

She spoke French fluently, pronouncing *les gens* (the servants) as if rhyming with *agence* and splitting *août* (august) in two syllables (*a-ou*). She naïvely translated the Russian *grab-ezhi* (robberies) as *les grabuges* (quarrels) and used some archaic French locutions that had somehow survived in old Russian families, but she rolled her r's most convincingly even though she had never been to France. Over the dresser in her Berlin room a postcard of Serov's portrait of the Tsar was fastened with a pin with a fake turquoise head. She was religious, but at times a fit of giggles would overcome her in church. She wrote verse with that terrifying facility typical of young Russian girls of her generation: patriotic verse, humorous verse, any kind of verse at all.

For about six years, that is until 1926, she resided in a boarding house on the Augsburgerstrasse (not far from the clock), together with her father, a broad-shouldered, beetle-browed old man with a yellowish mustache, and with tight, narrow trousers on his spindly legs. He had a job with some optimistic firm, was noted for his decency and kindness and was never one to turn down a drink.

In Berlin, Olga gradually acquired a large group of friends, all of them young Russians. A certain jaunty tone was established. 'Let's go to the cinemonkey,' or 'That was a heely deely German *Diele*, dance hall.' All sorts of popular sayings, cant phrases, imitations of imitations were much in demand. 'These cutlets are grim.' 'I wonder who's kissing her now?' Or, in a hoarse, choking voice 'Mes-sieurs les officiers...'

At the Zotovs', in their overheated rooms, she languidly danced the fox trot to the sound of the gramophone, shifting the elongated calf of her leg not without grace and holding away from her the cigarette she had just finished smoking, and when her eyes located the ashtray that revolved with the music she would shove the butt into it, without missing a step. How charmingly, how meaningfully she could raise the wine glass to her lips, secretly drinking to the health of a third party as she looked through her lashes at the one who had confided in her. How she loved to sit in the corner of the sofa, discussing with this person or that somebody else's affairs of the heart, the oscillation of chances, the probability of a declaration – all this indirectly, by hints – and how understandingly her eyes would smile, pure, wide-opened eyes with barely noticeable freckles on the thin, faintly bluish skin underneath and around them. But as for herself, no one fell in love with her, and this was why she long remembered the boor who pawed her at a charity ball and afterwards wept on her bare shoulder. He was challenged to a duel by the little Baron R., but refused to fight. The word 'boor', by the way, was used by Olga on any and every occasion. 'Such boors,' she would sing out in chest tones, languidly and affectionately. 'What a boor . . .' 'Aren't they boors?'

But presently her life darkened. Something was finished, people were already getting up to leave. How quickly! Her father died, she moved to another street. She stopped seeing her friends, knitted the little bonnets in fashion and gave cheap French lessons at some ladies' club or other. In this way her life dragged on to the age of thirty.

She was still the same beauty, with that enchanting slant of the widely spaced eyes and with that rarest line of lips into which the geometry of the smile seems to be already inscribed. But her hair lost its shine and was poorly cut. Her black tailored suit was in its fourth year. Her hands, with their glistening but untidy fingernails, were roped with veins and were shaking from nervousness and from her wretched continuous smoking. And we'd best pass over in silence the state of her stockings . . .

Now, when the silken insides of her handbag were in tatters (at least there was always the hope of finding a stray coin); now, when she was so tired; now, when putting on her only pair of shoes she had to force herself not to think of their soles, just as when, swallowing her pride, she entered the tobacconist's, she forbade herself to think of how much she already owed there; now that there was no longer the least hope of returning to Russia, and hatred had become so habitual that it almost ceased to be a sin; now that the sun was getting behind the chimney, Olga would occasionally be tormented by the luxury of certain advertisements, written in the saliva of Tantalus, imagining herself wealthy, wearing that dress, sketched with the aid of three or four insolent lines, on that ship-deck, under that palm tree, at the balustrade of that white terrace. And then there was also another thing or two that she missed.

One day, almost knocking her off her feet, her one-time friend Vera rushed like a whirlwind out of a telephone booth, in a hurry as always, loaded with parcels, with a shaggy-eyed terrier, whose leash immediately became wound twice around her skirt. She pounced upon Olga, imploring her to come and stay at their summer villa, saying that it was Fate itself, that it was wonderful and how have you been and are there many suitors. 'No, my dear, I'm no longer that age,' answered Olga, 'and besides . . .' She added a little detail and Vera burst out laughing, letting her parcels sink almost to the ground. 'No, seriously,' said Olga, with a smile. Vera continued coaxing her, pulling at the terrier, turning this way and that. Olga, starting all at once to speak through her nose, borrowed some money from her.

Vera adored arranging things, be it a party with punch, a visa or a wedding. Now she avidly took up arranging Olga's fate. 'The matchmaker within you has been aroused,' joked her husband, an elderly Balt (shaven head, monocle). Olga arrived on a bright August day. She was immediately dressed in one of Vera's frocks, her hairdo and make-up were changed. She swore languidly, but yielded, and how festively the floorboards creaked in the merry little villa! How the little mirrors, suspended in the green orchard to frighten off birds, flashed and sparkled!

A Russified German named Forstmann, a well-off athletic widower, author of books on hunting, came to spend a week. He had long been asking Vera to find him a bride, 'a real Russian beauty'. He had a massive, strong nose with a fine pink vein on its high bridge. He was polite, silent, at times even morose, but knew how to form, instantly and while no one noticed, an eternal friendship with a dog or with a child. With his arrival Olga became difficult. Listless and irritable, she did all the wrong things and she knew that they were wrong. When the conversation turned to old Russia (Vera tried to make her show off her past), it seemed to her that everything she said was a lie and that everyone understood that it was a lie, and therefore she stubbornly refused to say the things that Vera was trying to extract from her and in general would not cooperate in any way.

On the veranda, they would slam their cards down hard. Everyone would go off together for a stroll through the woods, but Forstmann conversed mostly with Vera's husband, and, recalling some pranks of their youth, the two of them would turn red with laughter, lag behind, and collapse on the moss. On the eve of Forstmann's departure they were playing cards on the veranda, as they usually did in the evening. Suddenly, Olga felt an impossible spasm in her throat. She still managed to smile and to leave without undue haste. Vera knocked on her door but she did not open. In the middle of the night, having swatted a multitude of sleepy flies and smoked continuously to the point where she was no longer able to inhale, irritated, depressed, hating herself and everyone, Olga went into the garden. There, the crickets stridulated, the branches swayed, an occasional apple fell with a taut thud, and the moon performed calisthenics on the white-washed wall of the chicken coop.

Early in the morning, she came out again and sat down on the porch step that was already hot. Forstmann, wearing a dark blue bathrobe, sat next to her and, clearing his throat, asked if she would consent to become his spouse – that was the very word he used 'spouse'. When they came to breakfast, Vera, her husband and his maiden cousin, in utter silence, were performing nonexistent dances, each in a different corner, and Olga drawled out in an affectionate voice 'What boors!' and next summer she died in childbirth.

That's all. Of course, there may be some sort of sequel, but it is not known to me. In such cases, instead of getting bogged down in guesswork, I repeat the words of the merry king in my favorite fairy tale: Which arrow flies for ever? The arrow that has hit its mark.

The Leonardo

'The Leonardo' ('Korolyok') was composed in Berlin, on the piney banks of the Grunewald Lake, in the summer of 1933. First published in *Posledniya Novosti*, Paris, 23 and 24 July 1933. Collected in *Vesna v Fialte*, New York, 1956.

Korolyok (literally: kinglet) is, or is supposed to be, a Russian cant term for 'counterfeiter'. I am deeply indebted to Professor Stephen Jan Parker for suggesting a corresponding American underground slang word which delightfully glitters with the kingly gold dust of the Old Master's name. Hitler's grotesque and ferocious shadow was falling on Germany at the time I imagined those two brutes and my poor Romantovski.

The English translation appeared in *Vogue*, April, 1973.

The objects that are being summoned assemble, draw near from different spots; in doing so, some of them have to overcome not only the distance of space but that of time: which nomad, you may wonder, is more bothersome to cope with, this one or that, the young poplar, say, that once grew in the vicinity but was cut down long ago, or the singled-out courtyard which still exists today but is situated far away from here? Hurry up, please.

Here comes the ovate little poplar, all punctuated with April greenery, and takes its stand where told, namely by the tall brick wall, imported in one piece from another city. Facing it, there grows up a dreary and dirty tenement house, with mean little balconies pulled out one by one like drawers. Other bits of scenery are distributed about the yard: a barrel, a second barrel, the delicate shade of leaves, an urn of sorts, and a stone cross propped at the foot of the wall. All this is only sketched and much has to be added and finished, and yet two live people – Gustav and his brother Anton – already come out on their tiny balcony, while rolling before him a little pushcart with a suitcase and a heap of books, Romantovski, the new lodger, enters the yard.

As seen from the yard, and especially on a bright day, the rooms of the house seem filled up with dense blackness (night is always with us, in this or that place, inside, during one part of twenty-four hours, outside, during the other). Romantovski looked up at the black open windows, at the two frog-eyed men watching him from their balcony, and shouldering his bag - with a forward lurch as if someone had banged him on the back of the head – plunged into the doorway. There remained, sunlit: the pushcart with the books, one barrel, another barrel, the nictating young poplar and an inscription in tar on the brick wall: VOTE FOR (illegible). Presumably it had been scrawled by the brothers before the elections.

Now this is the way we'll arrange the world: every man shall sweat, every man shall eat. There will be work, there will be belly-cheer, there will be a clean, warm, sunny –

(Romantovski became the occupant of the adjacent one. It was even drabber than theirs. But under the bed he discovered a small rubber doll. He concluded that his predecessor had been a family man.)

Despite the world's not having yet conclusively and totally turned into solid matter and still retaining sundry regions of an intangible and hallowed nature, the brothers felt snug and confident. The elder one, Gustav, had a furniture-moving job; the younger happened to be temporarily unemployed, but did not lose heart. Gustav had an evenly ruddy complexion, bristling fair eyebrows and an ample, cupboard-like torso always clothed in a pullover of coarse gray wool. He wore elastic bands to hold his shirt-sleeves at the joints of his fat arms, so as to keep his wrists free and prevent sloppiness. Anton's face was pockmarked, he trimmed his mustache in the shape of a dark trapezoid, and wore a dark red sweater over his spare wiry frame. But when they both leaned their elbows on the balcony railings, their backsides were exactly the same, big and triumphant, with identically checkered cloth enclosing tightly their prominent buttocks.

Repeat: the world shall be sweaty and well-fed. Idlers, parasites and musicians are not admitted. While one's heart pumps blood one should *live*, damn it! For two years now Gustav had been saving money to marry Anna, acquire a sideboard, a carpet.

She would come every other evening, that plump-armed buxom woman, with freckles on the broad bridge of her nose, a leaden shadow under her eyes, and spaced teeth, one of which, moreover, had been knocked out. The brothers and she would swill beer. She had a way of clasping her bare arms behind her nape, displaying the gleaming-wet red tufts of her armpits. With head thrown back, she opened her mouth so generously that one could survey her entire palate and uvula, which resembled the tail end of a boiled chicken. The anatomy of her mirth was greatly to the liking of the two brothers. They tickled her with zest.

In the daytime, while his brother worked, Anton sat in a friendly pub or sprawled among the dandelions on the cool, still vividly green grass along the canal bank and observed with envy exuberant roughs loading coal on a barge, or else stared stupidly at the empty blue of the sleep-inducing sky. But presently in the well-oiled life of the brothers some obstruction occurred.

From the very moment he had appeared, rolling his pushcart into the yard, Romantovski had provoked a mixture of irritation and curiosity in the two brothers. Their infallible flair let them sense that here was someone different from other people. Normally, one would not discern anything special in him at a casual glance, but the brothers did. For example, he walked differently: at every step he rose on a buoyant toe in a peculiar manner, stepping and flying up as if the mere act of treading allowed him a chance to perceive something uncommon over the common heads. He was what is termed a 'slank', very lean, with a pale sharp-nosed face and appallingly restless eyes. Out of the much too short sleeves of his doublebreasted jacket his long wrists protruded with a kind of annoying and nonsensical obviousness ('here we are what should we do?'). He went out and came home at unpredictable hours. On one of the first mornings Anton caught sight of him near a bookstand: he was pricing, or had actually bought something, because the vendor nimbly beat one dusty volume against another and carried them to his nook behind the stand. Additional eccentricities were noted: his light remained on practically until dawn; he was oddly unsociable.

We hear Anton's voice:

'That fine gentleman shows off. We should give him a closer look.'

'I'll sell him the pipe,' said Gustav.

The misty origins of the pipe. Anna had brought it over one day, but the brothers recognized only cigarillos. An expensive pipe, not yet blackened. It had a little steel tube inserted in its stem. With it came a suede case.

'Who's there? What do you want?' asked Romantovski through the door.

'Neighbors, neighbors,' answered Gustav in a deep voice.

And the neighbors entered, avidly looking around. A stump of sausage lay on the table next to an uneven pile of books; one of them was opened on a picture of ships with numerous sails and, flying above, in one corner, an infant with puffed-out cheeks.

'Let's get acquainted,' rumbled the brothers. 'Folks live side by side, one can say, but never meet somehow or other.'

The top of the commode was shared by an alcohol burner and an orange.

'Delighted,' said Romantovski softly. He sat down on the edge of the bed, and with bent forehead, its V-vein inflamed, started to lace his shoes.

'You were resting,' said Gustav with ominous courtesy. 'We come at the wrong time?'

Not a word, not a word, did the lodger say in reply; instead he straightened up suddenly, turned to the window, raised his finger and froze.

The brothers looked but found nothing unusual about that window; it framed a cloud, the tip of the poplar and part of the brick wall.

'Why, don't you see anything?' asked Romantovski.

Red sweater and gray went up to the window and actually leaned out, becoming identical twins. Nothing. And both had the sudden feeling that something was wrong, very wrong! They wheeled around. He stood near the chest of drawers in an odd attitude.

'I must have been mistaken,' said Romantovski, not looking at them. 'Something seemed to have flown by. I saw once an airplane fall.'

'That happens,' assented Gustav. 'Listen, we dropped in with a purpose. Would you care to buy this? Brand new. And there's a nice sheath.'

'Sheath? Is that so? Only, you know, I smoke very seldom.'

'Well, you'll smoke oftener. We sell it cheap. Three-fifty.'

'Three-fifty. I see.'

He fingered the pipe, biting his nether lip and pondering

something. His eyes did not really look at the pipe, they moved to and fro.

Meanwhile the brothers began to swell, to grow, they filled up the whole room, the whole house and then grew out of it. In comparison to them the young poplar was, by then, no bigger than one of those toy treelets, made of dyed cotton wool, that are so unstable on their round green supports. The dollhouse, a thing of dusty pasteboard with mica window-panes, barely reached up to the brothers' knees. Gigantic, imperiously reeking of sweat and beer, with beefy voices and senseless speeches, with fecal matter replacing the human brain, they provoke a tremor of ignoble fear. I don't know why they push against me; I implore you, do leave me alone. I'm not touching you, so don't you touch me either; I'll give in, only do leave me alone.

'All right, but I don't have enough change,' said Romantovski in a low voice. 'Now if you can give me six-fifty –'

They could, and went away, grinning. Gustav examined the ten-mark bill against the light and put it away in an iron money box.

Nevertheless, they did not leave their room neighbor in peace. It just maddened them that despite their having got acquainted with him, a man should remain as inaccessible as before. He avoided running into them: one had to waylay and trap him in order to glance fleetingly into his evasive eyes. Having discovered the nocturnal life of Romantovski's lamp, Anton could not bear it any longer. He crept up barefoot to the door (from under which showed a taut thread of golden light) and knocked.

Romantovski did not respond.

'Sleep, sleep,' said Anton slapping the door with his palm.

The light peered silently through the chink. Anton shook the door handle. The golden thread snapped.

Thenceforth both brothers (but especially Anton, thanks to his lacking a job) established a watch over their neighbor's insomnia. The enemy, however, was astute and endowed with a fine hearing. No matter how quietly one advanced toward his door, his light went out instantly, as if it never had been there; and only if one stood in the cold corridor for a goodish length of time, holding one's breath, could one hope to see the return of the sensitive lamp beam. Thus beetles faint and recover.

The task of detection turned out to be most exhausting. Finally, the brothers chanced to catch him on the stairs and jostled him.

'Suppose it's my habit to read at night. What business of yours is it? Let me pass, please.'

When he turned away, Gustav knocked off his hat in jest. Romantovski picked it up without a word.

A few days later, choosing a moment at nightfall – he was on his way back from the W.C. and failed to dart back into his room quickly enough – the brothers crowded around him. There were only two of them, yet they managed to form a crowd. They invited him to their room.

'There will be some beer,' said Gustav with a wink.

He tried to refuse.

'Oh, come along!' cried the brothers; they grabbed him under the arms and swept him off (while at it, they could feel how thin he was – that weakness, that slenderness below the shoulder offered an irresistible temptation – ah, to give a good squeeze so as to make him crunch, ah, hard to control oneself, let us, at least, dig into him on the move, just once, lightly . . .).

'You are hurting me,' said Romantovski. 'Leave me alone, I can walk by myself.'

The promised beer, the large mouth of Gustav's fiancée, a heavy smell in the room. They tried to make him drunk. Collarless, with a copper stud under his conspicuous and defenseless Adam's apple, long-faced and pale, with quivering eyelashes, he sat in a complicated pose, partly doubled up, partly bent out, and when he got up from his chair he seemed to unwind like a spiral. However, they forced him to fold up again and, upon their suggestion, Anna sat in his lap. He kept glancing askance at the swell of her instep in the harness of a tight shoe, but mastered his dull anguish as best he could, not daring to get rid of the inert red-haired creature.

There was a minute when it seemed to them that he was broken, that he had become one of them. In fact, Gustav said, 'You see, you were silly to look down on our company. We find offensive the way you have of keeping mum. What do you read all night?'

'Old, old tales,' replied Romantovski in such a tone of voice that the brothers suddenly felt very bored. The boredom was suffocating and grim, but drink prevented the storm from bursting out, and, on the contrary, weighed the eyelids down. Anna slipped off Romantovski's knee, brushing the table with a drowsy hip; empty bottles swayed like ninepins, one collapsed. The brothers stooped, toppled, yawned, still looking through sleepy tears at their guest. He, vibrating and diffusing rays, stretched out, thinned and gradually vanished.

This cannot go on. He poisons the life of honest folks. Why, it can well happen that he will move at the end of the month – intact, whole, never taken to pieces, proudly strutting about. It is not enough that he moves and breathes differently from other people; the trouble is that we just cannot put our finger upon the difference, cannot catch the tip of the ear by which to pull out the rabbit. Hateful is everything that cannot be palpated, measured, counted.

A series of trivial torments began. On Monday they managed to sprinkle his bedclothes with potato flour, which is said to provoke a maddening itch. On Tuesday they ambushed him at the corner of their street (he was carrying books hugged to his breast) and hustled him so neatly that his load landed in the puddle they had picked out for it. On Wednesday they painted the toilet seat with carpenter's glue. By Thursday the brothers' imagination was exhausted.

He said nothing, nothing whatever. On Friday, he overtook Anton, with his flying step, at the gate of the yard, and offered him an illustrated weekly – maybe you'd like to look at it? This unexpected courtesy perplexed the brothers and made them glow still hotter.

Gustav ordered his fiancée to stir up Romantovski, which would give one the opportunity to pick a quarrel with him. You involuntarily tend to set a football rolling before kicking it. Frolicsome animals also prefer a mobile object. And though Anna, no doubt, greatly repelled Romantovski with those bug-brown freckles on her milky skin, the vacant look in her light eyes and the little promontories of wet gums between her teeth, he found fit to conceal his distaste, fearing to infuriate Anna's lover by spurning her.

Since he went all the same to the cinema once a week, he took her with him on Saturday in the hope that this attention would be enough. Unnoticed, at a discreet distance, both wearing new caps and orange-red shoes, the brothers stole after the pair, and on those dubious streets, in that dusty dusk, there were hundreds of their likes but only one Romantovski.

In the small elongated movie house night had started to flicker, a self-manufactured lunar night, when the brothers, furtively hunching, seated themselves in the back row. They sensed the darkly delicious presence of Romantovski somewhere in front. On the way to the cinema, Anna failed to worm anything out of her disagreeable companion, nor did she quite understand what exactly Gustav wanted of him. As they walked, the mere sight of his lean figure and melancholy profile made her want to yawn. But once the picture started, she forgot about him, pressing an insensate shoulder against him. Specters conversed in trumpet tones on the newfangled speaking screen. The baron tasted his wine and carefully put his glass down—with the sound of a dropped cannon-ball.

And after a while the sleuths were pursuing the baron. Who would have recognized in him the master crook? He was hunted passionately, frenziedly. Automobiles sped with bursts of thunder. In a nightclub they fought with bottles, chairs, tables. A mother was putting an enchanting child to bed.

When it was all over, and Romantovski, with a little stumble, followed her out into the cool darkness, Anna exclaimed, 'Oh, that was wonderful!'

He cleared his throat and said after a pause, 'Let's not exaggerate. In real life, it is all considerably duller.'

'It's you who's dull,' she retorted crossly, and presently chuckled softly as she recalled the pretty child.

Behind them, gliding along at the same distance as before, came the brothers. Both were gloomy. Both were pumping themselves up with gloomy violence. Gloomily, Anton said, 'That's not done, after all – going out walking with another's bride.'

'And especially on Saturday night,' said Gustav.

A passer-by, coming abreast of them, happened to glance at their faces—and could not help walking faster.

The night wind chased rustling rubbish along the fences. It was a dark and desolate part of Berlin. Far to the left of the road, above the canal, blinked scattered lights. On the right were vacant lots from which a few hastily silhouetted houses had turned their black backs away. After a little while the brothers accelerated their step.

'My mother and sister live in the country,' Anna was telling him in a rather cosy undertone amid the velvety night. 'As soon as I get married, I hope to visit them with him. Last summer my sister –'

Romantovski suddenly looked back.

'– won a lottery prize,' continued Anna, mechanically looking back too.

Gustav emitted a sonorous whistle.

'Why, it's them!' exclaimed Anna, and joyfully burst out laughing. 'Ah, the rascals!'

'Good evening, good evening,' said Gustav hastily, in a panting voice. 'What are you doing here, you ass, with my girl?'

'I'm not doing anything. We have just been –'

'Now, now,' said Anton and, drawing back his elbow, hit Romantovski crisply in the lower ribs.

'Please, don't use your fists. You know perfectly well that –'

'Leave him alone, fellows,' said Anna with a soft snigger.

'Must teach him a lesson,' said Gustav, warming up and forefeeling with a poignant glow how he, too, would follow his brother's example and feel those cartilages, that crumpy backbone.

'Apropos, a funny thing happened to me one day,' Romantovski started to say, talking fast, but here Gustav began to jam and twist the huge lumps of his knuckles into his victim's side, causing utterly indescribable pain. In lurching back Romantovski slipped and nearly fell: to fall would have meant perishing then and there.

'Let him go,' said Anna.

He turned and, holding his side, walked off along the dark rustling fences. The brothers followed, all but treading upon

29

his heels. Gustav rumbled in the anguish of blood lust, and that rumble might turn any moment into a pounce.

Far away before him a bright twinkle promised safety; it meant a lighted street, and although what could be seen was probably one lone lamp, that slit in the blackness seemed a marvelous festive blaze, a blissful region of radiance, full of rescued men. He knew that if he started to run it would be the end, since he could not get there sufficiently fast; he should go at a quiet and smooth walk, then he might cover that distance, keeping silent the while and trying not to press his hand against his burning ribs. So he strode on, with his usual springy step, and the impression was that he did so on purpose, to mock non-flyers, and that next moment he might take off.

Anna's voice: 'Gustav, don't tangle with him. You know quite well you won't be able to stop. Remember what you did once to that bricklayer.'

'Hold your tongue, old bitch, don't teach him what must be done.' (That's Anton's voice.)

Now at last, the region of light – where one could distinguish a chestnut's foliage, and what looked like a Morris pillar, and farther still, to the left, a bridge – that breathlessly waiting imploring light, at last, was not so very remote ... And still one should not run. And though he knew he was making a fatal mistake, all at once, beyond the control of his will, he flew up and, with a sob, dashed forward.

He ran and seemed, as he ran, to be laughing exultingly. Gustav overtook him in a couple of leaps. Both fell, and amid the fierce rasping and crunching there occurred a special sound – smooth and moist, once, and a second time, up to the hilt – and then Anna instantly fled into the darkness, holding her hat in her hand.

Gustav stood up. Romantovski was lying on the ground and speaking in Polish. Abruptly his voice broke off.

'And now let's be gone,' said Gustav. 'I stuck him.'

'Take it out,' said Anton, 'take it out of him.'

'I did,' said Gustav. 'God, how I stuck him.'

They scurried off, though not toward the light, but across dark vacant lots. After skirting the cemetery they reached a back alley, exchanged glances and slowed down to a normal walk.

Upon coming home, they immediately fell asleep. Anton dreamed he was sitting on the grass and watching a barge drift by. Gustav did not dream of anything.

Early next morning police agents arrived; they searched the murdered man's room and briefly questioned Anton, who had come out into the passage. Gustav stayed in bed, replete and somnolent, his face the color of Westphalian ham, in contrast to the whitish tufts of his eyebrows.

Presently, the police left and Anton returned. He was in an unusual state of elation, choking with laughter, flexing his knees, noiselessly hitting his palm with his fist.

'What fun!' he said. 'Do you know who the fellow was? A leonardo!'

In their lingo a leonardo (from the name of the painter) meant a maker of counterfeit bills. And Anton related what he had managed to find out: the fellow, it appeared, belonged to a gang and had just got out of jail. Before that he had been designing fake paper money; an accomplice had knifed him, no doubt.

Gustav shook with mirth, too, but then his expression changed suddenly.

'He slipped us his slither, the rogue!' cried Gustav and ran, naked, to the wardrobe where he kept his money box.

'Doesn't matter, we'll pass it,' said his brother. 'A nonexpert won't see the difference.'

'Yes, but what a rogue!' Gustav kept repeating.

My poor Romantovski! And I who believed with them that you were indeed someone exceptional. I believed, let me confess, that you were a remarkable poet whom poverty obliged to dwell in that sinister district. I believed, on the strength of certain indices, that every night, by working on a line of verse or nursing a growing idea, you celebrated an invulnerable victory over the brothers. My poor Romantovski! It is all over now. Alas, the objects I had assembled wander away. The young poplar dims and takes off – to return where it had been fetched from. The brick wall dissolves. The house draws in its little balconies one by one, then turns, and floats away. Everything floats away. Harmony and meaning vanish. The world irks me again with its variegated void.

Torpid Smoke

'Torpid Smoke' ('Tyazhyolyy dym') appeared in the daily
Posledniya Novosti, Paris, 3 March 1935, and was reprinted
in *Vesna v Fialte*, New York, 1956. The present translation
has been published in *Triquarterly*, No. 27, Spring 1973. In
two or three passages brief phrases have been introduced to
elucidate points of habitus and locale, unfamiliar today not
only to foreign readers but to the incurious grandchildren of
the Russians who fled to western Europe in the first three or
four years after the Bolshevist Revolution; otherwise the
translation is acrobatically faithful – beginning with the title,
which in a coarse lexical rendering that did not take familiar
associations into account would read 'Heavy Smoke'.

The story belongs to that portion of my short fiction which
refers to émigré life in Berlin between 1920 and the late
thirties. Seekers of biographical tidbits should be warned
that my main delight in composing those things was to invent
ruthlessly assortments of exiles who in character, class,
exterior features and so forth were utterly unlike any of the
Nabokovs. The only two affinities here between author and
hero are that both wrote Russian verse and that I had lived
at one time or another in the same kind of lugubrious Berlin
apartment as he. Only very poor readers (or perhaps some
exceptionally good ones) will scold me for not letting them
into its parlor.

When the street lamps hanging in the dusk came on, practically in unison, all the way to Bayerischer Platz, every object in the unlit room shifted slightly under the influence of the outdoor rays, which started by taking a picture of the lace curtain's design. He had been lying supine (a long-limbed flat-chested youth with a pince-nez glimmering in the semi-obscurity) for about three hours, apart from a brief interval for supper, which had passed in merciful silence: his father and sister, after yet another quarrel, had kept reading at table. Drugged by the oppressive, protracted feeling so familiar to him, he lay and looked through his lashes, and every line, every rim, or shadow of a rim, turned into a sea horizon or a strip of distant land. As soon as his eye got used to the mechanics of these metamorphoses, they began to occur of their own accord (thus small stones continue to come alive, quite uselessly, behind the wizard's back), and now, in this or that place of the room's cosmos, an illusionary perspective was formed, a remote mirage enchanting in its graphic transparency and isolation: a stretch of water, say, and a black promontory with the minuscule silhouette of an araucaria.

At intervals scraps of indistinct, laconic speech came from the adjacent parlor (the cavernal centerpiece of one of those bourgeois flats which Russian émigré families used to rent in Berlin at the time), separated from his room by sliding doors, through whose ripply mat glass the tall lamp beyond shone yellow, while lower down there showed through, as if in deep water, the fuzzy dark back of a chair placed in that position to foil the propensity of the door-leaves to crawl apart in a series of jerks. In that parlor (probably on the divan at its farthest end) his sister sat with her boy friend, and, to judge by the mysterious pauses, resolving at last in a slight cough or a tender questioning laugh, the two were kissing. Other sounds could be heard from the street: the noise of a car would curl up like a wispy column to be capitaled by a honk at the crossing; or, vice versa, the honk would come first, followed by an approaching rumble in which the shudder of the door-leaves participated as best it could.

And in the same way as the luminosity of the water and its every throb pass through a medusa, so everything traversed his inner being, and that sense of fluidity became transfigured into something like second sight. As he lay flat on his couch, he felt carried sideways by the flow of shadows and, simultaneously, he escorted distant foot-passengers, and visualized now the sidewalk's surface right under his eyes (with the exhaustive accuracy of a dog's sight), now the design of bare branches against a sky still retaining some color, or else the alternation of shop windows: a hairdresser's dummy, hardly surpassing the queen of hearts in anatomic development; a picture framer's display, with purple heathscapes and the inevitable *Inconnue de la Seine*, so popular in the Reich, among numerous portraits of President Hindenburg; and then a lampshade shop with all bulbs aglow, so that one could not help wondering which of them was the workaday lamp belonging to the shop itself.

All at once it occurred to him, as he reclined mummylike in the dark, that it was all rather awkward – his sister might think that he was not at home, or that he was eavesdropping. To move was, however, incredibly difficult; difficult, because the very form of his being had now lost all distinctive marks, all fixed boundaries. For example, the lane on the other side of the house might be his own arm, while the long skeletal cloud that stretched across the whole sky with a chill of stars in the east might be his backbone. Neither the striped obscurity in his room nor the glass of the parlor door, which was transmuted into night-time seas shining with golden undulations, offered him a dependable method of measuring and marking himself off; that method he found only when in a burst of agility the tactile tip of his tongue, performing a sudden twist in his mouth (as if dashing to check, half-awake, if all was well), palpated and started to worry a bit of soft foreign matter, a

36

shred of boiled beef firmly lodged in his teeth; whereupon he reflected how many times, in some nineteen years, it had changed, that invisible but tangible householdry of teeth, which the tongue would get used to until a filling came out, leaving a great pit that presently would be refurnished.

He was now prompted to move not so much by the shame- lessly frank silence behind the door as by the urge to seek out a nice, pointed little tool, to aid the solitary blind toiler. He stretched, raised his head and switched on the light near his couch, thus entirely restoring his corporeal image. He per- ceived himself (the pince-nez, the thin, dark mustache, the bad skin on his forehead) with that utter revulsion he always ex- perienced on coming back to his body out of the languorous mist, promising – what? What shape would the force oppress- ing and teasing his spirit finally take? Where did it originate, this thing growing in me? Most of my day had been the same as usual – university, public library – but later, when I had to trudge to the Osipovs on Father's errand, there was that wet roof of some pub on the edge of a vacant lot, and the chimney smoke hugged the roof, creeping low, heavy with damp, sated with it, sleepy, refusing to rise, refusing to detach itself from beloved decay, and right then came that thrill, right then.

Under the table lamp gleamed an oilcloth-bound exercise book and next to it, on the ink-mottled blotter, lay a razor blade, its apertures encircled with rust. The light also fell on a safety pin. He unbent it, and following his tongue's rather fussy directions, removed the mote of meat, swallowed it – better than any dainties; after which the contented organ calmed down.

Suddenly a mermaid's hand was applied from the outside to the ripply glass of the door; then the leaves parted spasmodic- ally and his sister thrust in her shaggy head.

'Grisha dear,' she said, 'be an angel, do get some cigarettes from Father.'

He did not respond, and the bright slits of her furry eyes narrowed (she saw very poorly without her horn-rimmed glasses) as she tried to make out whether or not he was asleep on the couch.

'Get them for me, Grishenka,' she repeated, still more

entreatingly. 'Oh, please! I don't want to go to him after what happened yesterday.'

'Maybe I don't want to either,' he said.

'Hurry, hurry,' tenderly uttered his sister, 'come on, Grisha dear!'

'All right, lay off,' he said at last, and carefully reuniting the two halves of the door, she dissolved in the glass.

He examined again his lamp-lit island, remembering hopefully that he had put somewhere a pack of cigarettes which one evening a friend had happened to leave behind. The shiny safety pin had disappeared, while the exercise book now lay otherwise and was half-open (as a person changes position in sleep). Perhaps, between my books. The light just reached their spines on the shelves above the desk. Here was haphazard trash (predominantly), and manuals of political economy (I wanted something quite different, but Father won out); there were also some favorite books that at one time or another had done his heart good: Gumilyov's collection of poems *Shatyor* (*Tent*), Pasternak's *Sestra moya Zhizn'* (*Life, My Sister*), Gazdanov's *Vecher u Kler* (*Evening at Claire's*), Radiguet's *Le Bal du comte d'Orgel*, Sirin's *Zashchita Luzhina* (*Luzhin's Defense*), Ilf and Petrov's *Dvenadtsat' Stul'ev* (*Twelve Chairs*), Hoffmann, Hölderlin, Baratynski, and an old Russian guidebook. Again that gentle mysterious shock. He listened. Would the thrill be repeated? His mind was in a state of extreme tension, logical thought was eclipsed, and when he came out of his trance, it took him some time to recall why he was standing near the shelves and fingering books. The blue-and-white package that he had stuck between Professor Sombart and Dostoevski proved to be empty. Well, it had to be done, no getting out of it. There was, however, another possibility.

In worn bedroom slippers and sagging pants, listlessly, almost noiselessly, dragging his feet, he passed from his room to the hallway and groped for the switch. On the console under the looking-glass, next to the guest's smart beige cap, there remained a crumpled piece of soft paper: the wrappings of liberated roses. He rummaged in his father's overcoat, penetrating with squeamish fingers into the insensate world of a strange pocket, but did not find there the spare pack he had hoped to obtain, knowing as he did his father's heavyish providence. Nothing to be done, I must go to him.

Here, that is at some indeterminate point of his somnambulic itinerary, he again stepped into a zone of mist, and this time the renewed vibration within him possessed such power, and, especially, was so much more vivid than all external perceptions, that he did not immediately identify as his proper confines and countenance the stoop-shouldered youth with the pale, unshaven cheek and the red ear who glided soundlessly by in the mirror. He overtook his own self and entered the dining room.

There, at the table which long since, before going to bed, the maid had laid for late-evening tea, sat his father: one finger was grating in his black, gray-streaked beard; between the finger and thumb of his other hand he held aloft a pince-nez by its springy clips; he sat studying a large plan of Berlin badly worn at the folds. A few days ago, at the house of some friends, there had been a passionate, Russian-style argument about which was the shortest way to walk from a certain street to another, neither of which, incidentally, did any of the arguers ever frequent; and now, to judge by the expression of displeased astonishment on his father's inclined face, with those two pink figure-eights on the sides of his nose, the old man had turned out to be wrong.

'What is it?' he asked, glancing up at his son (with the secret hope, perhaps, that I would sit down, divest the teapot of its cozy, pour a cup for him, for myself). 'Cigarettes?' he went on in the same interrogatory tone, having noticed the direction in which his son gazed; the latter had started to go behind his father's back to reach for the box, which stood on the far side of the table, but his father was already handing it across so that there ensued a moment of muddle.

'Is he gone?' came the third question.

'No,' said the son, taking a silky handful of cigarettes.

On his way out of the dining room he noticed his father turn his whole torso in his chair to face the wall clock as if it had said something, and then begin turning back — but there the door I was closing closed, and I did not see that bit to the end. I did not see it to the end, I had other things on my mind, yet that, too, and the distant seas of a moment ago, and my sister's flushed little face, and the indistinct rumble on the circular rim of the transparent night – everything, somehow or other, helped to form what now had at last taken shape. With terrifying clarity, as if my soul were lit up by a noiseless explosion, I glimpsed a future recollection; it dawned upon me that exactly as I recalled such images of the past as the way my dead mother had of making a weepy face and clutching her temples when mealtime squabbles became too loud, so one day I would have to recall, with merciless, irreparable sharpness, the hurt look of my father's shoulders as he leaned over that torn map, morose, wearing his warm indoor jacket powdered with ashes and dandruff; and all this mingled creatively with the recent vision of blue smoke clinging to dead leaves on a wet roof.

Through a chink between the door-leaves, unseen, avid fingers took away what he held, and now he was lying again on his couch, but the former languor had vanished. Enormous, alive, a metrical line extended and bent; at the bend a rhyme was coming deliciously and hotly alight, and as it glowed forth, there appeared like a shadow on the wall when you climb upstairs with a candle, the mobile silhouette of another verse.

Drunk with the italianate music of Russian alliteration, with the longing to live, the new temptation of obsolete words (modern *bereg* reverting to *breg*, a farther 'shore', *holod* to *hlad,* a more classic 'chill', *veter* to *vetr*, a better Boreas), puerile, perishable poems, which, by the time the next were printed, would have been certain to wither as had withered one after the other all the previous ones written down in the black exercise book; but no matter: at this moment I trust the ravishing promises of the still breathing, still revolving verse, my face is wet with tears, my heart is bursting with happiness, and I know that this happiness is the greatest thing existing on earth.

Breaking the News

'Breaking the News' appeared under the title of
'Opoveshchenie' ('Notification') in an émigré periodical
around 1935 and was included in my collection *Soglyadatay*
(*Russkiya Zapiski*, Paris, 1938).

The milieu and the theme both correspond to those of
'Signs and Symbols', written ten years later in English (see
The New Yorker, 15 May 1948, and *Nabokov's Dozen*,
Doubleday, 1958).

Eugenia Isakovna Mints was an elderly émigré widow, who always wore black. Her only son had died on the previous day. She had not yet been told.

It was a March day in 1935, and after a rainy dawn, one horizontal section of Berlin was reflected in the other – variegated zigzags intermingling with flatter textures, *et cetera*. The Chernobylskis, old friends of Eugenia Isakovna, had received the telegram from Paris around 7 A.M., and a couple of hours later a letter had come by air-mail. The head of the factory office where Misha had worked announced that the poor young man had fallen into an elevator shaft from the top floor, and had remained in agony for forty minutes: although unconscious, he kept moaning horribly and uninterruptedly, till the very end.

In the meantime Eugenia Isakovna got up, dressed, flung with a crosswise flick a black woolen shawl over her sharp thin shoulders and made herself some coffee in the kitchen. The deep, genuine fragrance of her coffee was something she prided herself upon in relation to Frau Doktor Schwarz, her landlady, 'a stingy, uncultured beast': it had now been a whole week since Eugenia Isakovna had stopped speaking to her – and that was not their first quarrel by far – but, as she told her friends, she did not care to move elsewhere for a number of reasons, often enumerated and never tedious. A manifest advantage that she had over this or that person with whom she might decide to break off relations lay in her being able simply to switch off her hearing aid, a portable gadget resembling a small black handbag.

As she carried the pot of coffee back to her room across the hallway, she noticed the flutter of a postcard which, upon having been pushed by the mailman through a special slit, settled

43

on the floor. It was from her son, of whose death the Chernobylskis had just learned by more advanced postal means, in consequence of which the lines (virtually inexistent) that she now read, standing with the coffee pot in one hand, on the threshold of her sizable but inept room, could have been compared by an objective observer to the still visible beams of an already extinguished star. *My darling Moolik* (her son's pet-name for her since childhood), *I continue to be plunged up to the neck in work and when evening comes I literally fall off my feet, and I never go anywhere –*

Two streets away, in a similar grotesque apartment crammed with alien bagatelles, Chernobylski, not having gone downtown today, paced from one room to another, a large, fat, bald man, with huge arching eyebrows and a diminutive mouth. He wore a dark suit but was collarless (the hard collar with inserted tie hung yoke-like on the back of a chair in the dining room) and he gestured helplessly as he paced and spoke:

'How shall I tell her? What gradual preparation can there be when one has to yell? Good God, what a calamity. Her heart will not bear it, it will burst, her poor heart!'

His wife wept, smoked, scraped her head through her sparse gray hair, telephoned the Lipshteyns, Lenochka, Dr Orshanski – and could not make herself go to Eugenia Isakovna first. Their lodger, a woman pianist with a pince-nez, big-bosomed, very compassionate and experienced, advised the Chernobylskis not to hurry too much with the telling – 'all the same there will be that blow, so let it be later'.

'But on the other hand,' cried Chernobylski hysterically, 'neither can one postpone it! Clearly one cannot! She is the mother, she may want to go to Paris – who knows? I don't – or she may want him to be brought here. Poor, poor Mishuk, poor boy, not yet thirty, all life before him! And to think that it was I who helped him, found him a job, to think that, if it had not been for that lousy Paris –'

'Now, now, Boris Lvovich,' soberly countered the lady lodger, 'who could foresee? What have you to do with it? It is comical – In general, I must say, incidentally, that I don't understand how he could fall. You understand how?'

Having finished her coffee and rinsed her cup in the kitchen (while not paying any attention *whatsoever* to the presence of Frau Schwarz), Eugenia Isakovna, with black net bag, handbag and umbrella, went out. The rain, after hesitating a little, had stopped. She closed her umbrella and proceeded to walk along the shining sidewalk, still holding herself quite straight, on very thin legs in black stockings, the left sagging slightly. One also noted that her feet seemed disproportionately large and that she set them down somewhat draggingly, with toes turned out. When not connected with her hearing aid she was ideally deaf, and very deaf when connected. What she took for the hum of the town was the hum of her blood, and against this customary background, without ruffling it, there moved the surrounding world – rubbery pedestrians, cotton-wool dogs, mute tramcars – and overhead crept the ever so slightly rustling clouds through which, in this or that place, blabbed, as it were, a bit of blue. Amid the general silence, she passed, impassive, rather satisfied on the whole, black-coated, bewitched and limited by her deafness, and kept an eye on things, and reflected on various matters. She reflected that tomorrow, a holiday, so-and-so would drop in; that she ought to get the same little pink gaufrettes as last time, and also *marmelad* (candied fruit jellies) at the Russian store, and maybe a dozen dainties in that small pastry shop where one can always be sure that everything is fresh. A tall bowler-hatted man coming toward her seemed to her from a distance (quite some distance, in fact) frightfully like Vladimir Markovich Vilner, Ida's first husband, who had died alone, in a sleeping-car, of heart failure, so sad, and as she went by a watchmaker's she remembered that it was time to call for Misha's wristwatch, which he had broken in Paris and had sent her by *okaziya* (i.e. 'taking the opportunity of somebody's traveling that way'). She went in. Noiselessly, slipperily, never brushing against anything, pendelums swung, all different, all in discord. She took her purse-like gadget out of her larger, ordinary handbag, introduced with a quick movement that had been shy once the insert into her ear, and the familiar faraway voice of the watchmaker replied – began to vibrate – then faded away, then jumped at her with a crash *'Freitag ... Freitag –'*

'All right, I hear you, next Friday.'

Upon leaving the shop, she again cut herself off from the world. Her faded eyes with yellowish stains about the iris (as if its color had run) acquired once more a serene, even gay, expression. She went along streets which she had not only learned to know well during the half-dozen years since her escape from Russia, but which had now become as full of fond entertainment as those of Moscow or Kharkov. She kept casting casual looks of approval on kids, on small dogs, and presently she yawned as she went, affected by the resilient air of early spring. An awfully unfortunate man, with an unfortunate nose, in an awful old fedora, passed by: a friend of some friends of hers who always mentioned him, and by now she knew everything about him – that he had a deranged daughter, and a despicable son-in-law, and diabetes. Having reached a certain fruit stall (discovered by her last spring), she bought a bunch of wonderful bananas; then she waited quite a time for her turn in a grocery, with her eyes never leaving the profile of an impudent woman, who had come later than she but nevertheless had squeezed nearer than she to the counter: there came a moment when the profile opened like a nutcracker – but here Eugenia Isakovna took the necessary measures. In the pastry shop she carefully chose her cakes, leaning forward, straining on tiptoe like a little girl, and moving hither and thither a hesitant index – with a hole in the black wool of the glove. Hardly had she left and grown engrossed in a display of men's shirts next door than her elbow was grasped by Madame Shuf, a vivacious lady with a somewhat exaggerated make-up; whereupon Eugenia Isakovna, staring away into space, nimbly adjusted her complicated machine, and only then, with the world become audible, gave her friend a welcoming smile. It was noisy and windy, Madame Shuf stooped and exerted herself, red mouth all askew, as she endeavored to aim the point of her voice straight into the black hearing aid:

'Do you have – news – from Paris?'

'Oh I do, even most regularly,' answered Eugenia Isakovna softly, and added, 'Why don't you come to see me, why do you never ring me up?' – and a gust of pain rippled her gaze because well-meaning Madame Shuf shrieked back too piercingly.

They parted. Madame Shuf, who did not know anything yet, went home, while her husband, in his office, was uttering 'akhs' and 'tsks', and shaking his head with the receiver pressed to it, as he listened to what Chernobylski was telling him over the telephone.

'My wife has already gone to her,' said Chernobylski, 'and in a moment I'll go there also, though kill me if I know how to begin but my wife is after all a woman, maybe she'll somehow manage to pave the way.'

Shuf suggested they write on bits of paper, and give her to read, gradual communications: 'Sick.' 'Very sick.' 'Very, very sick.'

'Akh, I also thought about that, but it doesn't make it easier. What a calamity, eh? Young, healthy, exceptionally endowed. And to think that it was *I* who got that job for him, *I* who helped him with his living expenses! What? Oh, I understand all that perfectly, but still these thoughts drive me crazy. Okay, we're sure to meet there.'

Fiercely and agonizingly baring his teeth and throwing back his fat face, he finally got his collar fastened. He sighed as he started to go. He had already turned into her street when he saw her from behind walking quietly and trustfully in front of him, with a net bag full of her purchases. Not daring to overtake her, he slowed down. God grant she does not turn! Those dutifully moving feet, that narrow back, still suspecting nothing. Ah, it shall bend!

She noticed him only on the staircase. Chernobylski remained silent as he saw her ear was still bare.

'Why, how nice to drop in, Boris Lvovich. No, don't bother – I've been carrying my load long enough to bring it upstairs too; but hold this umbrella if you like, and then I'll unlock the door.'

They entered. Madame Chernobylski and the warm-hearted pianist had been waiting there for quite a long time. Now the execution would start.

Eugenia Isakovna liked visitors and her friends often called on her, so that now she had no reason to be astonished; she was only pleased, and without delay started fussing hospitably. They found it hard to arrest her attention while she dashed this way and that, changing her course at an abrupt angle (the plan that spread its glow within her was to fix a real lunch). At last the musician caught her in the corridor by the end of her shawl and the others heard the woman shouting to her that nobody, nobody would stay for lunch. So Eugenia Isakovna got out the fruit knives, arranged the gaufrettes in one little glass vase, bonbons in another ... She was made to sit down practically by force. The Chernobylskis, their lodger and a Miss Osipov who by that time had somehow managed to appear – a tiny creature, almost a dwarf – all sat down, too, at the oval table. In this way a certain array, a certain order had, at least, been attained.

'For God's sake, begin, Boris,' pleaded his wife, concealing her eyes from Eugenia Isakovna, who had begun to examine more carefully the faces around her, without interrupting, however, the smooth flow of her amiable, pathetic, completely defenseless words.

'*Nu, chto ya mogu!*' ('Well, what can I!'), cried Chernobylski, and spasmodically rising started to walk around the room.

The doorbell rang, and the solemn landlady, in her best dress, let in Ida and Ida's sister: their awful white faces expressed a kind of concentrated avidity.

'She doesn't know yet,' Chernobylski told them; he undid all three buttons of his jacket and immediately buttoned it up again.

Eugenia Isakovna, her eyebrows twitching but her lips still retaining their smile, stroked the hands of her new visitors and reseated herself, invitingly turning her little apparatus, which stood before her on the tablecloth, now toward this guest, now toward that, but the sounds slanted, the sounds crumbled. All of a sudden the Shufs came in, then lame Lipshteyn with his mother, then the Orshanskis, and Lenochka, and (by sheer chance) aged Madame Tomkin – and they all talked among themselves, but were careful to keep their voices away from her, though actually they collected around her in grim, oppressive groups, and somebody had already walked away to the window and was shaking and heaving there, and Dr Orshanski, who sat next to her at the table, attentively examined a gaufrette, matching it, like a domino, with another, and Eugenia Isakovna, her smile now gone and replaced by something akin to rancor, continued to push her hearing aid toward her visitors – and sobbing Chernobylski roared from a distant corner 'What's there to explain – dead, dead, dead!' but she was already afraid to look in his direction.

Lips to Lips

Mark Aldanov, who was closer than I to the *Posledniya Novosti* (with which I conducted a lively feud throughout the 1930s) informed me, some time in 1931 or 1932, that at the last moment, this story, 'Lips to Lips' ('Usta k Ustam'), which finally had been accepted for publication, would not be printed after all. *'Razbili nabor'* ('They broke up the type'), my friend muttered gloomily. It was published only in 1956, by the Chekhov Publishing House, New York, in my collection *Vesna v Fialte*, by which time everybody who might have been suspected of remotely resembling the characters in the story was safely and heirlessly dead. *Esquire* published the present translation in its September 1971 issue.

The violins were still weeping, performing, it seemed, a hymn of passion and love, but already Irina and the deeply moved Dolinin were rapidly walking toward the exit. They were lured by the spring night, by the mystery that had tensely stood up between them. Their two hearts were beating as one.

'*Give me your cloakroom ticket,*' *uttered Dolinin* (crossed out).

'*Please, let me get your hat and manteau*' (crossed out).

'*Please,*' *uttered Dolinin,* '*let me get your things*' ('and my' inserted between 'your' and 'things').

Dolinin went up to the cloakroom, and after producing his little ticket (corrected to 'both little tickets') –

Here Ilya Borisovich Tal grew pensive. It was awkward, most awkward, to dawdle there. Just now there had been an ecstatic surge, a sudden blaze of love between the lonely, elderly Dolinin and the stranger who happened to share his box, a girl in black, whereupon they decided to escape from the theater, far, far away from the décolletés and military uniforms. Somewhere beyond the theater the author dimly visualized the Kupecheskiy or Tsarskiy Park, locusts in bloom, precipices, a starry night. The author was terribly impatient to plunge with his hero and heroine into that starry night. Still one had to get one's coats, and that interfered with the glamour. Ilya Borisovich reread what he had written, puffed out his cheeks, stared at the crystal paperweight and finally made up his mind to sacrifice glamour to realism. This did not prove simple. His leanings were strictly lyrical, descriptions of nature and emotions came to him with surprising facility, but on the other hand he had a lot of trouble with routine items, such as, for instance, the opening and closing of doors, or shaking hands when there were numerous characters in a room, and one person or two persons saluted many people. Furthermore Ilya Borisovich tussled constantly with pronouns, as for example 'she', which had a teasing way of referring not only to the heroine but also to her mother or sister in the same sentence, so that in order to avoid repeating a proper name one was often compelled to put 'that lady' or 'her interlocutress' although no interlocution was taking place. Writing meant to him an unequal contest with indispensable objects; luxury goods appeared to be much more compliant, but even they rebelled now and then, got stuck, hampered one's freedom of movement – and now, having ponderously finished with the cloakroom fuss and being about to present his hero with an elegant cane, Ilya Borisovich naïvely delighted in the gleam of its rich knob, and did not foresee, alas, what claims that valuable article would make, how painfully it would demand mention, when Dolinin, his hands feeling the curves of a supple young body, would be carrying Irina across a vernal rill.

Dolinin was simply 'elderly'; Ilya Borisovich Tal would soon be fifty-five. Dolinin was 'colossally wealthy', without precise explanation of his source of income; Ilya Borisovich directed a company engaged in the installation of bathrooms (that year, incidentally, it had been appointed to panel with enameled tiles the cavernal walls of several underground stations) and was quite well-to-do. Dolinin lived in Russia – South Russia, probably – and first met Irina long before the Revolution. Ilya Borisovich lived in Berlin, whither he had migrated with wife and son in 1920. His literary output was of long standing, but not big: the obituary of a local merchant, famous for his liberal political views, in the *Kharkov Herald* (1910), two prose poems, *ibid.* (August 1914 and March 1917), and one book, consisting of that obituary and those two prose poems – a pretty volume that landed right in the raging middle of the civil war. Finally, upon reaching Berlin, Ilya Borisovich wrote a little étude, 'Travelers by Sea and Land', which appeared in a humble émigré daily published in Chicago; but that newspaper soon vanished like smoke, while other periodicals did not return manuscripts and never discussed rejections. Then followed two years of creative silence; his wife's illness and death, the *Inflationszeit*, a thousand business undertakings. His son finished high school in Berlin and entered Freiburg University. And now, in 1925, at the onset of old age, this prosperous and on the whole very lonely person experienced such an attack of writer's itch, such a longing – oh, not for fame, but simply for some warmth and heed on the part of readerdom – that he resolved to let himself go, write a novel and have it published at his own cost.

Already by the time that its protagonist, the heavy-hearted, world-weary Dolinin, hearkened to the clarion of a new life and (after that almost fatal stop at the cloakroom) escorted his young companion into the April night, the novel had acquired a title: *Lips to Lips*. Dolinin had Irina move to his flat, but nothing had happened yet in the way of love-making, for he desired that she come to his bed of her own accord, exclaiming:

'Take me, take my purity, take my torment. Your loneliness is my loneliness, and however long or short your love may be, I am prepared for everything, because around us spring summons us to humaneness and good, because the sky and the firmament radiate divine beauty, and because I love you.'

'A powerful passage,' observed Euphratski. *'Terra firma* meant, I dare say. Very powerful.'

'And it is not boring?' asked Ilya Borisovich Tal, glancing over his horn-rimmed glasses. 'Eh? Tell me frankly.'

'I suppose he'll deflower her,' mused Euphratski.

'Mimo, chitatel', mimo – wrong, reader, wrong!' answered Ilya Borisovich (misinterpreting Turgenev). He smiled rather smugly, gave his manuscript a resettling shake, crossed his fat-thighed legs more comfortably and continued his reading.

He read his novel to Euphratski bit by bit, at the rate of production. Euphratski, who had once swooped upon him on the occasion of a concert with a charitable purpose, was an émigré journalist 'with a name', or, rather, with a dozen pseudonyms. Hitherto Ilya Borisovich's acquaintances used to come from German industrial circles; now he attended émigré meetings, lectures, amateur theatricals and had learned to recognize some of the belles-lettres brethren. He was on especially good terms with Euphratski and valued his opinion as coming from a stylist, although Euphratski's style belonged to the topical sort we all know. Ilya Borisovich frequently invited him, they sipped cognac and talked about Russian literature, or more exactly Ilya Borisovich did the talking, and the guest avidly collected comical scraps with which to entertain his own cronies later. True, Ilya Borisovich's tastes were on the heavyish side. He gave Pushkin his due, of course, but knew him mainly through the medium of three or four operas, and in general found him 'olympically serene and incapable of stirring the reader'. His knowledge of more recent poetry was limited to his remembering two poems, both with a political slant, 'The Sea' by Veynberg (1830–1908) and the famous lines of Skitaletz (Stepan Petrov, born 1868) in which 'dangled' (on the gallows) rhymes with 'entangled' (in a revolutionary plot). Did Ilya Borisovich like to make mild fun of the 'decadents'? Yes, he did, but then, one must note that he frankly admitted his incomprehension of verse. Per contra, he was fond of discussing Russian fiction: he esteemed Lugovoy (a regional mediocrity of the 1900s), appreciated Korolenko, and considered that Artsybashev debauched young readers. In regard to the novels of modern émigré writers he would say, with the 'empty-handed' Russian gesture of inutility, 'Dull, dull!', which sent Euphratski into a kind of rapturous trance.

'An author should be soulful,' Ilya Borisovich would reiterate, 'and compassionate, and responsive, and fair. Maybe I'm a flea, a nonentity, but I have my credo. Let at least one word of my writings impregnate a reader's heart.' And Euphratski would fix reptilian eyes upon him, foretasting with agonizing tenderness tomorrow's mimetic report, A's belly laugh, Z's ventriloquistic squeak.

At last came the day when the first draft of the novel was finished. To his friend's suggestion that they repair to a café, Ilya Borisovich replied in a mysterious and weighty tone of voice,

'Impossible. I'm polishing my phrasing.'

The polishing consisted of his launching an attack on the too frequently occurring adjective *molodaya*, 'young' (feminine gender), replacing it here and there by 'youthful', *yunaya*, which he pronounced with a provincial doubling of the consonant as if it were spelled *yunnaya*.

One day later. Twilight. Café on the Kurfürstendamm.

Settee of red plush. Two gentlemen. To a casual eye: business-men. One – respectable-looking, even rather majestic, a non-smoker, with an expression of trust and kindliness on his fleshy face; the other – lean, beetle-browed, with a pair of fastidious folds descending from his triangular nostrils to the lowered corners of his mouth from which protrudes obliquely a cigarette not yet lit. The first man's quiet voice:

'I penned the end in one spurt. He dies, yes, he dies.'

Silence. The red settee is nice and soft. Beyond the picture window a translucent tram floats by like a bright fish in an aquarium tank.

Euphratski clicked his cigarette-lighter, expulsed smoke from his nostrils and said, 'Tell me, Ilya Borisovich, why not have a literary magazine run it as a serial before it comes out in book form?'

'But, look, I've no pull with that crowd. They publish always the same people.'

'Nonsense. I have a little plan. Let me think it over.'

'I'd be happy...' murmured Tal dreamily.

A few days later in I. B. Tal's room at the office. The unfolding of the little plan.

'Send your thing' (Euphratski narrowed his eyes and lowered his voice) 'to *Arion*.'

'*Arion*? What's that?' said I.B., nervously patting his manuscript.

'Nothing very frightening. It's the name of the best émigré review. You don't know it? Ay-ya-yay! The first number came out this spring, the second is expected in the fall. You should keep up with literature a bit closer, Ilya Borisovich!'

'But how to contact him? Just mail it?'

'That's right. Straight to the editor. It's published in Paris. Now don't tell me you've never heard Galatov's name?'

Guiltily Ilya Borisovich shrugged one fat shoulder. Euphratski, his face working wrily, explained: a writer, a master, new form of the novel, intricate construction, Galatov the Russian Joyce.

'Djoys,' meekly repeated Ilya Borisovich after him.

'First of all have it typed,' said Euphratski. 'And for God's sake acquaint yourself with the magazine.'

He acquainted himself. In one of the Russian bookshops of exile he was handed a plump pink volume. He bought it, thinking aloud, as it were: 'Young venture. Must be encouraged.'

'Finished, the young venture,' said the bookseller. 'One number was all that came out.'

'You are not in touch,' rejoined Ilya Borisovich with a smile. 'I definitely know that the next number will be out in autumn.'

Upon coming home, he took an ivory paperknife and neatly cut the magazine's pages. Therein he found an unintelligible piece of prose by Galatov, two or three short stories by vaguely familiar authors, a mist of poems, and an extremely capable article about German industrial problems signed Tigris.

'Oh, they'll never accept it,' reflected Ilya Borisovich with anguish. 'They all belong to one crew.'

Nevertheless he located one Madame Lubansky ('stenographer and typist') in the advertisement columns of a Russian-language newspaper and, having summoned her to his apartment, started to dictate with tremendous feeling, boiling with agitation, raising his voice – and glancing ever and ever again at the lady to see her reaction to his novel. Her pencil kept flitting as she bent over her writing pad – a small, dark woman with a rash on her forehead – and Ilya Borisovich paced his study in circles, and the circles would tighten around her at the approach of this or that spectacular passage. Toward the end of the first chapter the room vibrated with his cries.

'And his entire yore seemed to him a horrible error,' roared Ilya Borisovich, and then added, in his ordinary office voice, 'Type this out for tomorrow, five copies, wide margins, I shall expect you here at the same hour.'

That night, in bed, he kept thinking up what he would tell Galatov when sending the novel ('... awaiting your stern judgment ... my contributions have appeared in Russia and America...'), and on the following morning – such is the enchanting obligingness of fate – Ilya Borisovich received this letter from Paris:

Dear Boris Grigorievich,
I learn from a common friend that you have completed a

new opus. The editorial board of Arion *would be interested in seeing it, since we would like to have something 'refreshing' for our next issue.*

How strange! Only the other day I found myself recalling your elegant miniatures in the Kharkov Herald!

'I'm remembered, I'm wanted,' distractedly uttered Ilya Borisovich. Thereupon he rang up Euphratski, and throwing himself back in his armchair, sideways – with the uncouthness of triumph – leaning the hand that held the receiver upon his desk, while outlining an ample gesture with the other, and beaming all over, he drawled, 'Well, oh-old boy, well, oh-old boy' – and suddenly the various bright objects upon the desk began to tremble and twin and dissolve in a moist mirage. He blinked, everything resumed its right place, and Euphratski's languid voice replied, 'Oh come! Brother writers. Ordinary good turn.'

Five stacks of typed pages grew higher and higher. Dolinin, who with one thing and another had not yet possessed his fair companion, happened to discover that she was infatuated with another man, a young painter. Sometimes I.B. dictated in his office, and then the German typists in the other rooms, hearing that remote roar, wondered who on earth was being bawled out by the usually good-natured boss. Dolinin had a heart-to-heart talk with Irina, she told him she would never leave him, because she prized too highly his beautiful lonely soul, but, alas, she belonged physically to another, and Dolinin silently bowed. At last, the day came when he made a will in her favor, the day came when he shot himself (with a Mauser pistol), the day came when Ilya Borisovich, smiling blissfully, asked Madame Lubansky, who had brought the final portion of the typescript, how much he owed her, and attempted to overpay.

With ravishment he reread *Lips to Lips* and handed over one copy to Euphratski for corrections (some discreet editing had already been accomplished by Madame Lubansky at such points where chance omissions garbled her shorthand notes). All Euphratski did was to insert in one of the first lines a temperamental comma in red pencil. Ilya Borisovich religiously transported that comma to the copy destined for *Arion*, signed his novel with a pseudonym derived from 'Anna' (the name of his dead wife), fastened every chapter with a trim clip, added a lengthy letter, slipped all this into a huge solid envelope, weighed it, went to the post office himself and sent the novel by registered mail.

With the receipt tucked away in his wallet, Ilya Borisovich braced himself for weeks and weeks of tremulous waiting. Galatov's reply came, however, with miraculous promptness – on the fifth day.

Dear Ilya Grigorievich,

The editors are more than entranced with the material you sent us. Seldom have we had the occasion to peruse pages upon which a 'human soul' has been so clearly imprinted. Your novel moves the reader with a face's singular expression, to paraphrase Baratynski, the singer of the Finnish crags. It breathes 'bitterness and tenderness'. Some of the descriptions, such as for example that of the theater, in the very beginning, compete with analogous images in the works of our classical writers and in a certain sense gain the ascendancy. This I say with a full awareness of the 'responsibility' attached to such a statement. Your novel would have been a genuine adornment of our review.

As soon as Ilya Borisovich had somewhat recovered his composure, he walked over to the Tiergarten – instead of riding to his office – and sat there on a park bench, tracing arcs on the brown ground, thinking of his wife, and imagining how she would have rejoiced with him. After a while he went to see Euphratski. The latter lay in bed, smoking. They analyzed together every line of the letter. When they got to the last one, Ilya Borisovich meekly raised his eyes and asked, 'Tell me, why do you think he put "would have been" and not "will be"? Doesn't he understand that I'm overjoyed to give them my novel? Or is it simply a stylistic device?'

'I'm afraid there's another reason,' answered Euphratski. 'No doubt it's a case of concealing something out of sheer pride. In point of fact the magazine is folding up – yes, that's what I've just learned. The émigré public consumes as you

60

know all sorts of trash, and *Arion* is meant for the sophisticated reader. Well, that's the result.'

'I've also heard rumors,' said very much perturbed Ilya Borisovich, 'but I thought it was slander spread by competitors, or mere stupidity. Can it be really possible that no second issue will ever come out? It is awful!'

'They have no funds. The review is a disinterested, idealistic enterprise. Such publications, alas, perish.'

'But how, how can it be!' cried Ilya Borisovich, with a Russian splash-gesture of helpless dismay. 'Haven't they approved my thing, don't they want to print it?'

'Yes, too bad,' said Euphratski calmly. 'By the way, tell me –' and he changed the subject.

That night Ilya Borisovich did some hard thinking, conferred with his inner self and next morning phoned his friend to submit to him certain questions of a financial nature. Euphratski's replies were listless in tone but most accurate in sense. Ilya Borisovich pondered some more and on the following day made Euphratski an offer to be submitted to *Arion*. The offer was accepted, and Ilya Borisovich transferred to Paris a certain amount of money. In reply he got a letter with expressions of deep gratitude and a communication to the effect that the next issue of *Arion* would come out in a month's time. A postscript contained a courteous request: 'Allow us to put, "a novel by Ilya Annenski", and not, as you suggest, "I. Annenski", otherwise there might be some confusion with the "last swan of Tsarskoe Selo", as Gumilyov calls him.'

Ilya Borisovich answered:

Yes, of course, I just did not know that there already existed an author writing under that name. I am delighted my work will be printed. Please have the kindness to send me five specimens of your journal as soon as it is out. (He had in view an old female cousin and two or three business acquaintances. His son did not read Russian.)

Here began the era in his life which the wits denoted by the term 'apropos'. Either in a Russian bookshop, or at a meeting of the Friends of Expatriate Arts, or else simply on the sidewalk of a West Berlin street, you were amiably accosted ('Ah! How goes it?') by a person you knew slightly, a pleasant and dignified gentleman wearing horn-rimmed glasses and carrying a cane, who would engage you in casual conversation about this and that, would imperceptibly pass from this and that to the subject of literature and would suddenly say:

'Apropos, here's what Galatov writes me. Yes – Galatov. Galatov the Russian Djoys.'

You take the letter and scan it:

... editors are more than entranced ... our classical writers ... adornment of our review.

'He got my patronymic wrong,' adds Ilya Borisovich with a kindly chuckle. 'You know how writers are: absentminded! The journal will come out in September, you will read my little work.' And replacing the letter in his wallet, he takes leave of you and with a worried air hurries away.

Literary failures, hack journalists, special correspondents of forgotten newspapers derided him with savage volupty. Such hoots are emitted by delinquents torturing a cat; such a spark glows in the eyes of a no longer young, sexually unlucky fellow telling a particularly dirty story. Naturally, it was behind his back that they jeered, but they did so with the utmost sansgêne, disregarding the superb acoustics of every locus of tattle. Being, however, as deaf to the world as a grouse in courtship, he probably did not catch one sound of all this. He blossomed, he walked his cane with a new, novelistic stance, he started writing to his son in Russian with an interlinear German translation of most of the words. At the office one knew already that I. B. Tal was not only an excellent person but also a *Schriftsteller,* and some of his business friends confided their love secrets to him as themes he might use. To him, sensing a certain warm zephyr, there began to flock in, through front hall or back door, the motley mendicancy of emigration. Public figures addressed him with respect. The fact could not be denied: Ilya Borisovich was indeed surrounded by esteem and fame. Not a single party in a cultured Russian milieu passed without his name being mentioned. *How* it was mentioned, with *what* kind of snicker, hardly matters: the thing, not the way, is important, says true wisdom.

At the end of the month Ilya Borisovich had to leave town on a tedious business trip and so he missed the advertisements in Russian-language newspapers regarding the coming publication of *Arion* 2. When he returned to Berlin, a large cubical package awaited him on the hallway table. Without taking his topcoat off, he instantaneously undid the parcel. Pink, plump, cool tomes. And, on the covers, ARION in purple-red letters. Six copies.

Ilya Borisovich attempted to open one; the book crackled deliciously but refused to unclose. Blind, newborn! He tried again, and caught a glimpse of alien, alien versicles. He swung the mass of uncut pages from right to left – and happened to spot the table of contents. His eye raced through names and titles, but *he* was not there, *he* was not there! The volume endeavored to shut, he applied force, and reached the end of the list. Nothing! How could that be, good God? Impossible! Must have been omitted by chance from the table, such things happen, they happen! He was now in his study, and seizing his white knife, he stuck it into the thick, foliated flesh of the book. First Galatov, of course, then poetry, then two stories, then again poetry, again prose and farther on nothing but trivia – surveys, critiques and so forth. Ilya Borisovich was overwhelmed all at once by a sense of fatigue and futility. Well, nothing to be done. Maybe they had too much material. They'll print it in the next number. Oh, that's for certain! But a new period of waiting – Well, I'll wait. Mechanically he kept sifting the soft pages between finger and thumb. Fancy paper. Well, I've been at least of some help. One can't insist on being printed instead of Galatov or – And here, abruptly, there jumped out and whirled and went tripping, tripping along, hand on hip, in a Russian dance, the dear, heart-warm words '... her youthful, hardly formed bosom ... violins were still weeping ... both little tickets ... the spring night welcomed them with a car –' and on the reverse page, as inevitably as the continuation of rails after a tunnel: 'essing and passionate breath of wind –'

'How the deuce didn't I guess immediately!' ejaculated Ilya Borisovich.

It was entitled 'Prologue to a novel'. It was signed 'A. Ilyin', with, in parentheses, 'To be continued'. A small bit, three pages and a half, but what a *nice* bit! Overture. Elegant. 'Ilyin' is better than 'Annenski'. Might have been a mix-up even if they had put 'Ilya Annenski'. But why 'Prologue' and not simply: *Lips to Lips*, Chapter One? Oh, that's quite unimportant.

He reread the piece thrice. Then he laid the magazine aside, paced his study, whistling negligently the while, as if nothing whatever had happened: well, yes, there's that book lying there – some book or other – who cares? Whereupon he rushed toward it and reread himself eight times in a row. Then he looked up 'A. Ilyin, p. 205' in the table of contents, found p. 205 and, relishing every word, reread his 'Prologue'. He kept playing that way for quite a time.

The magazine replaced the letter. Ilya Borisovich constantly carried a copy of *Arion* under his arm, and upon running into any sort of acquaintance, opened the volume at a page that had grown accustomed to presenting itself. *Arion* was reviewed in the papers. The first of those reviews did not mention Ilyin at all. The second had: 'Mr Ilyin's "Prologue to a novel" must surely be a joke of some kind.' The third noted merely that Ilyin and another were newcomers to the magazine. Finally, a fourth reviewer (in a charming, modest little periodical appearing somewhere in Poland) wrote as follows 'Ilyin's piece attracts one by its sincerity. The author pictures the birth of love against a background of music. Among the indubitable qualities of the piece one should mention the good style of the narration.' A new era started (after the 'apropos' period and the book-carrying one): Ilya Borisovich would extract that review from his wallet.

He was happy. He purchased six more copies. He was happy. Silence was readily explained by inertia, detraction by enmity. He was happy. 'To be continued'. And then, one Sunday, came a telephone call from Euphratski:

'Guess,' he said, 'who wants to speak to you? Galatov! Yes, he's in Berlin for a couple of days. I pass the receiver.'

A voice never yet heard took over. A shimmering, urgeful, mellow, narcotic voice. A meeting was settled.

'Tomorrow at five at my place,' said Ilya Borisovich, 'what a pity you can't come tonight!'

'Very regrettable,' rejoined the shimmering voice; 'you see, I'm being dragged by friends to attend *The Black Panther* –

terrible play – but it's such a long time since I've seen dear Elena Dmitrievna.'

Elena Dmitrievna Garina, a handsome elderly actress, who had arrived from Riga to star in the repertoire of a Russian-language theater in Berlin. Beginning at half past eight. After a solitary supper Ilya Borisovich suddenly glanced at his watch, smiled a sly smile and took a taxi to the theater.

The 'theater' was really a large hall meant for lectures, rather than plays. The performance had not yet started. An amateur poster featured Garina reclining on the skin of a panther shot by her lover who was to shoot her later on. Russian speech crepitated in the cold vestibule. Ilya Borisovich relinquished into the hands of an old woman in black his cane, his bowler and his topcoat, paid for a numbered jetton, which he slipped into his waistcoat pocket, and leisurely rubbing his hands looked around the vestibule. Close to him stood a group of three people: a young reporter whom Ilya Borisovich knew slightly, the young man's wife (an angular lady with a lorgnette) and a stranger in a flashy suit, with a pale complexion, a little black beard, beautiful ovine eyes and a gold chainlet around his hairy wrist.

'But why, oh why,' the lady was saying to him vivaciously, 'why did you print it? 'Cause you know –'

'Now stop attacking that unfortunate fellow,' replied her interlocutor in an iridescent baritone voice. 'All right, he's a hopeless mediocrity, I grant you that, but evidently we had reasons –'

He added something in an undertone and the lady, with a click of her lorgnette, retorted in anger. 'Excuse me, but in my opinion, if you print him only because he supports you financially –'

'*Doucement, doucement.* Don't proclaim our editorial secrets.'

Here Ilya Borisovich caught the eye of the young reporter, the angular lady's husband, and the latter froze for an instant and then moaned with a start, and proceeded to push his wife away with his whole body, but she continued to speak at the top of her voice: 'I'm not concerned with the wretched Ilyin, I'm concerned with matters of principle –'

'Sometimes, principles have to be sacrificed,' coolly said the opal-voiced fop.

But Ilya Borisovich was no longer listening. He saw things through a haze, and being in a state of utter distress, not yet realizing fully the horror of the event, but instinctively striving to retreat as fast as possible from something shameful, odious, intolerable, he moved at first toward the vague spot where vague seats were being sold, but then abruptly turned back, almost collided with Euphratski who was hurrying toward him and made for the cloakroom.

Old woman in black. Number 79. Down there. He was in a desperate hurry, had already swept his arm back to get into a last coat sleeve, but here Euphratski caught up with him, accompanied by the other, the other —

'Meet our editor,' said Euphratski, while Galatov, rolling his eyes and trying not to let Ilya Borisovich regain his wits, kept catching the sleeve in a semblance of assistance and talking fast: 'Innokentiy Borisovich, how are you? Very glad to make your acquaintance. Pleasant occasion. Allow me to help you.'

'For God's sake, leave me alone,' muttered Ilya Borisovich, struggling with the coat and with Galatov. 'Go away. Disgusting. I can't. It's disgusting.'

'Obvious misunderstanding,' put in Galatov at top speed.

'Leave me alone,' cried Ilya Borisovich, wrenched himself free, scooped up his bowler from the counter and went out, still putting on his coat.

He kept whispering incoherently as he marched along the sidewalk; then he spread his hands: he had forgotten his cane!

Automatically he continued to walk, but presently with a quiet little stumble came to a stop as if the clockwork had run out.

He would go back for the thing once the performance had started. Must wait a few minutes.

Cars sped by, tramcars rang their bells, the night was clear, dry, spruced up with lights. He began to walk slowly toward the theater. He reflected that he was old, lonely, that his joys were few, and that old people must pay for their joys. He reflected that perhaps even tonight, and in any case, tomorrow,

Galatov would come with explanations, exhortations, justifica-
tions. He knew that he must forgive everything, otherwise the
'to be continued' would never materialize. And he also told
himself that he would be fully recognized after his death, and
he recollected, he gathered up in a tiny heap, all the crumbs of
praise he had received lately, and slowly walked to and fro,
and after a while went back for his cane.

The Visit to the Museum

'The Visit to the Museum' ('Poseshchenie muzeya') appeared in the émigré review *Sovremennyya Zapiski*, LXVIII, Paris, 1939, and in my collection *Vesna v Fialte*, Chekhov Publishing House, New York, 1959. The present English translation came out in *Esquire*, March 1963, and was included in *Nabokov's Quartet*, Phaedra, New York, 1968.

One explanatory note may be welcomed by non-Russian readers. At one point the unfortunate narrator notices a shop sign and realizes he is not in the Russia of his past, but in the Russia of the Soviets. What gives that shop sign away is the absence of the letter that used to decorate the end of a word after a consonant in old Russia but is omitted in the reformed orthography adopted by the Soviets today.

Several years ago a friend of mine in Paris – a person with oddities, to put it mildly – learning that I was going to spend two or three days at Montisert, asked me to drop in at the local museum where there hung, he was told, a portrait of his grandfather by Leroy. Smiling and spreading out his hands, he related a rather vague story to which I confess I paid little attention, partly because I do not like other people's obtrusive affairs, but chiefly because I had always had doubts about my friend's capacity to remain this side of fantasy. It went more or less as follows: after the grandfather died in their St Petersburg house back at the time of the Russo–Japanese War, the contents of his apartment in Paris were sold at auction. The portrait, after some obscure peregrinations, was acquired by the museum of Leroy's native town. My friend wished to know if the portrait was really there; if there, if it could be ransomed; and if it could, for what price. When I asked why he did not get in touch with the museum, he replied that he had written several times, but had never received an answer.

I made an inward resolution not to carry out the request – I could always tell him I had fallen ill or changed my itinerary. The very notion of seeing sights, whether they be museums or ancient buildings, is loathsome to me; besides, the good freak's commission seemed absolute nonsense. It so happened, however, that, while wandering about Montisert's empty streets in search of a stationery store, and cursing the spire of a long-necked cathedral, always the same one, that kept popping up at the end of every street, I was caught in a violent downpour which immediately went about accelerating the fall of the maple leaves, for the fair weather of a southern October was holding on by a mere thread. I dashed for cover and found myself on the steps of the museum.

It was a building of modest proportions, constructed of many-colored stones, with columns, a gilt inscription over the frescoes of the pediment, and a lion-legged stone bench on either side of the bronze door. One of its leaves stood open, and the interior seemed dark against the shimmer of the shower. I stood for a while on the steps, but, despite the overhanging roof, they were gradually growing speckled. I saw that the rain had set in for good, and so, having nothing better to do, I decided to go inside. No sooner had I trod on the smooth, resonant flagstones of the vestibule than the clatter of a moved stool came from a distant corner, and the custodian – a banal pensioner with an empty sleeve – rose to meet me, laying aside his newspaper and peering at me over his spectacles. I paid my franc and, trying not to look at some statues at the entrance (which were as traditional and as insignificant as the first number in a circus program), I entered the main hall.

Everything was as it should be: gray tints, the sleep of substance, matter dematerialized. There was the usual case of old, worn coins resting in the inclined velvet of their compartments. There was, on top of the case, a pair of owls, Eagle Owl and Long-eared, with their French names reading 'Grand Duke' and 'Middle Duke' if translated. Venerable minerals lay in their open graves of dusty papier-mâché; a photograph of an astonished gentleman with a pointed beard dominated an assortment of strange black lumps of various sizes. They bore a great resemblance to frozen frass, and I paused involuntarily over them, for I was quite at a loss to guess their nature, composition and function. The custodian had been following me with felted steps, always keeping a respectful distance; now, however, he came up, with one hand behind his back and the ghost of the other in his pocket, and gulping, if one judged by his Adam's apple.

'What are they?' I asked.

'Science has not yet determined,' he replied, undoubtedly having learned the phrase by rote. 'They were found,' he continued in the same phony tone, 'in 1895, by Louis Pradier, Municipal Councillor and Knight of the Legion of Honor,' and his trembling finger indicated the photograph.

'Well and good,' I said, 'but who decided, and why, that they merited a place in the museum?'

'And now I call your attention to this skull!' the old man cried energetically, obviously changing the subject.

'Still, I would be interested to know what they are made of,' I interrupted.

'Science...' he began anew, but stopped short and looked crossly at his fingers, which were soiled with dust from the glass.

I proceeded to examine a Chinese vase, probably brought back by a naval officer; a group of porous fossils; a pale worm in clouded alcohol; a red-and-green map of Montisert in the seventeenth century; and a trio of rusted tools bound by a funeral ribbon – a spade, a mattock and a pick. 'To dig in the past,' I thought absentmindedly, but this time did not seek clarification from the custodian, who was following me noiselessly and meekly, weaving in and out among the display cases. Beyond the first hall there was another, apparently the last, and in its center a large sarcophagus stood like a dirty bathtub, while the walls were hung with paintings.

At once my eye was caught by the portrait of a man between two abominable landscapes (with cattle and 'atmosphere'). I moved closer and, to my considerable amazement, found the very object whose existence had hitherto seemed to me but the figment of an unstable mind. The man, depicted in wretched oils, wore a frock coat, whiskers and a large pince-nez on a cord; he bore a likeness to Offenbach, but, in spite of the work's vile conventionality, I had the feeling one could make out in his features the horizon of a resemblance, as it were, to my friend. In one corner, meticulously traced in carmine against a black background, was the signature *Leroy* in a hand as commonplace as the work itself.

I felt a vinegarish breath near my shoulder, and turned to meet the custodian's kindly gaze. 'Tell me,' I asked, 'supposing someone wished to buy one of these paintings, whom should he see?'

'The treasures of the museum are the pride of the city,' replied the old man, 'and pride is not for sale.'

Fearing his eloquence, I hastily concurred, but nevertheless asked for the name of the museum's director. He tried to distract me with the story of the sarcophagus, but I insisted. Finally he gave me the name of one M. Godard and explained where I could find him.

Frankly, I enjoyed the thought that the portrait existed. It is fun to be present at the coming true of a dream, even if it is not one's own. I decided to settle the matter without delay. When I get in the spirit, no one can hold me back. I left the museum with a brisk, resonant step, and found that the rain had stopped, blueness had spread across the sky, a woman in besplattered stockings was spinning along on a silver-shining bicycle, and only over the surrounding hills did clouds still hang. Once again the cathedral began playing hide-and-seek with me, but I outwitted it. Barely escaping the onrushing tires of a furious red bus packed with singing youths, I crossed the asphalt thoroughfare and a minute later was ringing at the garden gate of M. Godard. He turned out to be a thin, middle-aged gentleman in high collar and dickey, with a pearl in the knot of his tie, and a face very much resembling a Russian wolfhound; as if that were not enough, he was licking his chops in a most doglike manner, while sticking a stamp on an envelope, when I entered his small but lavishly furnished room with its malachite inkstand on the desk and a strangely familiar Chinese vase on the mantel. A pair of fencing foils hung crossed over the mirror, which reflected the narrow gray back of his head. Here and there photographs of a warship pleasantly broke up the blue flora of the wallpaper.

'What can I do for you?' he asked, throwing the letter he had just sealed into the wastebasket. This act seemed unusual to me; however, I did not see fit to interfere. I explained in brief my reason for coming, even naming the substantial sum with which my friend was willing to part, though he had asked me not to mention it, but wait instead for the museum's terms.

'All this is delightful,' said M. Godard. 'The only thing is, you are mistaken – there is no such picture in our museum.'

'What do you mean there is no such picture? I have just seen it! Portrait of a Russian nobleman, by Gustave Leroy.'

'We do have one Leroy,' said M. Godard when he had

leafed through an oilcloth notebook and his black fingernail had stopped at the entry in question. 'However, it is not a portrait but a rural landscape: The Return of the Herd.'

I repeated that I had seen the picture with my own eyes five minutes before and that no power on earth could make me doubt its existence.

'Agreed,' said M. Godard, 'but I am not crazy either. I have been curator of our museum for almost twenty years now and know this catalogue as well as I know the Lord's Prayer. It says here Return of the Herd and that means the herd is returning, and unless perhaps your friend's grandfather is depicted as a shepherd, I cannot conceive of his portrait's existence in our museum.'

'He is wearing a frock coat,' I cried. 'I swear he is wearing a frock coat!'

'And how did you like our museum in general?' M. Godard asked suspiciously. 'Did you appreciate the sarcophagus?'

'Listen,' I said (and I think there was already a tremor in my voice), 'do me a favor – let's go there this minute, and let's make an agreement that if the portrait is there, you will sell it.'

'And if not?' inquired M. Godard.

'I shall pay you the sum anyway.'

'All right,' he said. 'Here, take this red-and-blue pencil and using the red – the red, please – put it in writing for me.'

In my excitement I carried out his demand. Upon glancing at my signature, he deplored the difficult pronunciation of Russian names. Then he appended his own signature and, quickly folding the sheet, thrust it into his waistcoat pocket.

'Let's go,' he said, freeing a cuff.

On the way he stepped into a shop and bought a bag of sticky-looking caramels which he began offering me insistently; when I flatly refused, he tried to shake out a couple of them into my hand. I pulled my hand away. Several caramels fell on the sidewalk; he stopped to pick them up and then overtook me at a trot. When we drew near the museum we saw the red tourist bus (now empty) parked outside.

'Aha,' said M. Godard, pleased. 'I see we have many visitors today.'

He doffed his hat and, holding it in front of him, walked decorously up the steps.

All was not well at the museum. From within issued rowdy cries, lewd laughter, and even what seemed like the sound of a scuffle. We entered the first hall; there the elderly custodian was restraining two sacrilegists who wore some kind of festive emblems in their lapels and were altogether very purple-faced and full of pep as they tried to extract the municipal councillor's merds from beneath the glass. The rest of the youths, members of some rural athletic organization, were making noisy fun, some of the worm in alcohol, others of the skull. One joker was in rapture over the pipes of the steam radiator, which he pretended was an exhibit; another was taking aim at an owl with his fist and forefinger. There were about thirty of them in all, and their motion and voices created a condition of crush and thick noise.

M. Godard clapped his hands and pointed at a sign reading 'Visitors to the Museum must be decently attired.' Then he pushed his way, with me following, into the second hall. The whole company immediately swarmed after us. I steered Godard to the portrait; he froze before it, chest inflated, and then stepped back a bit, as if admiring it, and his feminine heel trod on somebody's foot.

'Splendid picture,' he exclaimed with genuine sincerity. 'Well, let's not be petty about this. You were right, and there must be an error in the catalogue.'

As he spoke, his fingers, moving as it were on their own, tore up our agreement into little bits which fell like snowflakes into a massive spittoon.

'Who's the old ape?' asked an individual in a striped jersey, and, as my friend's grandfather was depicted holding a glowing cigar, another funster took out a cigarette and prepared to borrow a light from the portrait.

'All right, let us settle on the price,' I said, 'and, in any case, let's get out of here.'

'Make way, please!' shouted M. Godard, pushing aside the curious.

There was an exit, which I had not noticed previously, at the end of the hall and we thrust our way through to it.

'I can make no decision,' M. Godard was shouting above the din. 'Decisiveness is a good thing only when supported by law. I must first discuss the matter with the mayor, who has just died and has not yet been elected. I doubt that you will be able to purchase the portrait but nonetheless I would like to show you still other treasures of ours.'

We found ourselves in a hall of considerable dimensions. Brown books, with a half-baked look and coarse, foxed pages, lay open under glass on a long table. Along the walls stood dummy soldiers in jack boots with flared tops.

'Come, let's talk it over,' I cried out in desperation, trying to direct M. Godard's evolutions to a plush-covered sofa in a corner. But in this I was prevented by the custodian. Flailing his one arm, he came running after us, pursued by a merry crowd of youths, one of whom had put on his head a copper helmet with a Rembrandtesque gleam.

'Take it off, take it off!' shouted M. Godard, and someone's shove made the helmet fly off the hooligan's head with a clatter.

'Let us move on,' said M. Godard, tugging at my sleeve, and we passed into the section of Ancient Sculpture.

I lost my way for a moment among some enormous marble legs, and twice ran around a giant knee before I again caught sight of M. Godard, who was looking for me behind the white ankle of a neighboring giantess. Here a person in a bowler, who must have clambered up her, suddenly fell from a great height to the stone floor. One of his companions began helping him up, but they were both drunk, and, dismissing them with a wave of the hand, M. Godard rushed on to the next room, radiant with Oriental fabrics; there hounds raced across azure carpets, and a bow and quiver lay on a tiger skin.

Strangely, though, the expanse and motley only gave me a feeling of oppressiveness and imprecision, and, perhaps because new visitors kept dashing by or perhaps because I was impatient to leave the unnecessarily spreading museum and amid calm and freedom conclude my business negotiations with M. Godard, I began to experience a vague sense of alarm. Meanwhile we had transported ourselves into yet another hall, which must have been really enormous, judging by the fact that it housed the entire skeleton of a whale, resembling a frigate's frame; beyond were visible still other halls, with the oblique sheen of large paintings, full of storm clouds, among which floated the delicate idols of religious art in blue and pink vestments: and all this resolved itself in an abrupt turbulence of misty draperies, and chandeliers came aglitter and fish with translucent frills meandered through illuminated aquariums. Racing up a staircase, we saw, from the gallery above, a crowd of gray-haired people with umbrellas examining a gigantic mock-up of the universe.

At last, in a somber but magnificent room dedicated to the history of steam machines, I managed to halt my carefree guide for an instant.

'Enough!' I shouted. 'I'm leaving. We'll talk tomorrow.'

He had already vanished. I turned and saw, scarcely an inch from me, the lofty wheels of a sweaty locomotive. For a long time I tried to find the way back among models of railroad stations. How strangely glowed the violet signals in the gloom beyond the fan of wet tracks, and what spasms shook my poor heart! Suddenly everything changed again: in front of me stretched an infinitely long passage, containing numerous office cabinets and elusive, scurrying people. Taking a sharp turn, I found myself amid a thousand musical intruments; the walls, all mirror, reflected an enfilade of grand pianos, while in the center there was a pool with a bronze Orpheus atop a green rock. The aquatic theme did not end here as, racing back, I ended up in the Section of Fountains and Brooks, and it was difficult to walk along the winding slimy edges of those waters.

Now and then, on one side or the other, stone stairs, with puddles on the steps, which gave me a strange sensation of fear, would descend into misty abysses, whence issued whistles, the rattle of dishes, the clatter of typewriters, the ring of hammers and many other sounds, as if, down there, were exposition halls of some kind or other, already closing or not yet completed. Then I found myself in darkness and kept bumping into unknown furniture until I finally saw a red light and walked out onto a platform that clanged under me – and suddenly, beyond it, there was a bright parlor, tastefully furnished in Empire style, but not a living soul, not a living soul ... By now I was indescribably terrified, but every time I turned and tried to retrace my steps along the passages, I found myself in hitherto unseen places – a greenhouse with hydrangeas and broken windowpanes with the darkness of artificial night showing through beyond; or a deserted laboratory with dusty alembics on its tables. Finally I ran into a room of some sort with coatracks monstrously loaded down with black coats and astrakhan furs; from beyond a door came a burst of applause, but when I flung the door open, there was no theater, but only a soft opacity and splendidly counterfeited fog with the perfectly convincing blotches of indistinct streetlights. More than convincing! I advanced, and immediately a joyous and unmistakable sensation of reality at last replaced all the unreal trash amid which I had just been dashing to and fro. The stone beneath my feet was real sidewalk, powdered with wonderfully fragrant, newly fallen snow, in which the infrequent pedestrians had already left fresh black tracks. At first the quiet and the snowy coolness of the night, somehow strikingly familiar, gave me a pleasant feeling after my feverish wanderings. Trustfully, I started to conjecture just where I had come out, and why the snow, and what were those lights exaggeratedly but indistinctly beaming here and there in the brown darkness. I examined and, stooping, even touched a round spur stone on the curb, then glanced at the palm of my hand, full of wet granular cold, as if hoping to read an explanation there. I felt how lightly, how naïvely I was clothed, but the distinct realization that I had escaped from the museum's maze was still so strong that, for the first two or three minutes, I experienced neither surprise nor fear. Continuing my leisurely examination, I looked up at the house beside which I was standing and was immediately struck by the sight of iron steps and railings that descended into the snow on their way to the cellar. There was a twinge in my heart, and it was with a new, alarmed curiosity that I glanced at the pavement, at its white cover along which stretched black lines, at the brown sky across which there kept sweeping a mysterious light, and at the massive parapet some distance away. I sensed that there was a drop beyond it; something was creaking and gurgling down there. Further on, beyond the murky cavity, stretched a chain of fuzzy lights. Scuffling along the snow in my soaked shoes, I walked a few paces, all the time glancing at the dark house on my right; only in a single window did a lamp glow softly under its green-glass shade. Here, a locked wooden gate ... There, what must be the shutters of a sleeping shop ... And by the light of a streetlamp whose shape had long been shouting to me its impossible message, I made out the ending of a sign – '... *inka Sapog*' ('... *oe Repair*') – but no, it was not the snow that had obliterated the 'hard sign' at the end. 'No, no, in a minute I shall wake up,' I said aloud, and, trembling, my heart pounding, I turned, walked on, stopped again. From somewhere came the receding sound of hooves, the snow sat like a skullcap on a slightly leaning spur stone and indistinctly showed white on the woodpile on the other side of the fence, and already I knew, irrevocably, where I was. Alas, it was not the Russia I remembered, but the factual Russia of today, forbidden to me, hopelessly slavish, and hopelessly my own native land. A semiphantom in a light foreign suit, I stood on the impassive snow of an October night, somewhere on the Moyka or the Fontanka Canal, or perhaps on the Obvodny, and I had to do something, go somewhere, run; desperately protect my fragile, illegal life. Oh, how many times in my sleep I had experienced a similar sensation! Now, though, it was reality. Everything was real – the air that seemed to mingle with scattered snowflakes, the still unfrozen canal, the floating fish house, and that peculiar squareness of the darkened and the yellow windows. A man in a fur cap, with a briefcase under his arm, came toward me out of the fog, gave me a startled glance, and turned to look again when he had passed me. I waited for him to disappear and then, with a tremendous haste, began pulling out everything I had in my pockets, ripping up papers, throwing them into the snow and stamping them down. There were some documents, a letter from my sister in Paris, five hundred francs, a handkerchief, cigarettes; however, in order to shed all the integument of exile, I would have to tear off and destroy my clothes, my linen, my shoes, everything, and remain ideally naked; and, even though I was already shivering from my anguish and from the cold, I did what I could.

But enough. I shall not recount how I was arrested, nor tell of my subsequent ordeals. Suffice it to say that it cost me incredible patience and effort to get back abroad, and that, ever since, I have foresworn carrying out commissions entrusted one by the insanity of others.

An Affair of Honor

'An Affair of Honor' appeared under the title of 'Podlets'
('The Cur'), in the émigré daily *Rul*, Berlin, around 1927, and
was included in my first collection *Vozvrashchenie Chorba*,
Slovo, Berlin, 1930. The present translation was published in
The New Yorker, 3 September 1966, and was included in
Nabokov's Quartet, Phaedra, New York, 1966.

The story renders in a drab expatriate setting a belated
variation on the romantic theme whose decline started with
Chekhov's magnificent novella *Single Combat* (1891).

1

The accursed day when Anton Petrovich made the acquaintance of Berg existed only in theory, for his memory had not affixed to it a date label at the time, and now it was impossible to identify that day. Broadly speaking, it happened last winter around Christmas, 1926. Berg arose out of nonbeing, bowed in greeting and settled down again – into an armchair instead of his previous nonbeing. It was at the Kurdyumovs', who lived on St Mark Strasse, way off in the sticks, in the Moabit section of Berlin, I believe. The Kurdyumovs remained the paupers they had become after the Revolution, while Anton Petrovich and Berg, although also expatriates, had since grown somewhat richer. Now, when a dozen similar ties of a smoky, luminous shade – say that of a sunset cloud – appeared in a haberdasher's window, together with a dozen handkerchiefs in exactly the same tints, Anton Petrovich would buy both the fashionable tie and fashionable handkerchief, and every morning, on his way to the bank, would have the pleasure of encountering the same tie and the same handkerchief, worn by two or three gentlemen who were also hurrying to their offices. At one time he had business relations with Berg; Berg was indispensable, would call up five times a day, began frequenting their house and would crack endless jokes – God, how he loved to crack jokes. The first time he came, Tanya, Anton Petrovich's wife, found that he resembled an Englishman and was very amusing. 'Hello, Anton!' Berg would roar, swooping down on Anton's hand with outspread fingers (the way Russians do), and then shaking it vigorously. Berg was broad-shouldered, well-built, clean-shaven and liked to compare himself to an athletic angel. He once showed Anton Petrovich a little old black notebook. The pages were all covered with crosses, exactly five hundred twenty-three in number. 'Civil war in the

Crimea – a souvenir,' said Berg with a slight smile, and coolly added, 'Of course, I counted only those Reds I killed outright.' The fact that Berg was an ex-cavalry man and had fought under General Denikin aroused Anton Petrovich's envy, and he hated when Berg would tell, in front of Tanya, of reconnaissance forays and midnight attacks. Anton Petrovich himself was short-legged, rather plump and wore a monocle, which, in its free time, when not screwed into his eye socket, dangled on a narrow black ribbon and, when Anton Petrovich sprawled in an easy chair, would gleam like a foolish eye on his belly. A boil excised two years before had left a scar on his left cheek. This scar, as well as his coarse, cropped mustache and fat Russian nose, would twitch tensely when Anton Petrovich screwed the monocle home. 'Stop making faces,' Berg would say, 'you won't find an uglier one.'

In their glasses a light vapor floated over the tea; a half-squashed chocolate eclair on a plate released its creamy inside; Tanya, her bare elbows resting on the table and her chin leaning on her interlaced fingers, gazed upwards at the drifting smoke of her cigarette, and Berg was trying to convince her that she must wear her hair short, that all women, from time immemorial, had done so, that the Venus de Milo had short hair, while Anton Petrovich heatedly and circumstantially objected, and Tanya only shrugged her shoulder, knocking the ash off her cigarette with a tap of her nail.

And then it all came to an end. One Wednesday at the end of July Anton Petrovich left for Kassel on business, and from there sent his wife a telegram that he would return on Friday. On Friday he found that he had to remain at least another week, and sent another telegram. On the following day, however, the deal fell through, and without bothering to wire a third time Anton Petrovich headed back to Berlin. He arrived about ten, tired and dissatisfied with his trip. From the street he saw that the bedroom windows of his flat were aglow, conveying the soothing news that his wife was at home. He went up to the fifth floor, with three twirls of the key unlocked the thrice-locked door, and entered. As he passed through the front hall, he heard the steady noise of running water from the bathroom. 'Pink and moist,' Anton Petrovich thought with fond anticipation, and carried his bag on into the bedroom. In the bedroom, Berg was standing before the wardrobe mirror, putting on his tie.

Anton Petrovich mechanically lowered his little suitcase to the floor, without taking his eyes off Berg, who tilted up his impassive face, flipped back a bright length of tie and passed it through the knot. 'Above all, don't get excited,' said Berg, carefully tightening the knot. 'Please don't get excited. Stay perfectly calm.'

Must do something, Anton Petrovich thought, but what? He felt a tremor in his legs, an absence of legs – only that cold, aching tremor. Do something quick ... He started pulling a glove off one hand. The glove was new and fit snugly. Anton Petrovich kept jerking his head and muttering mechanically, 'Go away immediately. This is dreadful. Go away ...'

'I'm going, I'm going, Anton,' said Berg, squaring his broad shoulders as he leisurely got into his jacket.

'If I hit him, he'll hit me too,' Anton Petrovich thought in a flash. He pulled off the glove with a final yank and threw it awkwardly at Berg. The glove slapped against the wall and dropped into the washstand pitcher.

'Good shot,' said Berg.

He took his hat and cane, and headed past Anton Petrovich toward the door. 'All the same, you'll have to let me out,' he said. 'The downstairs door is locked.'

Scarcely aware of what he was doing, Anton Petrovich followed him. As they started to go down the stairs, Berg, who was in front, suddenly began to laugh. 'Sorry,' he said without turning his head, 'but this is awfully funny – being kicked out with such complications.' At the next landing he chuckled again and accelerated his step. Anton Petrovich also quickened his pace. That dreadful rush was unseemly ... Berg was deliberately making him go down in leaps and bounds. What torture ... Third floor ... second ... When will these stairs end? Berg flew down the remaining steps and stood waiting for Anton Petrovich, lightly tapping the floor with his cane. Anton Petrovich was breathing heavily, and had trouble getting the dancing key into the trembling lock. At last it opened.

'Try not to hate me,' said Berg from the sidewalk. 'Put yourself in my place...'

Anton Petrovich slammed the door. From the very beginning he had had a ripening urge to slam some door or other. The noise made his ears ring. Only now, as he climbed the stairs, did he realize that his face was wet with tears. As he passed through the front hall, he heard again the noise of running water. Hopefully waiting for the tepid to grow hot. But now above that noise he could also hear Tanya's voice. She was singing loudly in the bathroom.

With an odd sense of relief, Anton Petrovich returned to the bedroom. He now saw what he had not noticed before – that both beds were tumbled and that a pink nightgown lay on his wife's. Her new evening dress and a pair of silk stockings were laid out on the sofa: evidently, she was getting ready to go dancing with Berg. Anton Petrovich took his expensive fountain pen out of his breast pocket. I cannot bear to see you. I cannot trust myself if I see you. He wrote standing up, bending awkwardly over the dressing table. His monocle was blurred by a large tear ... the letters swam.... Please go away. I am leaving you some cash. I'll talk it over with Natasha tomorrow. Sleep at her house or at a hotel tonight – only please do not stay here. He finished writing and placed the paper against the mirror, in a spot where she would be sure to see it. Beside it he put a hundred-mark note. And, passing through the front hall, he again heard his wife singing in the bathroom. She had a gypsy kind of voice, a bewitching voice ... happiness, a summer night, a guitar ... she sang that night seated on a cushion in the middle of the floor, and slitted her smiling eyes as she sang ... He had just proposed to her ... yes, happiness, a summer night, a moth bumping against the ceiling, 'my soul I surrender to you, I love you with infinite passion...' 'How dreadful! How dreadful!' He kept repeating as he walked down the street. The night was very mild, with a swarm of stars. It did not matter which way he went. By now she had probably come out of the bathroom and found the note. Anton Petrovich winced as he remembered the glove. A brand-new glove afloat in a brimming pitcher. The vision of this brown wretched thing cause him to utter a cry that made a passerby start. He saw the dark shapes of huge poplars around a square and thought, 'Mityushin lives here someplace.' Anton Petrovich called him up from a bar, which arose before him as in a dream and then receded into the distance like the tail light of a train. Mityushin let him in but he was drunk, and at first paid no attention to Anton Petrovich's livid face. A person unknown to Anton Petrovich sat in the small dim room, and a black-haired lady in a red dress lay on the couch with her back to the table, apparently asleep. Bottles gleamed on the table. Anton Petrovich had arrived in the middle of a birthday celebration, but he never understood whether it was being held for Mityushin, the fair sleeper or the unknown man (who turned out to be a Russified German with the strange name of Gnushke). Mityushin, his rosy face beaming, introduced him to Gnushke, and, indicating with a nod the generous back of the sleeping lady, remarked casually, 'Adelaida Albertovna, I want you to meet a great friend of mine.' The lady did not stir; Mityushin, however, did not show the least surprise, as if he had never expected her to wake up. All of this was a little bizarre and nightmarish – that empty vodka bottle with a rose stuck into its neck, that chess board on which a higgledy-piggledy game was in progress, the sleeping lady, the drunken but quite peaceful Gnushke...

'Have a drink,' said Mityushin, and then suddenly raised his eyebrows. 'What's the matter with you, Anton Petrovich? You look very ill.'

'Yes, by all means, have a drink,' with idiotic earnestness said Gnushke, a very long-faced man in a very tall collar, who resembled a dachshund.

Anton Petrovich gulped down half a cup of vodka and sat down.

'Now tell us what's happened,' said Mityushin. 'Don't be embarrassed in front of Henry – he is the most honest man on earth. My move, Henry, and I warn you, if after this you grab my bishop, I'll mate you in three moves. Well, out with it, Anton Petrovich.'

'We'll see about that in a minute,' said Gnushke, revealing a big starched cuff as he stretched out his arm. 'You forgot about the pawn at h5.'

'H5 yourself,' said Mityushin. 'Anton Petrovich is going to tell us his story.'

Anton Petrovich had some more vodka and the room went into a spin. The gliding chessboard seemed on the point of colliding with the bottles; the bottles, together with the table, set off toward the couch; the couch with mysterious Adelaida Albertovna headed for the window; and the window also started to move. This accursed motion was somehow connected with Berg, and had to be stopped – stopped at once, trampled upon, torn, destroyed . . .

'I want you to be my second,' began Anton Petrovich, and was dimly aware that the phrase sounded oddly truncated but could not correct that flaw.

'Second what?' said Mityushin absently, glancing askance at the chessboard, over which Gnushke's hand hung, its fingers wriggling.

'No, you listen to me,' Anton Petrovich exclaimed with anguish in his voice. 'You just listen! Let us not drink any more. This is serious, very serious.'

Mityushin fixed him with his shiny blue eyes. 'The game is canceled, Henry,' he said, without looking at Gnushke. 'This sounds serious.'

'I intend to fight a duel,' whispered Anton Petrovich, trying by mere optical force to hold back the table that kept floating away. 'I wish to kill a certain person. His name is Berg – you may have met him at my place. I prefer not to explain my reasons . . .'

'You can explain everything to your second,' said Mityushin smugly.

'Excuse me for interfering,' said Gnushke suddenly, and raised his index finger. 'Remember, it has been said: "Thou shalt not kill!" '

'The man's name is Berg,' said Anton Petrovich. 'I think you know him. And I need two seconds.' The ambiguity could now be ignored.

'A duel,' said Gnushke.

Mityushin nudged him with his elbow. 'Don't interrupt, Henry.'

'And that is all,' Anton Petrovich concluded in a whisper

and, lowering his eyes, feebly fingered the ribbon of his totally useless monocle.

Silence. The lady on the couch snored comfortably. A car passed in the street, its horn blaring.

'I'm drunk, and Henry's drunk,' muttered Mityushin, 'but apparently something very serious has happened.' He chewed on his knuckles and looked at Gnushke. 'What do you think, Henry?' Gnushke sighed.

'Tomorrow you two will call on him,' said Anton Petrovich. 'Select the spot, and so on. He did not leave me his card. According to the rules he should have given me his card. I threw my glove at him.'

'You are acting like a noble and courageous man,' said Gnushke with growing animation. 'By a strange coincidence, I am not unfamiliar with these matters. A cousin of mine was also killed in a duel.'

'Why "also"?' Anton Petrovich wondered in anguish. 'Can this be a portent?'

Mityushin took a swallow from his cup and said jauntily:

'As a friend, I cannot refuse. We'll go see Mr Berg in the morning.'

'As far as the German laws are concerned,' said Gnushke, 'if you kill him, they'll put you in jail for several years; if, on the other hand, you are killed, they won't bother you.'

'I have taken all that into consideration,' Anton Petrovich said solemnly.

Then there appeared again that beautiful expensive implement, that shiny black pen with its delicate gold nib, which in normal times would glide like a wand of velvet across the paper; now, however, Anton Petrovich's hand shook, and the table heaved like the deck of a storm-tossed ship ... On a sheet of foolscap that Mityushin produced, Anton Petrovich wrote a cartel of defiance to Berg, three times calling him a scoundrel and concluding with the lame sentence: 'One of us must perish.'

Having done, he burst into tears, and Gnushke, clucking his tongue, wiped the poor fellow's face with a large red-checked handkerchief, while Mityushin kept pointing at the chessboard, repeating ponderously, 'You finish him off like that king there – mate in three moves and no questions asked.' Anton Petrovich sobbed, and tried to brush away Gnushke's friendly hands, repeating with childish intonations, 'I loved her so much, so much!'

And a new sad day was dawning.

'So at nine you will be at his house,' said Anton Petrovich, lurching out of his chair.

'At nine we'll be at his house,' Gnushke replied like an echo.

'We'll get in five hours of sleep,' said Mityushin.

Anton Petrovich smoothed his hat into shape (he had been sitting on it all the while), caught Mityushin's hand, held it for a moment, lifted it and pressed it to his cheek.

'Come, come, you shouldn't,' mumbled Mityushin and, as before, addressed the sleeping lady, 'Our friend is leaving, Adelaida Albertovna.'

This time she stirred, awakened with a start, and turned over heavily. Her face was full and creased by sleep, with slanting, excessively made-up eyes. 'You fellows better stop drinking,' she said calmly, and turned back toward the wall.

At the corner of the street Anton Petrovich found a sleepy taxi, which whisked him with ghostly speed through the wastes of the blue-gray city and fell asleep again in front of his house. In the front hall he met Elspeth the maid, who opened her mouth and looked at him with unkind eyes, as if about to say something; but she thought better of it, and shuffled off down the corridor in her carpet slippers.

'Wait,' said Anton Petrovich. 'Is my wife gone?'

'It's shameful,' the maid said with great emphasis. 'This is a madhouse. Lug trunks in the middle of the night, turn everything upside down...'

'I asked if my wife was gone,' Anton Petrovich shouted in a high-pitched voice.

'She is,' glumly answered Elspeth.

Anton Petrovich went on into the parlor. He decided to sleep there. The bedroom, of course, was out of the question. He turned on the light, lay down on the sofa and covered himself with his overcoat. For some reason his left wrist felt uncomfortable. Oh, of course – my watch. He took it off and wound it, thinking at the same time, 'Extraordinary, how this man retains his composure – does not even forget to wind his watch.' And, since he was still drunk, enormous, rhythmic waves immediately began rocking him, up and down, up and down, and he began to feel very sick. He sat up ... the big copper ashtray ... quick ... His insides gave such a heave that a pain shot through his groin ... and it all missed the ashtray. He fell asleep right away. One foot in its black shoe and gray spat dangled from the couch, and the light (which he had quite forgotten to turn off) lent a pale gloss to his sweaty forehead.

2

Mityushin was a brawler and a drunkard. He could go and do all kinds of things at the least provocation. A real daredevil. One also recalls having heard about a certain friend of his who, to spite the post office, used to throw lighted matches into mailboxes. He was nicknamed the Gnut. Quite possibly it was Gnushke. Actually, all Anton Petrovich had intended to do was to spend the night at Mityushin's place. Then, suddenly, for no reason at all that talk about duels had started ... Oh, of course Berg must be killed; only the matter ought to have been carefully thought out first, and, if it had come to choosing seconds, they should in any case have been gentlemen. As it was, the whole thing had taken on an absurd, improper turn. Everything had been absurd and improper – beginning with the glove and ending with the ashtray. But now, of course, there was nothing to be done about it – he would have to drain this cup ...

He felt under the couch, where his watch had landed. Eleven. Mityushin and Gnushke have already been at Berg's. Suddenly a pleasant thought darted among the others, pushed them apart, and disappeared. What was it? Oh, of course! They had been drunk yesterday, and he had been drunk too. They must have overslept, then come to their senses and thought that he had been babbling nonsense; but the pleasant thought flashed past and vanished. It made no difference – the thing had been started and he would have to repeat to them what he had said yesterday. Still it was odd that they had not

93

shown up yet. A duel. What an impressive word, 'duel'! I am
having a duel. Hostile meeting. Single combat. Duel. 'Duel'
sounds best. He got up, and noticed that his trousers were
terribly wrinkled. The ashtray had been removed. Elspeth must
have come in while he was sleeping. How embarrassing. Must
go see how things look in the bedroom. Forget his wife. She did
not exist any more. Never had existed. All of that was gone.
Anton Petrovich took a deep breath and opened the bedroom
door. He found the maid there stuffing a crumpled newspaper
into the wastebasket.

'Bring me some coffee, please,' he said, and went to the
dressing table. There was an envelope on it. His name; Tanya's
hand. Beside it, in disorder, lay his hairbrush, his comb, his
shaving brush and an ugly, stiff glove. Anton Petrovich opened
the envelope. The hundred marks and nothing else. He turned
it this way and that, not knowing what to do with it.

'Elspeth . . .'

The maid approached, glancing at him suspiciously.

'Here, take it. You were put to so much inconvenience last
night, and then those other unpleasant things . . . Go on, take it.'

'One hundred marks?' the maid asked in a whisper, and
then suddenly blushed crimson. Heaven only knows what
rushed through her head, but she banged the wastebasket down
on the floor and shouted, 'No! You can't bribe me, I'm an
honest woman. Just you wait, I'll tell everybody you wanted to
bribe me. No! This is a madhouse . . .' And she went out,
slamming the door.

'What's wrong with her? God Lord, what's wrong with
her?' muttered Anton Petrovich in confusion, and, stepping
rapidly to the door, shrieked after the maid, 'Get out this minute, get out of this house!'

'That's the third person I've thrown out,' he thought, his
whole body trembling. 'And now there is no one to bring me
my coffee.'

He spent a long time washing and changing, and then sat in
the café across the street, glancing every so often to see if
Mityushin and Gnushke were not coming. He had lots of business to attend to in town, but he could not be bothered with
business. Duel. A glamorous word.

In the afternoon Natasha, Tanya's sister, appeared. She was so upset that she could barely speak. Anton Petrovich paced back and forth, giving little pats to the furniture. Tanya had arrived at her sister's flat in the middle of the night, in a terrible state, a state you simply could not imagine. Anton Petrovich suddenly found it strange to be saying '*ty*' (thou) to Natasha. After all, he was no longer married to her sister.

'I shall give her a certain sum every month under certain conditions,' he said, trying to keep a rising hysterical note out of his voice.

'Money isn't the point,' answered Natasha, sitting in front of him and swinging her glossily stockinged leg. 'The point is that this is an absolutely awful mess.'

'Thanks for coming,' said Anton Petrovich, 'we'll have another chat some time, only right now I'm very busy.' As he saw her to the door, he remarked casually (or at least he hoped it sounded casual), 'I'm fighting a duel with him.' Natasha's lips quivered; she quickly kissed him on the cheek and went out. How strange that she did not start imploring him not to fight. By all rights she ought to have implored him not to fight. In our time nobody fights duels. She is wearing the same perfume as ... As who? No, no, he had never been married.

A little later still, at about seven, Mityushin and Gnushke arrived. They looked grim. Gnushke bowed with reserve and handed Anton Petrovich a sealed business envelope. He opened it. It began: 'I have received your extremely stupid and extremely rude message ...' Anton Petrovich's monocle fell out, he reinserted it. 'I feel very sorry for you, but since you have adopted this attitude, I have no choice but to accept your challenge. Your seconds are pretty awful. Berg.'

Anton Petrovich's throat went unpleasantly dry, and there was again that ridiculous quaking in his legs.

'Sit down, sit down,' he said, and himself sat down first. Gnushke sank back into an armchair, caught himself and sat up on its edge.

'He's a highly insolent character,' Mityushin said with feeling. 'Imagine – he kept laughing all the while, so that I nearly punched him in the teeth.'

Gnushke cleared his throat and said, 'There is only one thing I can advise you to do: take careful aim, because he is also going to take careful aim.'

Before Anton Petrovich's eyes flashed a notebook page covered with X's: diagram of a cemetery.

'He is a dangerous fellow,' said Gnushke, leaning back in his armchair, sinking again, and again wriggling out.

'Who's going to make the report, Henry, you or I?' asked Mityushin, chewing on a cigarette as he jerked at his lighter with his thumb.

'You'd better do it,' said Gnushke.

'We've had a very busy day,' began Mityushin, goggling his baby-blue eyes at Anton Petrovich. 'At exactly eight-thirty Henry, who was still as tight as a drum, and I . . .'

'I protest,' said Gnushke.

'. . . went to call on Mr Berg. He was sipping his coffee. Right off we handed him your little note. Which he read. And what did he do, Henry? Yes, he burst out laughing. We waited for him to finish laughing, and Henry asked what his plans were.'

'No, not his plans, but how he intended to react,' Gnushke corrected.

'. . . to react. To this, Mr Berg replied that he agreed to fight and that he chose pistols. We have settled all the conditions: the combatants will be placed facing each other at twenty paces. Firing will be regulated by a word of command. If nobody is dead after the first exchange, the duel may go on. And on. What else was there, Henry?'

'If it is impossible to procure real dueling pistols, then Browning automatics will be used,' said Gnushke.

'Browning automatics. Having established this much, we asked Mr Berg how to get in touch with his seconds. He went out to telephone. Then he wrote the letter you have before you. Incidentally, he kept joking all the time. The next thing we did was to go to a café to meet his two chums. I bought Gnushke a carnation for his buttonhole. It was by this carnation that they recognized us. They introduced themselves, and, well, to put it in a nutshell, everything is in order. Their names are Marx and Engels.'

'That's not quite exact,' interjected Gnushke. 'They are Markov and Colonel Arkhangelski.'

'No matter,' said Mityushin and went on. 'Here begins the epic part. We went out of town with these chaps to look for a suitable spot. You know Weissdorf, just beyond Wannsee. That's it. We took a walk through the woods there and found a glade, where, it turned out, these chaps had had a little picnic with their girls the other day. The glade is small, and all around there is nothing but woods. In short, the ideal spot – although, of course, you don't get the grand mountain decor as in Lermontov's fatal affair. See the state of my boots – all white with dust.'

'Mine too,' said Gnushke. 'I must say that trip was quite a strenuous one.'

There followed a pause.

'It's hot today,' said Mityushin. 'Even hotter than yesterday.'

'Considerably hotter,' said Gnushke.

With exaggerated thoroughness Mityushin began crushing his cigarette in the ashtray. Silence. Anton Petrovich's heart was beating in his throat. He tried to swallow it, but it started pounding even harder. When would the duel take place? Tomorrow? Why didn't they tell him? Maybe the day after tomorrow? It would be better the day after tomorrow ...

Mityushin and Gnushke exchanged glances and got up.

'We shall call for you tomorrow at six-thirty A.M.,' said Mityushin. 'There is no point in leaving sooner. There isn't a damn soul out there anyway.'

Anton Petrovich got up too. What should he do? Thank them?

'Well, thank you, gentlemen ... Thank you, gentlemen ... Everything is settled, then. All right, then.'

The others bowed.

'We must still find a doctor and the pistols,' said Gnushke.

In the front hall Anton Petrovich took Mityushin by the elbow and mumbled, 'You know, it's awfully silly, but you see, I don't know how to shoot, so to speak, I mean, I know how, but I've had no practice at all ...'

'Hm,' said Mityushin, 'that's too bad. Today is Sunday,

otherwise you could have taken a lesson or two. That's really bad luck.'

'Colonel Arkhangelski gives private shooting lessons,' put in Gnushke.

'Yes,' said Mityushin. 'You're the smart one, aren't you? Still, what are we to do, Anton Petrovich? You know what – beginners are lucky. Put your trust in God and just press the trigger.'

They left. Dusk was falling. Nobody had lowered the blinds. There must be some cheese and graham bread in the sideboard. The rooms were deserted and motionless, as if all the furniture had once breathed and moved about but had now died. A ferocious cardboard dentist bending over a panic stricken patient of cardboard – this he had seen such a short time ago, on a blue, green, violet, ruby night, shot with fireworks, at the Luna Amusement Park. Berg took a long time aiming, the air rifle popped, the pellet hit the target, releasing a spring, and the cardboard dentist yanked out a huge tooth with a quadruple root. Tanya clapped her hands, Anton Petrovich smiled, Berg fired again, and the cardboard discs rattled as they spun, the clay pipes were shattered one after another, and the ping-pong ball dancing on a slender jet of water disappeared. How awful ... And, most awful of all, Tanya had then said jokingly, 'It wouldn't be much fun fighting a duel with you.' Twenty paces. Anton Petrovich went from door to window, counting the paces. Eleven. He inserted his monocle, and tried to estimate the distance. Two such rooms. Oh, if only he could manage to disable Berg at the first fire. But he did not know how to aim the thing. He was bound to miss. Here, this letter opener, for example. No, better take this paperweight. You are supposed to hold it like this and take aim. Or like this, perhaps, right up near your chin – it seems easier to do it this way. And at this instant, as he held before him the paperweight in the form of a parrot, pointing it this way and that, Anton Petrovich realized that he would be killed.

At about ten he decided to go to bed. The bedroom, though, was taboo. With great effort he found some clean bedclothes in the dresser, recased the pillow and spread a sheet over the leather couch in the parlor. As he undressed, he thought, 'I am going to bed for the last time in my life.' 'Nonsense,' faintly squeaked some little particle of Anton Petrovich's soul, the same particle that had made him throw the glove, slam the door and call Berg a scoundrel. 'Nonsense!' Anton Petrovich said in a thin voice, and at once told himself it was not right to say such things. If I think that nothing will happen to me, then the worst will happen. Everything in life always happens the other way around. It would be nice to read something – for the last time – before going to sleep.

'There I go again,' he moaned inwardly. 'Why for the last time? I am in a terrible state. I must take hold of myself. Oh, if only I were given some sign. Cards?'

He found a deck of cards on a near-by console and took the top card, a three of diamonds. What does the three of diamonds mean chiromantically? No idea. Then he drew, in that order, the queen of diamonds, the eight of clubs, the ace of spades. Ah! That's bad. The ace of spades – I think that means death. But then that's a lot of nonsense, superstitious nonsense ... Midnight. Five past. Tomorrow has become today. I have a duel today.

He sought peace in vain. Strange things kept happening: the book he was holding, a novel by some German writer or other, was called *The Magic Mountain,* and mountain, in German, is 'Berg'; he decided that if he counted to three and a streetcar went by at 'three' he would be killed, and a streetcar obliged. And then Anton Petrovich did the very worst thing a man in his situation could have done: he decided to reason out what death really meant. When he had thought along these lines for a minute or so, everything lost sense. He found it difficult to breathe. He got up, walked about the room and took a look out the window at the pure and terrible night sky. 'Must write my testament,' thought Anton Petrovich. But to make a will was, so to speak, playing with fire; it meant inspecting the contents of one's own urn in the columbarium. 'Best thing is to get some sleep,' he said aloud. But as soon as he closed his eyelids, Berg's grinning face would appear before him, purposively slitting one eye. He would turn on the light again, attempt to read, smoke, though he was not a regular smoker. Trivial memories floated by – a toy pistol, a path in the park, that sort of thing – and he would immediately cut short his recollections with the thought that those who are about to die always remember trifles from their past. Then the opposite thing frightened him: he realized that he was not thinking of Tanya, that he was numbed by a strange drug that made him insensitive to her absence. She was my life and she has gone, he thought. I have already, unconsciously, bid life farewell, and everything is now indifferent to me, since I shall be killed ... The night, meanwhile, was beginning to wane.

At about four he shuffled into the dining room and drank a glass of soda water. A mirror near which he passed reflected his striped pajamas and thinning, wispy hair. 'I'm going to look like my own ghost,' he thought. 'But how can I get some sleep? How?'

He wrapped himself in a lap robe, for he noticed that his teeth were chattering, and sat down in an armchair in the middle of the dim room that was slowly ascertaining itself. How will it all be? I must dress soberly, but elegantly. Tuxedo? No, that would be idiotic. A black suit, then ... and, yes, a black tie. The new black suit. But if there's a wound, a shoulder wound, say ... The suit will be ruined ... The blood, the hole and, besides, they may start cutting off the sleeve. Nonsense, nothing of the sort is going to happen. I must wear my new black suit. And when the duel starts, I shall turn up my jacket collar – that's the custom, I think, in order to conceal the whiteness of one's shirt, probably, or simply because of the morning damp. That's how they did it in that film I saw. Then I must keep absolutely cool, and address everyone politely and calmly. Thank you, I have already fired. It is your turn now. If you do not remove that cigarette from your mouth I shall not fire. I am ready to continue. 'Thank you, I have already laughed' – that's what you say to a stale joker ... Oh, if one could only imagine all the details! They would arrive – he, Mityushin and Gnushke – in a car, leave the car on the road, walk into the woods. Berg and his seconds would probably be waiting there already, they always do in books. Now, there was a question: does one salute one's opponent? What does Onegin do in the opera? Perhaps a discreet tip of the hat from a distance would be just right. Then they would probably start marking off the yards and loading the pistols. What would he do meanwhile? Yes, of course – he would place one foot on a stump somewhere a little way off, and wait in a casual attitude. But what if Berg also put one foot on a stump? Berg was capable of it ... Mimicking me to embarrass me. That would be awful. Other possibilities would be to lean against a tree trunk, or simply sit down on the grass. Somebody (in a Pushkin story?) ate cherries from a paper bag. Yes, but you have to bring that bag to the dueling ground – looks silly. Oh, well, he would decide when the time came. Dignified and nonchalant. Then we would take our positions. Twenty yards between us. It would be then that he should turn up his collar. He would grasp the pistol like this. Colonel Angel would wave a handkerchief or count till three. And then, suddenly, something utterly terrible, something absurd would happen – an unimaginable thing, even if one thought about it for nights on end, even if one lived to be a hundred in Turkey ... Nice to travel, sit in cafés ... What does one feel when a bullet hits one between the ribs or in the forehead? Pain? Nausea? Or is there simply a bang followed by total darkness? The tenor Sobinov once crashed down so realistically that his pistol flew into the orchestra. And what if, instead, he received a ghastly wound of some kind – in one eye, or in the groin? No, Berg would kill him outright. Of course, here I've counted only the ones I killed outright. One more cross in that little black book. Unimaginable ...

The dining-room clock struck five: ding-dawn. With a tremendous effort, shivering and clutching at the lap robe, Anton Petrovich got up, then paused again, lost in thought, and suddenly stamped his foot, as Louis XVI stamped his when told it was time, Your Majesty, to go to the scaffold. Nothing to be done about it. Stamped his soft clumsy foot. The execution was inevitable. Time to shave, wash and dress. Scrupulously clean underwear and the new black suit. As he inserted the opal links into his shirt cuffs, Anton Petrovich mused that opals were the stones of fate and that it was only two or three hours before the shirt would be all bloody. Where would the hole be? He stroked the shiny hairs that went down his fat warm chest, and felt so frightened that he covered his eyes with his hand. There was something pathetically independent about the way everything within him was moving now – the heart pulsating, the lungs swelling, the blood circulating, the intestines contracting – and he was leading to slaughter this tender, defenseless, inner creature, that lived so blindly, so trustingly ... Slaughter! He grabbed his favorite shirt, undid one button and grunted as he plunged head first into the cold, white darkness of the linen enveloping him. Socks, tie. He awkwardly shined his shoes with a chamois rag. As he searched for a clean handkerchief he stumbled on a stick of rouge. He glanced into the mirror at his hideously pale face, and then tentatively touched his cheek with the crimson stuff. At first it made him look even worse than before. He licked his finger and rubbed his cheek, regretting that he had never taken a close look at how women apply make-up. A light, brick hue was finally imparted to his cheeks, and he decided it looked all right. 'There, I'm ready now,' he said, addressing the mirror; then came an agonizing yawn, and the mirror dissolved into tears. He rapidly scented his handkerchief, distributed papers, handkerchief, keys, and fountain pen in various pockets and slipped into the black noose of his monocle. Pity I don't have a good pair of gloves. The pair I had was nice and new, but the left glove is widowed. The drawback inherent in duels. He sat down at his writing desk, placed his elbows on it, and began waiting, glancing now out of the window, now at the traveling clock in its folding leather case.

It was a beautiful morning. The sparrows twittered like mad in the tall linden tree under the window. A pale-blue velvet shadow covered the street, and here and there a roof would flash silver. Anton Petrovich was cold and had an unbearable headache. A nip of brandy would be paradise. None in the house. House already deserted; master going away forever. Oh, nonsense. We insist on calmness. The front door bell will ring in a moment. I must keep perfectly calm. The bell is going to ring right now. They are already three minutes late. Maybe they won't come? Such a marvelous summer morning ... Who was the last person killed in a duel in Russia? A Baron Manteuffel, twenty years ago. No, they won't come. Good. He would wait another half-hour, and then go to bed – the bedroom was losing its horror and becoming definitely attractive. Anton Petrovich opened his mouth wide, preparing to squeeze out a huge lump of yawn – he felt the crunch in his ears, the swelling under his palate – and it was then that the door bell brutally rang. Spasmodically swallowing the unfinished yawn, Anton Petrovich went into the front hall, unlocked the door and Mityushin and Gnushke ushered each other across the threshold.

'Time to go,' said Mityushin, gazing intently at Anton Petrovich. He was wearing his usual pistachio-colored tie, but Gnushke had put on an old frock coat.

'Yes, I am ready,' said Anton Petrovich, 'I'll be right with you . . .'

He left them standing in the front hall, rushed into the bedroom, and, in order to gain time, started washing his hands, while he kept repeating to himself, 'What is happening? My God, what is happening?' Just five minutes ago there had still been hope, there might have been an earthquake, Berg might have died of a heart attack, fate might have intervened, suspended events, saved him.

'Anton Petrovich, hurry up,' called Mityushin from the front hall. Quickly he dried his hands and joined the others.

'Yes, yes, I'm ready, let's go.'

'We'll have to take the train,' said Mityushin when they were outside. 'Because if we arrive by taxi in the middle of the forest, and at this hour, it might seem suspicious, and the driver might tell the police. Anton Petrovich, please don't start losing your nerve.'

'I'm not – don't be silly,' replied Anton Petrovich with a helpless smile.

Gnushke, who had remained silent until this point, loudly blew his nose and said matter-of-factly:

'Our adversary is bringing the doctor. We were unable to find dueling pistols. However, our colleagues did procure two identical Brownings.'

In the taxi that was to take them to the station, they seated themselves thus: Anton Petrovich and Mityushin in back, and Gnushke facing them on the jump seat, with his legs pulled in. Anton Petrovich was again overcome by a nervous fit of yawning. That revengeful yawn he had suppressed. Again and again came that humpy spasm, so that his eyes watered. Mityushin and Gnushke looked very solemn, but at the same time seemed exceedingly pleased with themselves.

Anton Petrovich clenched his teeth and yawned with his nostrils only. Then, abruptly, he said, 'I had an excellent night's sleep.' He tried to think of something else to say . . .

'Quite a few people in the streets,' he said, and added, 'In spite of the early hour.' Mityushin and Gnushke were silent. Another fit of yawning. Oh, God . . .

They soon arrived at the station. It seemed to Anton Petrovich that he had never traveled so fast. Gnushke bought the tickets, and, holding them fanwise, went ahead. Suddenly he looked around at Mityushin and cleared his throat significantly. By the refreshment booth stood Berg. He was getting some change out of his trouser pocket, thrusting his left hand deep inside it, and holding the pocket in place with his right, the way Anglo-Saxons do in cartoons. He produced a coin in the palm of his hand, and, as he handed it to the woman vendor, said something that made her laugh. Berg laughed too. He stood with legs slightly spread. He was wearing a gray flannel suit.

'Let's go around that booth,' said Mityushin. 'It would be awkward passing right next to him.'

A strange numbness came over Anton Petrovich. Totally unconscious of what he was doing, he boarded the coach, took a window seat, removed his hat, donned it again. Only when the train jerked and began to move did his brain start working again, and in this instant he was possessed by the feeling that comes in dreams when, speeding along in a train from nowhere to nowhere, you suddenly realize that you are traveling clad only in your underpants.

'They are in the next coach,' said Mityushin taking out a cigarette case. 'Why on earth do you keep yawning all the time, Anton Petrovich? It gives one the creeps.'

'I always do in the morning,' mechanically answered Anton Petrovich.

Pine trees, pine trees, pine trees. A sandy slope. More pine trees. Such a marvelous morning . . .

104

'That frock coat, Henry, is not a success,' said Mityushin. 'No question about it – to put it bluntly – it just isn't.'

'That is my business,' said Gnushke.

Lovely, those pines. And now a gleam of water. Woods again. How touching, the world, how fragile ... If I could only keep from yawning again ... jaws aching. If you restrain the yawn, your eyes begin watering. He was sitting with his face turned toward the window, listening to the wheels beating out the rhythm 'Abattoir ... abattoir ... abattoir ...'

'Here's what I advise you to do,' said Gnushke. 'Blaze at once. I advise you to aim at the center of his body – you have more of a chance that way.'

'It's all a question of luck,' said Mityushin. 'If you hit him, fine, and if not, don't worry – he might miss too. A duel becomes real only after the first exchange. It is then that the interesting part begins, so to speak.'

A station. Did not stop long. Why did they torture him so? To die today would be unthinkable. What if I faint? You have to be a good actor ... What can I try? What shall I do? Such a marvelous morning ...

'Anton Petrovich, excuse me for asking,' said Mityushin, 'but it's important. You don't have anything to entrust to us? I mean, papers, documents. A letter, maybe, or a will? It's the usual procedure.'

Anton Petrovich shook his head.

'Pity,' said Mityushin. 'Never know what might happen. Take Henry and me – we're all set for a sojourn in jail. Are your affairs in order?'

Anton Petrovich nodded. He was no longer able to speak. The only way to keep from screaming was to watch the pines that kept flashing past.

'We get off in a minute,' said Gnushke, and rose. Mityushin rose also. Clenching his teeth, Anton Petrovich wanted to rise too, but a jolt of the train made him fall back into his seat.

'Here we are,' said Mityushin.

Only then did Anton Petrovich manage to separate himself from the seat. Pressing his monocle into his eye socket, he cautiously descended to the platform. The sun welcomed him warmly.

'They are behind,' said Gnushke. Anton Petrovich felt his back growing a hump. No, this is unthinkable, I must wake up.

They left the station and set out along the highway, past tiny brick houses with petunias in the windows. There was a tavern at the intersection of the highway and of a soft, white road leading off into the forest. Suddenly Anton Petrovich stopped.

'I'm awfully thirsty,' he muttered. 'I could do with a drop of something.'

'Yes, wouldn't hurt,' said Mityushin. Gnushke looked back and said, 'They have left the road and turned into the woods.'

'It will only take a minute,' said Mityushin.

The three of them entered the tavern. A fat woman was wiping the counter with a rag. She scowled at them and poured three mugs of beer.

Anton Petrovich swallowed, choked slightly and said, 'Excuse me for a second.'

'Hurry,' said Mityushin, putting his mug back on the bar.

Anton Petrovich turned into the passage, followed the arrow to men, mankind, human beings, marched past the toilet, past the kitchen, gave a start when a cat darted under his feet, quickened his step, reached the end of the passage, pushed open a door and a shower of sunlight splashed his face. He found himself in a little green yard, where hens walked about and a boy in a faded bathing suit sat on a log. Anton Petrovich rushed past him, past some elder bushes, down a couple of wooden steps and into more bushes, then suddenly slipped, for the ground sloped. Branches whipped against his face, and he pushed them aside awkwardly, diving and slipping; the slope, overgrown with elder, kept growing steeper. At last his headlong descent became uncontrollable. He slid down on tense, outspread legs, warding off the springy twigs. Then he embraced an unexpected tree at full speed, and began moving obliquely. The bushes thinned out. Ahead was a tall fence. He saw a loophole in it, rustled through the nettles and found himself in a pine grove, where shadow-dappled laundry hung between the tree trunks near a shack. With the same purposefulness he traversed the grove and presently realized that he was again sliding downhill. Ahead of him water shimmered among the trees. He stumbled, then saw a path to his right. It led him to the lake.

An old fisherman, suntanned, the color of smoked flounder and wearing a straw hat, indicated the way to the Wannsee station. The road at first skirted the lake, then turned into the forest, and he wandered through the woods for about two hours before emerging at the railroad tracks. He trudged to the nearest station, and as he reached it a train approached. He boarded a car and squeezed in between two passengers, who glanced with curiosity at this fat, pale, moist man in black, with painted cheeks and dirty shoes, a monocle in his begrimed eye socket. Only upon reaching Berlin did he pause for a moment, or at least he had the sensation that, up to that moment, he had been fleeing continuously and only now had stopped to catch his breath and look around him. He was in a familiar square. Beside him an old flower woman with an enormous woolen bosom was selling carnations. A man in an armor-like coating of newspapers was touting the title of a local scandal sheet. A shoeshine man gave Anton Petrovich a fawning look. Anton Petrovich sighed with relief and placed his foot firmly on the stand; whereupon the man's elbows began working lickety-split.

'It is all horrible, of course,' he thought, as he watched the tip of his shoe begin to gleam. 'But I am alive, and for the moment that is the main thing.' Mityushin and Gnushke had probably traveled back to town and were standing guard before his house, so he would have to wait a while for things to blow over. In no circumstances must he meet them. Much later he would go to fetch his things. And he must leave Berlin that very night . . .

'*Dobryy den*' (Good day), Anton Petrovich,' came a gentle voice right above his ear.

He gave such a start that his foot slipped off the stand. No, it was all right – false alarm. The voice belonged to a certain Leontiev, a man he had met three or four times, a journalist or something of the sort. A talkative but harmless fellow. They said his wife deceived him right and left.

'Out for a stroll?' asked Leontiev, giving him a melancholy handshake.

'Yes. No, I have various things to do,' replied Anton Petrovich, thinking at the same time, 'I hope he proceeds on his way, otherwise it will be quite dreadful.'

Leontiev looked around, and said, as if he had made a happy discovery, 'Splendid weather!'

Actually he was a pessimist and, like all pessimists, a ridiculously unobservant man. His face was ill-shaven, yellowish and long, and all of him looked clumsy, emaciated and lugubrious, as if nature had suffered from toothache when creating him.

The shoeshine man jauntily clapped his brushes together. Anton Petrovich looked at his revived shoes.

'Which way are you headed?' asked Leontiev.

'And you?' asked Anton Petrovich.

'Makes no difference to me. I'm free right now. I can keep you company for a while.' He cleared his throat and added insinuatingly, 'If you allow me, of course.'

'Of course, please do,' mumbled Anton Petrovich. Now he's attached himself, he thought. Must find some less familiar street, or else more acquaintances will turn up. If I can only avoid meeting those two ...

'Well, how is life treating you?' asked Leontiev. He belonged to the breed of people who ask how life is treating you only to give a detailed account of how it is treating them.

'Oh, well, I am all right,' Anton Petrovich replied. Of course he'll find out all about it afterwards. Good Lord, what a mess. 'I am going this way,' he said aloud, and turned sharply. Smiling sadly at his own thoughts, Leontiev almost ran into him and swayed slightly on lanky legs. 'This way? All right, it's all the same to me.'

'What shall I do?' thought Anton Petrovich. 'After all, I can't just keep strolling with him like this. I have to think things over and decide so much ... And I'm awfully tired, and my corns hurt.'

As for Leontiev, he had already launched into a long story. He spoke in a level, unhurried voice. He spoke of how much he paid for his room, how hard it was to pay, how hard life was for him and his wife, how rarely one got a good landlady, how insolent theirs was with his wife.

'Adelaida Albertovna, of course, has a quick temper herself,' he added with a sigh. He was one of those middle-class Russians who use the patronymic when speaking of their spouses.

They were walking along an anonymous street where the pavement was being repaired. One of the workmen had a dragon tattooed on his bare chest. Anton Petrovich wiped his forehead with his handkerchief and said:

'I have some business near here. They are waiting for me. A business appointment.'

'Oh, I'll walk you there,' said Leontiev sadly.

Anton Petrovich surveyed the street. A sign said 'Hotel'. A squalid and squat little hotel between a scaffolded building and a warehouse.

'I have to go in here,' said Anton Petrovich. 'Yes, this hotel. A business appointment.'

Leontiev took off his torn glove and gave him a soft handshake. 'Know what? I think I'll wait a while for you. Won't be long, will you?'

'Quite long, I'm afraid,' said Anton Petrovich.

'Pity. You see, I wanted to talk something over with you, and ask your advice. Well, no matter. I'll wait around for a while, just in case. Maybe you'll get through early.'

Anton Petrovich went into the hotel. He had no choice. It was empty and darkish inside. A disheveled person materialized from behind a desk and asked what he wanted.

'A room,' Anton Petrovich answered softly.

The man pondered this, scratched his head and demanded a deposit. Anton Petrovich handed over ten marks. A red-haired maid, rapidly wiggling her behind, led him down a long corridor and unlocked a door. He entered, heaved a deep sigh and sat down in a low armchair of ribbed velvet. He was alone. The furniture, the bed, the washstand seemed to awake, to give him a frowning look, and go back to sleep. In this drowsy, totally unremarkable hotel room, Anton Petrovich was at last alone.

Hunching over, covering his eyes with his hand, he lapsed into thought, and before him bright, speckled images passed by, patches of sunny greenery, a boy on a log, a fisherman, Leontiev, Berg, Tanya. And, at the thought of Tanya, he moaned and hunched over even more tensely. Her voice, her dear voice. So light, so girlish, quick of eye and limb, she would perch on the sofa, tuck her legs under her, and her skirt would float up around her like a silk dome and then drop back. Or else, she would sit at the table, quite motionless, only blinking now and then, and blowing out cigarette smoke with her face upturned. It's senseless ... Why did you cheat? For you did cheat. What shall I do without you? Tanya! ... Don't you see – you cheated. My darling – why? Why?

Emitting little moans and cracking his finger joints, he began pacing up and down the room, bumping against the furniture without noticing it. He happened to stop by the window and glance out into the street. At first he could not see the street because of the mist in his eyes, but presently the street appeared, with a truck at the curb, a bicyclist, an old lady gingerly stepping off the sidewalk. And along the sidewalk slowly strolled Leontiev, reading a newspaper as he went; he passed and turned the corner. And, for some reason, at the sight of Leontiev, Anton Petrovich realized just how hopeless his situation was – yes, hopeless, for there was no other word for it. Only yesterday he had been a perfectly honorable man, respected by friends, acquaintances, and fellow workers at the bank. His job! There was not even any question of it. Everything was different now: he had run down a slippery slope, and now he was at the bottom.

'But how can it be? I must decide to do something,' Anton Petrovich said in a thin voice. Perhaps there was a way out? They had tormented him for a while, but enough was enough. Yes, he had to decide. He remembered the suspicious gaze of the man at the desk. What should one say to that person? Oh, obviously: 'I'm going to fetch my luggage – I left it at the station.' So. Goodbye for ever, little hotel! The street, thank God, was now clear: Leontiev had finally given up and left. How do I get to the nearest streetcar stop? Oh, just go straight, my dear sir, and you will reach the nearest streetcar stop. No, better take a taxi. Off we go. The streets grow familiar again. Calmly, quite calmly. Tip the taxi driver. Home! Five floors. Calmly, quite calmly he went into the front hall. Then quickly opened the parlor door. My, what a surprise!

In the parlor, around the circular table, sat Mityushin, Gnushke and Tanya. On the table stood bottles, glasses, and cups. Mityushin beamed – pink-faced, shiny-eyed, drunk as an owl. Gnushke was drunk too, and also beamed, rubbing his hands together. Tanya was sitting with her bare elbows on the table, gazing at him motionlessly . . .

'At last!' exclaimed Mityushin, and took him by the arm. 'At last you've shown up!' He added in a whisper, with a mischievous wink, 'You sly-boots, you!'

Anton Petrovich now sits down and has some vodka. Mityushin and Gnushke keep giving him the same mischievous but good-natured looks. Tanya says:

'You must be hungry. I'll get you a sandwich.'

Yes, a big ham sandwich, with the edge of fat overlapping. She goes to make it and then Mityushin and Gnushke rush to him and begin to talk, interrupting each other.

'You lucky fellow! Just imagine – Mr Berg also lost his nerve. Well, not "also" but lost his nerve anyhow. While we were waiting for you at the tavern, his seconds came in and announced that Berg had changed his mind. Those broad-shouldered bullies always turn out to be cowards. "Gentlemen, we ask you to excuse us for having agreed to act as seconds for this scoundrel." That's how lucky you are, Anton Petrovich! So everything is now just dandy. And you came out of it honorably, while he is disgraced forever. And, most important, your wife, when she heard about it, immediately left Berg and returned to you. And you must forgive her.'

Anton Petrovich smiled broadly, got up and started fiddling with the ribbon of his monocle. His smile slowly faded away. Such things don't happen in real life.

He looked at the moth-eaten plush, the plump bed, the washstand, and this wretched room in this wretched hotel seemed to him to be the room in which he would have to live from that day on. He sat down on the bed, took off his shoes, wiggled his toes with relief and noticed that there was a blister on his heel, and a corresponding hole in his sock. Then he rang the bell and ordered a ham sandwich. When the maid placed the plate on the table, he deliberately looked away but as soon as the door had shut, he grabbed the sandwich with both hands, immediately soiled his fingers and chin with the hanging margin of fat, and, grunting greedily, began to munch.

Terra Incognita

The Russian original of 'Terra Incognita' appeared under the same title in *Posledniya Novosti*, Paris, 22 November 1931, and was reprinted in my collection *Soglyadatay*, Paris, 1938. The present English translation was published in *The New Yorker*, 18 May 1963.

The sound of the waterfall grew more and more muffled, until it finally dissolved altogether, and we moved on through the wildwood of a hitherto unexplored region. We walked, and had been walking, for a long time already – in front, Gregson and I; our eight native porters behind, one after the other; last of all, whining and protesting at every step, came Cook. I knew that Gregson had recruited him on the advice of a local hunter. Cook had insisted that he was ready to do anything to get out of Zonraki, where they pass half the year brewing their 'von-gho' and the other half drinking it. It remained unclear, however – or else I was already beginning to forget many things, as we walked on and on – exactly who this Cook was (a runaway sailor, perhaps?).

Gregson strode on beside me, sinewy, lanky, with bare, bony knees. He held a long-handled green butterfly net like a banner. The porters, big, glossy-brown Badonians with thick manes of hair and cobalt arabesques between their eyes, whom we had also engaged in Zonraki, walked with a strong, even step. Behind them straggled Cook, bloated, red-haired, with a drooping underlip, hands in pockets and carrying nothing. I recalled vaguely that at the outset of the expedition he had chattered a lot and made obscure jokes, in a manner he had, a mixture of insolence and servility, reminiscent of a Shakespearean clown; but soon his spirits fell and he grew glum and began to neglect his duties, which included interpreting, since Gregson's understanding of the Badonian dialect was still poor.

There was something languorous and velvety about the heat. A stifling fragrance came from the inflorescences of *Vallieria mirifica*, mother-of-pearl in color and resembling clusters of soap bubbles, that arched across the narrow, dry stream bed along which we proceeded. The branches of porphyroferous trees intertwined with those of the Black-Leafed Limia to form a tunnel, penetrated here and there by a ray of hazy light. Above, in the thick mass of vegetation, among brilliant pendulous racemes and strange dark tangles of some kind, hoary monkeys snapped and chattered, while a cometlike bird flashed like Bengal light, crying out in its small, shrill voice. I kept telling myself that my head was heavy from the long march, the heat, the medley of colors and the forest din, but secretly I knew that I was ill. I surmised it to be the local fever. I had resolved, however, to conceal my condition from Gregson, and had assumed a cheerful, even merry air, when disaster struck.

'It's my fault,' said Gregson. 'I should never have got involved with him.'

We were now alone. Cook and all eight of the natives, with tent, folding boat, supplies and collections, had deserted us and vanished noiselessly while we busied ourselves in the thick bush, chasing fascinating insects. I think we tried to catch up with the fugitives – I do not recall clearly, but, in any case, we failed. We had to decide whether to return to Zonraki or continue our projected itinerary, across as yet unknown country, toward the Gurano Hills. The unknown won out. We moved on. I was already shivering all over and deafened by quinine, but still went on collecting nameless plants, while Gregson, though fully realizing the danger of our situation, continued catching butterflies and Diptera as avidly as ever.

We had scarcely walked half a mile when suddenly Cook overtook us. His shirt was torn – apparently by himself, deliberately – and he was panting and gasping. Without a word Gregson drew his revolver and prepared to shoot the scoundrel, but he threw himself at Gregson's feet and, shielding his head with both arms, began to swear that the natives had led him away by force and had wanted to eat him (which was a lie, for the Badonians are not cannibals). I suspect that he had easily incited them, stupid and timorous as they were, to abandon the dubious journey, but had not taken into account that he could not keep up with their powerful stride, and, having fallen hopelessly behind, had returned to us. Because of him invaluable collections were lost. He had to die. But Gregson put away the revolver and we moved on, with Cook wheezing and stumbling behind.

The woods were gradually thinning. I was tormented by strange hallucinations. I gazed at the weird tree trunks, around some of which were coiled thick, flesh-colored snakes; suddenly I thought I saw, between the trunks, as though through my fingers, the mirror of a half-open wardrobe with dim reflections, but then I took hold of myself, looked more carefully and found that it was only the deceptive glimmer of an acreana bush (a curly plant with large berries resembling plump prunes). After a while the trees parted altogether and the sky rose before us like a solid wall of blue. We were at the top of a steep incline. Below shimmered and steamed an enormous marsh, and, far beyond, one distinguished the tremulous silhouette of a mauve-colored range of hills.

'I swear to God we must turn back,' said Cook in a sobbing voice. 'I swear to God we'll perish in these swamps – I've got seven daughters and a dog at home. Let's turn back – we know the way ...'

He wrung his hands, and the sweat rolled from his fat, red-browed face. 'Home, home,' he kept repeating. 'You've caught enough bugs. Let's go home!'

Gregson and I began to descend the stony slope. At first Cook remained standing above, a small white figure against the monstrously green background of forest; but suddenly he threw up his hands, uttered a cry, and started to slither down after us.

The slope narrowed, forming a rocky crest that reached out like a long promontory into the marshes; they sparkled through the steamy haze. The noonday sky, now freed of its leafy veils, hung oppressively over us with its blinding darkness – yes, its blinding darkness, for there is no other way to describe it. I tried not to look up; but in this sky, at the very verge of my field of vision, there floated, always keeping up with me, whitish phantoms of plaster, stucco curlicues and rosettes, like those used to adorn European ceilings; however, I had only to look directly at them and they would vanish, and again the tropical sky would boom, as it were, with even, dense blueness. We were still walking along the rocky promontory, but it kept tapering and betraying us. Around it grew golden marsh reeds, like a million bared swords gleaming in the sun. Here and there flashed elongated pools, and over them hung dark swarms of midges. A large swamp flower, presumably an orchid, stretched toward me its drooping, downy lip, which seemed smeared with egg yolk. Gregson swung his net – and sank to his hips in the brocaded ooze as a gigantic swallowtail, with a flap of its satin wing, sailed away from him over the reeds, toward the shimmer of pale emanations where the indistinct folds of a window curtain seemed to hang. *I must not,* I said to myself, *I must not* ... I shifted my gaze and walked on beside Gregson, now over rock, now across hissing and lip-smacking soil. I felt chills, in spite of the greenhouse heat. I foresaw that in a moment I would collapse altogether, that the contours and convexities of delirium, showing through the sky and through the golden reeds, would gain complete control of my consciousness. At times Gregson and Cook seemed to grow transparent, and I thought I saw, through them, wallpaper with an endlessly repeated design of reeds. I took hold of myself, strained to keep my eyes open and moved on. Cook by now was crawling on all fours, yelling, and snatching at Gregson's legs, but the latter would shake him off and keep walking. I looked at Gregson, at his stubborn profile, and felt, to my horror, that I was forgetting who Gregson was, and why I was with him.

Meanwhile we kept sinking into the ooze more and more frequently, deeper and deeper; the insatiable mire would suck at us; and, wriggling, we would slip free. Cook kept falling down and crawling, covered with insect bites, all swollen and soaked, and, dear God, how he would squeal when disgusting bevies of minute, bright-green hydrotic snakes, attracted by our sweat, would take off in pursuit of us, tensing and uncoiling to sail two yards and then another two. I, however, was much more frightened by something else: now and then, on my left (always, for some reason, on my left), listing among the repetitious reeds, what seemed a large armchair but was actually a strange, cumbersome gray amphibian, whose name Gregson refused to tell me, would rise out of the swamp.

'A break,' said Gregson abruptly, 'let's take a break.'

By a stroke of luck we managed to scramble onto an islet of rock, surrounded by the swamp vegetation. Gregson took off his knapsack and issued us some native patties, smelling of ipecacuanha, and a dozen acreana fruit. How thirsty I was, and how little help was the scanty, astringent juice of the acreana...

'Look, how odd,' Gregson said to me, not in English, but in some other language, so that Cook would not understand. 'We must get through to the hills, but look, how odd – could the hills have been a mirage? – they are no longer visible.'

I raised myself up from my pillow and leaned my elbow on the resilient surface of the rock ... Yes, it was true that the hills were no longer visible; there was only the quivering vapor hanging over the marsh. Once again everything around me assumed an ambiguous transparency. I leaned back and said softly to Gregson, 'You probably can't see, but something keeps trying to come through.'

'What are you talking about?' asked Gregson.

I realized that what I was saying was nonsense and stopped. My head was spinning and there was a humming in my ears; Gregson, down on one knee, rummaged through his knapsack, but found no medicine there, and my supply was exhausted. Cook sat in silence, morosely picking at a rock. Through a rent in his shirtsleeve there showed a strange tattoo on his arm: a crystal tumbler with a teaspoon, very well executed.

'Vallière is sick – haven't you got some tablets?' Gregson said to him. I did not hear the exact words, but I could guess the general sense of their talk, which would grow absurd and somehow spherical when I tried to listen more closely.

Cook turned slowly and the glassy tattoo slid off his skin to one side, remaining suspended in mid-air; then it floated off, floated off, and I pursued it with my frightened gaze, but, as I turned away, it lost itself in the vapor of the swamp, with a last faint gleam.

'Serves you right,' muttered Cook. 'It's just too bad. The same will happen to you and me. Just too bad ...'

In the course of the last few minutes – that is, ever since we had stopped to rest on the rocky islet – he seemed to have grown larger, had swelled, and there was now something mocking and dangerous about him. Gregson took off his sun helmet and, pulling out a dirty handkerchief, wiped his forehead, which was orange over the brows, and white above that. Then he put on his helmet again, leaned over to me, and said, 'Pull yourself together, please' (or words to that effect). 'We shall try to move on. The vapor is hiding the hills, but they are there. I am certain we have covered about half the swamp.' (This is all very approximate.)

'Murderer,' said Cook under his breath. The tattoo was now again on his forearm; not the entire glass, though, but one side of it – there was not quite enough room for the remainder, which quivered in space, casting reflections. 'Murderer,' Cook repeated with satisfaction, raising his inflamed eyes. 'I told you we would get stuck here. Black dogs eat too much carrion. Mi, re, fa, sol.'

'He's a clown,' I softly informed Gregson, 'a Shakespearean clown.'

'Clow, clow, clow,' Gregson answered, 'clow, clow – clo, clo, clo . . . Do you hear,' he went on, shouting in my ear. 'You must get up. We have to move on.'

The rock was as white and as soft as a bed. I raised myself a little, but promptly fell back on the pillow.

'We shall have to carry him,' said Gregson's faraway voice. 'Give me a hand.'

'Fiddlesticks,' replied Cook (or so it sounded to me). 'I suggest we enjoy some fresh meat before he dries up. Fa, sol, mi, re.'

'He's sick, he's sick too,' I cried to Gregson. 'You're here with two lunatics. Go ahead alone. You'll make it . . . Go.'

'Fat chance we'll let him go,' said Cook.

Meanwhile delirious visions, taking advantage of the general confusion, were quietly and firmly finding their places. The lines of a dim ceiling stretched and crossed in the sky. A large armchair rose, as if supported from below, out of the swamp. Glossy birds flew through the haze of the marsh and, as they settled, one turned into the wooden knob of a bedpost, another into a decanter. Gathering all my will power, I focused my gaze and drove off this dangerous trash. Above the reeds flew real birds with long flame-colored tails. The air buzzed with insects. Gregson was waving away a varicolored fly, and at the same time trying to determine its species. Finally he could contain himself no longer and caught it in his net. His motions underwent curious changes, as if someone kept reshuffling them. I saw him in different poses simultaneously; he was divesting himself of himself, as if he were made of many glass Gregsons whose outlines did not coincide. Then he condensed again, and stood up firmly. He was shaking Cook by the shoulder.

'You are going to help me carry him,' Gregson was saying distinctly. 'If you were not a traitor, we would not be in this mess.'

Cook remained silent, but slowly flushed purple.

'See here, Cook, you'll regret this,' said Gregson. 'I'm telling you for the last time –'

At this point occurred what had been ripening for a long time. Cook drove his head like a bull into Gregson's stomach. They both fell; Gregson had time to get his revolver out, but Cook managed to knock it out of his hand. Then they clutched each other and started rolling in their embrace, panting deafeningly. I looked at them, helpless. Cook's broad back would grow tense and the vertebrae would show through his shirt; but suddenly, instead of his back, ·a leg, also his, would appear, covered with coppery hairs, and with a blue vein running up the skin, and Gregson was rolling on top of him. Gregson's helmet flew off and wobbled away, like half of an enormous cardboard egg. From somewhere in the labyrinth of their bodies Cook's fingers wriggled out, clenching a rusty but sharp knife; the knife entered Gregson's back as if it were clay, but Gregson only gave a grunt, and they both rolled over several times; when I next saw my friend's back the handle and top half of the blade protruded, while his hands had locked around Cook's thick neck, which crunched as he squeezed, and Cook's legs were twitching. They made one last full revolution, and now only a quarter of the blade was visible – no, a fifth – no, now not even that much showed: it had entered completely. Gregson grew still after having piled on top of Cook, who had also become motionless.

I watched, and it seemed to me (fogged as my senses were by

fever) that this was all a harmless game, that in a moment they would get up and, when they had caught their breath, would peacefully carry me off across the swamp toward the cool blue hills, to some shady place with babbling water. But suddenly, at this last stage of my mortal illness – for I knew that in a few minutes I would die – in these final minutes everything grew completely lucid: I realized that all that was taking place around me was not the trick of an inflamed imagination, not the veil of delirium, through which unwelcome glimpses of my supposedly real existence in a distant European city (the wallpaper, the armchair, the glass of lemonade) were trying to show. I realized that the obtrusive room was fictitious, since everything beyond death is, at best, fictitious: an imitation of life hastily knocked together, the furnished rooms of nonexistence. I realized that reality was here, here beneath that wonderful, frightening tropical sky, among those gleaming sword-like reeds, in that vapor hanging over them, and in the thick-lipped flowers clinging to the flat islet, where, beside me, lay two clinched corpses. And, having realized this, I found within me the strength to crawl over to them and pull the knife from the back of Gregson, my leader, my dear friend. He was dead, quite dead, and all the little bottles in his pockets were broken and crushed. Cook, too, was dead, and his ink-black tongue protruded from his mouth. I pried open Gregson's fingers and turned his body over. His lips were half-open and bloody; his face, which already seemed hardened, appeared badly shaven; the bluish whites of his eyes showed between the lids. For the last time I saw all this distinctly, consciously, with the seal of authenticity on everything – their skinned knees, the bright flies circling over them, the females of those flies, already seeking a spot for oviposition. Fumbling with my enfeebled hands, I took a thick notebook out of my shirt pocket, but here I was overcome by weakness; I sat down and my head drooped. And yet I conquered this impatient fog of death and looked around. Blue air, heat, solitude . . . And how sorry I felt for Gregson, who would never return home – I even remembered his wife and the old cook, and his parrots, and many other things. Then I thought about our discoveries, our precious finds, the rare, still undescribed plants and animals that now would never be named by us. I was alone. Hazier flashed the reeds, dimmer flamed the sky. My eyes followed an exquisite beetle that was crawling across a stone, but I had no strength left to catch it. Everything around me was fading, leaving bare the scenery of death – a few pieces of realistic furniture and four walls. My last motion was to open the book, which was damp with my sweat, for I absolutely had to make a note of something; but, alas, it slipped out of my hand. I groped all along the blanket, but it was no longer there.

A Dashing Fellow

'The Dashing Fellow', 'Khvat' in Russian, was first published
in the early 1930s. The two leading émigré papers, *Rul*
(Berlin) and *Posledniya novosti* (Paris), rejected it as improper
and brutal. It appeared in *Segodnya* (Riga), exact date to be
settled, and in 1938 was included in my collection of short
stories *Soglyadatay* (*Russkie Zapiski*, Paris). The present
translation appeared in *Playboy* for December, 1971.

Our suitcase is carefully embellished with bright-colored stickers: 'Nürnberg', 'Stuttgart', 'Köln' – and even 'Lido' (but that one is fraudulent). We have a swarthy complexion, a network of purple-red veins, a black mustache, trimly clipped and hairy nostrils. We breathe hard through our nose as we try to solve a crossword puzzle in an émigré paper. We are alone in a third-class compartment – alone and, therefore, bored.

Tonight we arrive in a voluptuous little town. Freedom of action! Fragrance of commercial travels! A golden hair on the sleeve of one's coat! Oh, woman, thy name is Goldie! That's how we called Mamma and, later, our wife Katya. Psychoanalytic fact: every man is Oedipus. During the last trip we were unfaithful to Katya three times, and that cost us thirty Reichsmarks. Funny – they all look a fright in the place one lives in, but in a strange town they are as lovely as antique hetaerae. Even more delicious, however, might be the elegancies of a chance encounter: your profile reminds me of the girl for whose sake years ago ... After one single night we shall part like ships ... Another possibility: she might turn out to be Russian. Allow me to introduce myself: Konstantin ... Better omit the family name – or maybe invent one? Obolenski. Yes, relatives.

We do not know any famous Turkish general and can guess neither the father of aviation nor an American rodent. It is also not very amusing to look at the view. Fields. A road. Birches-smirches. Cottage and cabbage patch. Country lass, not bad, young.

Katya is the very type of a good wife. Lacks any sort of passion, cooks beautifully, washes her arms as far as the shoulders every morning and is not overbright: therefore, not jealous. Given the sterling breadth of her pelvis one is surprised that for the second time now she has produced a still-born babikins. Laborious years. Uphill all the way. *Absolut Marasmus* in business. Sweating twenty times before persuading one customer. Then squeezing out the commission drop by drop. God, how one longs to tangle with a graceful gold-bright little devil in a fantastically lit hotel room! Mirrors, orgies, a couple of drinks. Another five hours of travel. Railroad riding, it is proclaimed, disposes one to this kind of thing. Am extremely disposed. After all, say what you will, but the mainspring of life is robust romance. Can't concentrate on business unless I take care first of my romantic interests. So here is the plan: starting point, the café which Lange told me about. Now if I don't find anything there –

Crossing gate, warehouse, big station. Our traveler let down the window and leaned upon it, elbows wide apart. Beyond a platform, steam was issuing from under some sleeping cars. One could vaguely make out the pigeons changing perches under the lofty glass dome. Hotdogs cried out in treble, beer in baritone. A girl, her bust enclosed in white wool, stood talking to a man, now joining her bare arms behind her back, swaying slightly and beating her buttocks with her handbag, now folding her arms on her chest and stepping with one foot upon the other, or else holding her handbag under her arm and with a small snapping sound thrusting nimble fingers under her glossy black belt; thus she stood and laughed, and sometimes touched her companion in a valedictory gesture, only to resume at once her twisting and turning: a suntanned girl with a heaped-up hairdo that left her ears bare, and a quite ravishing scratch on her honey-hued upper arm. She does not look at us, but never mind, let us ogle her fixedly. In the beam of the gloating tense glance she starts to shimmer and seems about to dissolve. In a moment the background will show through her – a refuse bin, a poster, a bench; but here, unfortunately, our crystalline lens had to return to its normal condition, for everything shifted, the man jumped into the next carriage, the train jerked into motion, and the girl took a handkerchief out of her handbag. When, in the course of her receding glide, she came exactly in front of his window, Konstantin, Kostya, Kostenka, thrice kissed with gusto the palm of his hand, but his salute passed unnoticed: with rhythmical weaves of her handkerchief, she floated away.

He shut the window, and, on turning around, saw with pleased surprise that during his mesmeric activities the compartment had managed to fill up: three men with their newspapers, and, in the far corner, a brunette with a powdered face. Her shiny coat was of gelatin-like translucency – resisting rain, maybe, but not a man's gaze. Decorous humor and correct eye-reach – that's our motto.

Ten minutes later he was deep in conversation with the passenger in the opposite window seat, a neatly dressed old gentleman; the prefatory theme had sailed by in the guise of a factory chimney; certain statistics came to be mentioned, and both men expressed themselves with melancholic irony regarding industrial trends; meanwhile the white-faced woman dismissed a sickly bouquet of forget-me-nots to the baggage rack, and having produced a magazine from her traveling bag became engrossed in the transparent process of reading: through it comes our caressive voice, our commonsensical speech. The second male passenger joined in: he was engagingly fat, wore checked knickerbockers stuck into green stockings and talked about pig breeding. What a good sign – she adjusts every part you look at. The third man, an arrogant recluse, hid behind his paper. At the next stop the industrialist and the expert on hogs got out, the recluse retired to the dining car and the lady moved to the window seat.

Let us appraise her point by point. Funeral expression of eyes, lascivious lips. First-rate legs, artificial silk. What is better: the experience of a sexy thirty-year-old brunette, or the silly young bloom of a bright-curled romp? Today the former is better, and tomorrow we shall see. Next point: through the gelatin of her raincoat glimmers a beautiful nude, like a mermaid seen through the yellow waves of the Rhine. Spasmodically rising, she shed her coat, but revealed only a beige dress with a piqué collaret. Arrange it. That's right.

'May weather,' affably said Konstantin, 'and yet the trains are still heated.'

Her left eyebrow went up, and she answered, 'Yes, it *is* warm here, and I'm mortally tired. My contract is finished, I'm going home now. They all toasted me – the station buffet there is tops. I drank too much, but I never get tipsy, just a heaviness in my stomach. Life has grown hard, I receive more flowers than money and a month's rest will be most welcome; after that I have a new contract, but of course, it's impossible to lay anything by. The pot-bellied chap who just left behaved obscenely. How he stared at me! I feel as if I have been on this train for a long, long time, and I am so very anxious to return to my cosy little apartment far from all that flurry and claptrap and rot.'

'Allow me to offer you,' said Kostya, 'something to palliate the offense.'

He pulled from under his backside a square pneumatic cushion, its rubber covered in speckled satin: he always had it under him during his flat, hard, hemorrhoidal trips.

'And what about yourself?' she inquired.

'We'll manage, we'll manage. I must ask you to rise a little. Excuse me. Now sit down. Soft, isn't it? That part is especially sensitive on the road.'

'Thank you,' she said. 'Not all men are so considerate. I've lost quite a bit of flesh lately. Oh, how nice! Just like traveling second class.'

'*Galanterie, Gnädigste*,' said Kostenka, 'is an innate property with us. Yes, I'm a foreigner. Russian. Here's an example: one day my father had gone for a walk on the grounds of his manor with an old pal, a well-known general. They happened to meet a peasant woman – a little old hag, you know, with a bundle of firewood on her back – and my father took off his hat. This surprised the general, and then my father said, "Would Your Excellency really want a simple peasant to be more courteous than a member of the gentry?"'

'I know a Russian – I'm sure you've heard his name, too – let me see, what was it? Baretski ... Baratski ... From Warsaw. He now owns a drugstore in Chemnitz. Baratski ... Baritski. I'm sure you know him?'

'I do not. Russia is a big country. Our family estate was about as large as your Saxony. And all has been lost, all has been burnt down. The glow of the fire could be seen at a distance of seventy kilometers. My parents were butchered in my

130

presence. I owe my life to a faithful retainer, a veteran of the Turkish campaign.'

'How terrible,' she said, 'how very terrible!'

'Yes, but it inures one. I escaped, disguised as a country girl. In those days I made a very cute little maiden. Soldiers pestered me. Especially one beastly fellow ... And thereby hangs a most comic tale.'

He told his tale. '*Pfui!*' she uttered, smiling.

'Well, after that came the era of wanderings, and a multitude of trades. At one time I even used to shine shoes – and would see in my dreams the precise spot in the garden where the old butler, by torchlight, had buried our ancestral jewels. There was, I remember, a sword, studded with diamonds –'

'I'll be back in a minute,' said the lady.

The resilient cushion had not yet had time to cool when she again sat down upon it and with mellow grace recrossed her legs.

'– and moreover two rubies, that big, then stocks in a golden casket, my father's epaulets, a string of black pearls –'

'Yes, many people are ruined at present,' she remarked with a sigh, and continued, again raising that left eyebrow: 'I too have experienced all sorts of hardships. I had a husband, it was a dreadful marriage, and I said to myself: enough! I'm going to live my own way. For almost a year now I'm not on speaking terms with my parents – old people, you know, don't understand the young – and it affects me deeply. Sometimes I pass by their house and sort of dream of dropping in – and my second husband is now, thank goodness, in Argentina, he writes me absolutely marvelous letters, but I will never return to him. There was another man, the director of a factory, a very sedate gentleman, he adored me, wanted me to bear him a child, and his wife was also such a dear, so warm-hearted – much older than he – oh, we three were such friends, went boating on the lake in summer, but then they moved to Frankfort. Or take actors – such good, gay people – and affairs with them are so *kameradschaftlich*, there's no pouncing upon you, at once, at once, at once ...'

In the meantime Kostya reflected: we know all those parents and directors. She's making up everything. Very attractive, though. Breasts like a pair of piggies, slim hips. Likes to tipple, apparently. Let's order some beer from the diner.

'Well, some time later, there was a lucky break, brought me heaps of money. I had four apartment houses in Berlin. But the man whom I trusted, my friend, my partner, deceived me ... Painful recollections. I lost a fortune but not my optimism, and now, again, thank God, despite the depression ... Apropos, let me show you something, madam.'

The suitcase with the swanky stickers contained (among other meretricious articles) samples of a highly fashionable kind of vanity-bag looking glass: little things neither round, nor square, but *Phantasie*-shaped, say, like a daisy or a butterfly or a heart. Meanwhile came the beer. She examined the little mirrors and looked in them at herself; blinks of light shot across the compartment. She downed the beer like a trooper, and with the back of her hand removed the foam from her orange-red lips. Kostenka fondly replaced the samples in the valise and put it back on the shelf. All right, let's begin.

'Do you know – I keep looking at you, and imagining that we met once years ago. You resemble to an absurd degree a girl – she died of consumption – whom I loved so much that I almost shot myself. Yes, we Russians are sentimental eccentrics, but believe me we can love with the passion of a Rasputin and the naïveté of a child. You are lonely, and I am lonely. You are free, and I am free. Who, then, can forbid us to spend several pleasant hours in a sheltered love nest?'

Her silence was enticing. He left his seat and sat next to her. He leered, and rolled his eyes, and knocked his knees together, and rubbed his hands, as he gaped at her profile.

'What is your destination?' she asked.

Kostenka told her.

'And I am returning to –'

She named a city famous for its cheese production.

'All right, I'll accompany you, and tomorrow continue my journey. Though I dare not predict anything, madam, I have all grounds to believe that neither you nor I will regret it.'

The smile, the eyebrow.

'You don't even know my name yet.'

'Oh, who cares, who cares? Why should one have a name?'

'Here's mine,' she said, and produced a visiting card: Sonja Bergmann.

'And I'm just Kostya. Kostya, and no nonsense. Call me Kostya, right?'

An enchanting woman! A nervous, supple, interesting woman! We'll be there in half an hour. Long live Life, Happiness, Ruddy Health! A long night of double-edged pleasures. See our complete collection of caresses! Amorous Hercules!

The person we nicknamed the recluse returned from the diner, and flirtation had to be suspended. She took several snapshots out of her handbag and proceeded to show them: 'This girl's just a friend. Here's a very sweet boy, his brother works for the radio station. In this one I came out appallingly. That's my leg. And here – do you recognize this person? I've put spectacles on and a bowler – cute, isn't it?'

We are on the point of arriving. The little cushion has been returned with many thanks. Kostya deflated it and slipped it into his valise. The train began braking.

'Well, so long,' said the lady.

Energetically and gaily he carried out both suitcases – hers, a small fiber one, and his, of a nobler make. The glass-topped station was shot through by three beams of dusty sunlight. The sleepy recluse and the forgotten forget-me-nots rode away.

'You're completely mad,' she said with a laugh.

Before checking his bag, he extracted from it a pair of flat folding slippers. At the taxi stand there still remained one cab.

'Where are we going?' she asked. 'To a restaurant?'

'We'll fix something to eat at your place,' said terribly impatient Kostya. 'That will be much cosier. Get in. It's a better idea. I suppose he'll be able to change fifty marks? I've got only big bills. No, wait a sec, here's some small cash. Come on, come on, tell him where to go.'

The inside of the cab smelt of kerosene. We must not spoil our fun with the small fry of osculatory contacts. Shall we get there soon? What a dreary town. Soon? Urge becoming intolerable. That firm I know. Ah, we've arrived.

The taxi pulled up in front of an old, coal-black house with green shutters. They climbed to the fourth landing and there she stopped and said, 'And what if there's somebody else there? How do you know that I'll let you in? What's that on your lip?'

'A cold sore,' said Kostya, 'just a cold sore. Hurry up. Open. Let's dismiss the whole world and its troubles. Quick. Open.'

They entered. A hallway with a large wardrobe, a kitchen, and a small bedroom.

'No, please wait. I'm hungry. We shall first have supper. Give me that fifty-mark note, I'll take the occasion to change it for you.'

'All right, but for God's sake, hurry,' said Kostya, rummaging in his wallet. 'There's no need to change anything, here's a nice tenner.'

'What would you like me to buy?'

'Oh, anything you want. I only beseech you to make haste.'

She left. She locked him in, using both keys. Taking no chances. But what loot could one have found here? None. In the middle of the kitchen floor a dead cockroach lay on its back, brown legs stretched out. The bedroom contained one chair and a lace-covered wooden bed. Above it, the photograph of a man with fat cheeks and waved hair was nailed to the spotty wall. Kostya sat down on the chair and in a twinkle substituted the morocco slippers for his mahogany-red street shoes. Then he shed his Norfolk jacket, unbuttoned his lilac braces and took off his starched collar. There was no toilet, so he quickly used the kitchen sink, then washed his hands and examined his lip. The doorbell rang.

He tiptoed fast to the door, placed his eye to the peephole, but could see nothing. The person behind the door rang again, and the copper ring was heard to knock. No matter – we can't let him in even if we wished to.

'Who's that?' asked Kostya insinuatingly through the door.

A cracked voice inquired, 'Please, is Frau Bergmann back?'

'Not yet,' replied Kostya; 'why?'

'Misfortune,' said the voice and paused. Kostya waited.

The voice continued, 'You don't know when she will be back in town? I was told she was expected to return today. You are Herr Seidler, I believe?'

'What's happened? I'll pass her the message.'

A throat was cleared and the voice said as if over the telephone, 'Franz Loschmidt speaking. She does not know me, but tell her please –'

Another pause and an uncertain query: 'Perhaps you can let me come in?'

'Never mind, never mind,' said Kostya impatiently, 'I'll tell her everything.'

'Her father is dying, he won't live through the night: he has had a stroke in the shop. Tell her to come over at once. When do you think she'll be back?'

'Soon,' answered Kostya, 'soon. I'll tell her. Good-bye.'

After a series of receding creaks the stairs became silent. Kostya made for the window. A gangling youth, death's apprentice, raincloaked, hatless, with a small close-cropped smoke-blue head crossed the street and vanished around the corner. A few moments later from another direction appeared the lady with a well-filled net bag.

The door's upper lock clicked, then its lower one.

'Phew!' she said, entering. 'What a load of things I bought!'

'Later, later,' cried Kostya, 'we'll sup later. Quick to the bedroom. Forget those parcels, I beseech you.'

'I want to eat,' she replied in a long-drawn-out voice.

She smacked his hand away, and went into the kitchen. Kostya followed her.

'Roast beef,' she said. 'White bread. Butter. Our celebrated cheese. Coffee. A pint of cognac. Goodness me, can't you wait a little? Let me go, it's indecent.'

Kostya, however, pressed her against the table, she started to giggle helplessly, his fingernails kept catching in the knit silk of her green undies, and everything happened very ineffectually, uncomfortably and prematurely.

'*Pfui!*' she uttered, smiling.

No, it was not worth the trouble. Thank you kindly for the treat. Wasting my strength. I'm no longer in the bloom of youth. Rather disgusting. Her perspiring nose, her faded mug. Might have washed her hands before fingering eatables. What's that on your lip? Impudence! Still to be seen, you know, who catches what from whom. Well, nothing to be done.

'Bought that cigar for me?' he inquired.

She was busy taking knives and forks out of the cupboard and did not hear.

'What about that cigar?' he repeated.

'Oh, sorry, I didn't know you smoked. Shall I run down to get one?'

'Never mind, I'll go myself,' he replied gruffly and passed into the bedroom where he put on his shoes and coat. Through the open door he could see her moving gracelessly as she laid the table.

'The tobacconist's right on the corner,' she sang out, and choosing a plate arranged upon it with loving care the cool, rosy slices of roast beef which she had not been able to afford since quite a time.

'Moreover, I'll get some pastry,' said Konstantin, and went out. 'Pastry, and whipped cream, and a chunk of pineapple, and chocolates with brandy filling,' he added mentally.

Once in the street, he looked up, seeking out her window (the one with the cactuses, or the next?), then turned right, walked around the back of a furniture van, nearly got struck by the front wheel of a cyclist and showed him his fist. Further on there was a small public garden and some kind of stone *Herzog*. He made another turn, and saw at the very end of the street, outlined against a thundercloud and lit up by a gaudy sunset, the brick tower of the church, past which, he recalled, they had driven. From there it was but a step to the station. A convenient train could be had in a quarter of an hour: in this respect, at least, luck was on his side. Expenses: bag-check, 30 pfennigs, taxi, 1.40, she, 10 marks (5 would have been enough). What else? Yes, the beer, 55 pfennigs, with tip. In all: 12 marks and 25 pfennigs. Idiotic. As to the bad news, she was sure to get it sooner or later. I spared her several sad minutes by a deathbed. Still, maybe, I should send her a message from here? But I've forgotten the house number. No, I remember 27. Anyway, one may assume I forgot it – nobody is obliged to have such a good memory. I can imagine what a rumpus there would have been if I had told her at once! The old bitch. No, we like only small blondes – remember that once for all.

The train was crammed, the heat stifling. We feel out of sorts, but do not quite know if we are hungry or drowsy. But when we have fed and slept, life will regain its looks, and the American instruments will make music in the merry café described by our friend Lange. And then, sometime later, we die.

Ultima Thule

The winter of 1939–40 was my last season of Russian prose writing. In spring I left for America where I was to spend twenty years in a row writing fiction solely in English. Among the works of those farewell months in Paris was a novel which I did not complete before my departure, and to which I never went back. Except for two chapters and a few notes, I destroyed the unfinished thing. Chapter One, entitled 'Ultima Thule', appeared in 1942 (*Novyy Zhurnal*, I, New York). It had been preceded by the publication of Chapter Two, 'Solus Rex', in early 1940 (*Sovremennyya Zapiski*, LXX, Paris). The present translation, made in February 1971, by my son with my collaboration, is scrupulously faithful to the original text, including the restoration of a scene that had been marked in the *Sovremennyya Zapiski* by suspension points.

Perhaps, had I finished my book, readers would not have been left wondering about a few things: was Falter a quack? Was he a true seer? Was he a medium whom the narrator's dead wife might have been using to come through with the blurry outline of a phrase which her husband did or did not recognize? Be that as it may, one thing is clear enough. In the course of evolving an imaginary country (which at first merely diverted him from his grief, but then grew into a self-contained artistic obsession), the widower becomes so engrossed in Thule that the latter starts to develop its own reality. Sineusov mentions in Chapter One that he is moving from the Riviera to his former apartment in Paris; actually, he moves into a bleak palace on a remote northern island. His art helps him to resurrect his wife in the disguise of Queen Belinda, a pathetic act which does not let him triumph over death even in the world of free fancy. In Chapter Three she was to die again, killed by a bomb meant for her husband, on the new bridge across the Egel, a few minutes after returning from the Riviera. That is about all I can make out through the dust and debris of my old fancies.

A word about K. The translators had some difficulty about that designation because the Russian for 'king', *korol*, is abbreviated as 'Kr' in the sense it is used here, which sense can be rendered only by 'K' in English. To put it rather neatly, my 'K' refers to a chessman, not to a Czech. As to the title of the fragment, let me quote Blackburne, *Terms & Themes of Chess Problems* (London, 1907): 'If the King is the only Black man on the board, the problem is said to be of the *"Solus Rex"* variety.'

Prince Adulf, whose physical aspect I imagined, for some reason, as resembling that of S. P. Diaghilev (1872–1929), remains one of my favorite characters in the private museum of stuffed people that every grateful writer has somewhere on the premises. I do not remember the details of poor Adulf's death, except that he was dispatched, in some horrible, clumsy manner, by Sien and his companions, exactly five years before the inauguration of the Egel bridge.

Freudians are no longer around, I understand, so I do not need to warn them not to touch my circles with their symbols. The good reader, on the other hand, will certainly distinguish garbled English echoes of this last Russian novel of mine in *Bend Sinister* (1947) and, especially, *Pale Fire* (1962); I find those echoes a little annoying, but what really makes me regret its non-completion is that it promised to differ radically, by the quality of its coloration, by the amplitude of its style, by something undefinable about its powerful underflow, from all my other works in Russian. The present translation of 'Ultima Thule' appeared in *The New Yorker*, April 7, 1973.

Do you remember the day you and I were lunching (partaking of nourishment) a couple of years before your death? Assuming, of course, that memory can live without its headdress? Let us imagine – just an 'apropositional' thought – some totally new handbook of epistolary samples. To a lady who has lost her right hand: I kiss your ellipsis. To a deceased: Respecterfully yours. But enough of these sheepish vignettes. If you don't remember, then I remember for you: the memory of you can pass, grammatically speaking at least, for your memory, and I am perfectly willing to grant for the sake of an ornate phrase that if, after your death, I and the world will still endure, it is only because you recollect the world and me. I address you now for the following reason. I address you now on the following occasion. I address you now simply to chat with you about Falter. What a fate! What a mystery! What a handwriting! When I tire of trying to persuade myself that he is a halfwit or a *kvak* (as you used to Russianize the English synonym for 'charlatan'), he strikes me as a person who ... who, because he survived the bomb of truth that exploded in him ... became a god! Beside him, how paltry seem all the bygone clairvoyants: the dust raised by the herd at sunset, the dream within a dream (when you dream you have awakened), the crack students in this our institute of learning hermetically closed to outsiders; for Falter stands *outside* our world, in the true reality. Reality! – that is the pouter-pigeon throat of the snake that fascinates me. Remember the time we lunched at the hotel managed by Falter near the luxuriant, many-terraced Italian border, where the asphalt is infinitely exalted by the wisteria, and the air smells of rubber and paradise? Adam Falter was still one of us then, and, if nothing about him presaged ... what shall I call it? – say, seerhood – nevertheless his whole strong cast (the caromlike co-ordination of his bodily movements, as though he had ball bearings for cartilages, his precision, his aquiline aloofness) now, in retrospect, explains why he survived the shock: the original figure was large enough to withstand the subtraction.

Oh my love, how your presence smiles from that fabled bay – and nevermore! – oh, I bite my knuckles so as not to start shaking with sobs, but there is no holding them back; down I slide with locked brakes, making 'hoo' and 'boo-hoo' sounds, and it is all such humiliating physical nonsense: the hot blinking, the feeling of suffocation, the dirty handkerchief, the convulsive yawning alternating with the tears – I just can't, can't live without you. I blow my nose, swallow and then all over again try to persuade the chair which I clutch, the desk which I pound, that I can't boohoo without you. Are you able to hear me? That's from a banal questionnaire, which ghosts do not answer, but how willingly our death-cell-mates respond for them; 'I know!' (pointing skyward at random), 'I'll be glad to tell you!' Your darling head, the hollow of your temple, the forget-me-not gray of an eye squinting at an incipient kiss, the placid expression of your ears when you would lift up your hair ... how can I reconcile myself to your disappearance, to this gaping hole, into which slides everything – my whole life, wet gravel, objects and habits – and what tombal railings can prevent me from tumbling, with silent relish, into this abyss? Vertigo of the soul. Remember how, right after you died, I hurried out of the sanatorium, not walking but sort of stamping and even dancing with pain (life having got jammed in the door like a finger), alone on that winding road among the exaggeratedly scaly pines and the prickly shields of agaves, in a green armored world that quietly drew in its feet so as not to catch my disease. Ah, yes – everything around me kept warily, attentively silent, and only when I looked at something did that something give a start and begin ostentatiously to move, rustle or buzz, pretending not to notice me. 'Indifferent nature,' says Pushkin. Nonsense! A continuous shying-away would be a more accurate description.

What a shame, though. You were such a darling. And, holding on to you from within by a little button, our child went with you. But, my poor sir, one does not make a child to a woman when she has tuberculosis of the throat. Involuntary translation from French into Hadean. You died in your sixth month and took the remaining twelve weeks with you, not paying off your debt in full, as it were. How much I wanted her to bear me a child, the red-nosed widower informed the walls. *Êtes-vous tout à fait certain, docteur, que la science ne connaît pas de ces cas exceptionnels où l'enfant naît dans la tombe?* And the dream I had: that garlicky doctor (who was at the same time Falter, or was it Alexander Vasilievich?) replying with exceptional readiness, that yes, of course it sometimes did happen, and that such children (i.e., the posthumously born) were known as cadaverkins.

As to you, never once since you died have you appeared in my dreams. Perhaps the authorities intercept you, or you yourself avoid such prison visits with me. At first, base ignoramus that I was, I feared – superstitiously, humiliatingly – the small cracklings that a room always emits at night, but that were now reflected within me by terrifying flashes which made my clucking heart scuttle away faster with low-spread wings. Even worse, however, was the nighttime waiting, when I would lie in bed, trying not to think how you might suddenly give me an answering knock if I thought about it, but this only meant complicating the mental parenthesization, placing brackets within braces (thinking about trying not to think), and the fear within them grew and grew. Oh how awful was the dry tap of the phantasmal fingernail inside the table top, and how little it resembled, of course, the intonation of your soul, of your life. A vulgar ghost with the tricks of a woodpecker, a disincarnate humorist, a corny cobold taking advantage of my stark-naked grief! In the daytime, on the other hand, I was fearless, and would challenge you to manifest your responsiveness in any way you liked, as I sat on the pebbles of the beach, where once your golden legs had been extended; and, as before, a wave would arrive, all out of breath, but, as it had nothing to report, it would disperse in apologetic salaams. Pebbles like cuckoo eggs, a piece of tile shaped like a pistol clip, a fragment of topaz-colored glass, something quite dry resembling a whisk of bast, my tears, a microscopic bead, an empty cigarette package with a yellow-bearded sailor in the center of a life buoy, a stone like a Pompeian's foot, some creature's small bone or a spatula, a kerosene can, a shiver of garnet-red glass, a nutshell, a nondescript rusty thingum related to nothing, a shard of porcelain, of which the companion fragments must inevitably exist somewhere – and I imagined an eternal torment, a convict's task, that would serve as the best punishment for such as I, whose thoughts had ranged too far during their life span: namely, to find and gather all these parts, so as to recreate that gravy boat or soup tureen – hunch-backed wanderings along wild, misty shores. And, after all, if one is supremely lucky, one might restore the dish on the first morning instead of the trillionth – and there it is, that most agonizing question of *luck*, of Fortune's Wheel, of the right lottery ticket, without which a given soul might be denied eternal felicity beyond the grave.

On these early-spring days the narrow strip of shingle is unadorned and forlorn, but strollers would pass along the promenade above, and this person or that, no doubt, must have said, on observing my shoulder blades, 'There's Sineusov, the artist – lost his wife the other day.' And I would probably have sat like that forever, picking at the desiccated jetsam, watching the stumbling foam, noting the sham tenderness of elongated serial cloudlets all along the horizon and the wine-dark washes of warmth in the chill blue-green of the sea, if someone indeed had not recognized me from the sidewalk.

However (as I fumble among the torn silks of phrase), let me return to Falter. As you have by now remembered, we went there once, on a torrid day, crawling like two ants up a flower-basket ribbon, because I was curious to take a look at my former tutor (whose lessons were limited to witty polemics with the compilers of my manuals), a resilient-looking, well-groomed man with a large white nose and a glossy parting in his hair; and it was along this straight line that he later traveled to business success, while his father, Ilya Falter, was only the senior chef at Ménard's in St Petersburg: *il y a pauvre Ilya*, turning on *povar*, which is 'man cook' in Russian. My angel, oh my angel, perhaps our whole earthly existence is now but a pun to you, or a grotesque rhyme, something like 'dental' and 'transcendental' (remember?), and the true meaning of reality, of that piercing term, purged of all our strange, dreamy, masquerade interpretations, now sounds so pure and sweet that you, angel, find it amusing that we could have taken the dream seriously (although you and I did have an inkling of why everything disintegrated at one furtive touch – words, conventions of everyday life, systems, persons – so, you know, I think laughter is some chance little ape of truth astray in our world).

I was now seeing him after an interval of twenty years; and how right I had been, when approaching the hotel, to construe all of its classical ornaments – the cedar of Lebanon, the eucalyptus, the banana tree, the terra cotta tennis court, the enclosure for cars beyond the lawn – as a ceremonial of fortunate fate, as a symbol of the corrections that the former image of Falter now required! During our years of separation (quite painless for us both) he had changed from a poor, wiry student with animated night-dark eyes and a beautiful, strong, sinistral handwriting into a dignified, rather corpulent gentleman, though the liveliness of his glance and the beauty of his large hands were undiminished – only I would never have recognized him from the back, for, instead of the thick, sleek hair and shaven nape, there was now a nimbus of black fluff encircling a sun-browned bald spot akin to a tonsure. With his silk shirt, the color of stewed rutabaga, his checked tie, his wide pearl-gray pants, and his piebald shoes, he struck me as being dressed up for a fancy-dress ball; but his large nose was the same as ever, and with it he infallibly caught the light scent of the past when I came up, slapped him on his muscular shoulder, and posed him my riddle. You were standing a little way off, your bare ankles pressed together on their high cobalt-blue heels, examining with restrained but mischievous interest the furnishings of the enormous hall, empty at that hour – the hippopotamus hide of the armchairs, the austere bar, the British magazines on the glass-topped table, the frescoes, of studied simplicity, depicting scanty-breasted bronzed girls against a golden background, one of whom, with parallel strands of stylized hair falling along her cheek, had for some reason gone down on one knee. Could we conceive that the master of all this splendor would ever cease to see it? My angel ... Meanwhile, taking my hands in his, squeezing them, puckering the skin between his brows and fixing me with dark, narrowed eyes, he was observing that life-suspending pause observed by those who are about to sneeze but are not quite sure if they will succeed ... but he succeeded, the past burst into light, and he loudly pronounced my nickname. He kissed your hand, without bending his head, and then, in a benevolent fuss, obviously enjoying the fact that I, a person who had seen better days, had now found him in the full glory of the life he had himself created by the power of his sculptitory will, he seated us on the terrace, ordered cocktails and lunch, introduced us to his brother-in-law, Mr L., a cultured man in a dark business suit that contrasted oddly with Falter's exotic foppishness. We drank, we ate, we talked about the past as about someone gravely ill, I managed to balance a knife on the back of a fork, you petted the wonderful nervous dog that feared its master, and after a minute of silence, in the midst of which Falter suddenly uttered a distinct 'Yes,' as if concluding a diagnostic deliberation, we parted, making each other promises that neither he nor I had the least intention of keeping.

You didn't find anything remarkable about him, did you? And to be sure – that type has been done to death: throughout a drab youth supported his alcoholic father by giving lessons, and then slowly, obstinately, buoyantly achieved prosperity; for, in addition to the not very profitable hotel, he had flourishing interests in the wine business. But, as I understood later, you were wrong when you said that it was all somewhat dull and that energetic, successful fellows like him always reek of sweat. Actually, I am madly envious now of the early Falter's basic trait: the precision and power of his 'volitional substance', as – you remember? – poor Adolf put it in a quite different context. Whether sitting in a trench or in an office, whether catching a train or getting up on a dark morning in an unheated room, whether arranging business connections or pursuing someone in friendship or enmity, Adam Falter not only was always in possession of all his faculties, not only lived every moment cocked like a pistol, but was always certain of unfailingly achieving today's aim, and tomorrow's, and the whole gradual progression of his aims, at the same time working economically, for he did not aim high, and knew his limitations exactly. His greatest service to himself was that he deliberately disregarded his talents and banked on the ordinary, the commonplace; for he was endowed with strange, mysteriously fascinating gifts, which some other, less circumspect person might have tried to put to practical use. Perhaps only in the very beginning of life had he sometimes been unable to control himself, intermixing the humdrum coaching of a schoolboy in a humdrum subject with unusually elegant manifestations of mathematical thought, which left a certain chill of poetry hanging about my schoolroom after he had hurried away to his next lesson. I think with envy that if my nerves were as strong as his, my soul as resilient, my will-power as condensed, he would have imparted to me nowadays the essence of the superhuman discovery he recently made – that is, he would not have feared that the information would crush me; I, on the other hand, would have been sufficiently persistent to make him tell me everything to the end.

A slightly husky voice hailed me discreetly from the promenade, but, as more than a year had passed since our luncheon with Falter, I did not immediately recognize his humble brother-in-law in the person who now cast a shadow on my stones. Out of mechanical politeness I went up to join him on the sidewalk, and he expressed his deepest *et cetera:* he had happened to stop by at my *pension*, he said, and the good people there had not only informed him of your death, but also indicated to him from afar my figure upon the deserted beach, a figure that had become a kind of local curiosity (for a moment I felt ashamed that the round back of my grief should be visible from every terrace).

'We met at Adam Ilyich's,' he said, showing the stumps of his incisors and taking his place in my limp consciousness. I must have proceeded to ask him something about Falter.

'Oh, so you haven't heard?' the prattler said in surprise, and it was then that I learned the whole story.

It happened that the previous spring Falter had gone on business to a particularly viny Riviera town, and, as usual, stopped at a quiet little hotel, whose proprietor was a debtor of his of long standing. One must picture this hotel, tucked up in the feathered armpit of a hill overgrown with mimosa, and the little lane, not fully built up yet, with its half-dozen tiny villas, where radio sets sang in the small human space between the stardust and the sleeping oleanders, while crickets zinked the night with their stridulation in the vacant lot under Falter's open third-story window. After having passed a hygienic evening in a small bordello on the Boulevard de la Mutualité, he returned at about eleven to the hotel, in an excellent mood, clear of head and light of loin, and immediately went up to his room. The star-ashed brow of night; her expression of gentle insanity; the swarming of lights in the old town; an amusing mathematical problem about which he had corresponded the year before with a Swedish scholar; the dry, sweet smell that seemed to loll, without thought or task, here and there in the hollows of the darkness; the metaphysical taste of a wine, well bought and well sold; the news, recently received from a remote, unattractive country, of the death of a half-sister, whose image had long since wilted in his memory – all of this, I imagine, was floating through Falter's mind as he walked up the street and then mounted to his room; and while taken separately none of these reflections and impressions was in the least new or unusual for this hard-nosed, not quite ordinary, but superficial man (for, on the basis of our human core, we are divided into professionals and amateurs; Falter, like me, was an amateur), in their totality they formed perhaps the most favorable medium for the flash, the unearthly lightning, as catastrophic as a sweepstakes win, monstrously fortuitous, in no way foretold by the normal function of his reason, that struck him that night in that hotel.

About half an hour had passed since his return when the collective slumber of the small white building, with its barely rippling crape-like mosquito netting and wall flowers, was abruptly – no, not interrupted, but rent, split, blasted by sounds that remained unforgettable to the hearers, my darling – those sounds, those dreadful sounds. They were not the porcine squeals of a mollycoddle being dispatched by hasty villains in a ditch, not the roar of a wounded soldier whom a savage surgeon relieves of a monstrous leg – no, they were worse, far worse ... And if, said later the innkeeper, Monsieur Paon, one were going to make comparisons, those sounds resembled most of all the paroxysmal, almost exultant screams of a woman in the throes of infinitely painful childbirth – a woman, however, with a man's voice and a giant in her womb. It was hard to identify the dominant note amid the storm rending that human throat – whether it was pain, fear, or the clarion of madness, or again, and most likely of all, the expression of an unfathomable sensation, whose very unknowability imparted to the ex-ululation bursting from Falter's room something that aroused in the hearers a panical desire to put an immediate stop to it. The newlyweds who were toiling in the nearest bed paused, diverting their eyes in parallel and holding their breath; the Dutchman living downstairs scuttled out into the garden, which already contained the housekeeper and the white shimmer of eighteen maids (only two, really, multiplied by their darting to and fro). The hotel keeper, who, according to his own account, had retained full presence of mind, rushed upstairs and ascertained that the door behind which continued the hurricane of howling, so mighty that it seemed to thrust one back, was locked from within and would yield neither to thump nor entreaty. Roaring Falter, insofar as one could assume it was indeed he that roared (his open window was dark, and the intolerable sounds issuing from within did not bear the imprint of anyone's personality), spread out far beyond the limits of the hotel, and neighbors gathered in the surrounding darkness, and one rascal had five cards in his hand, all trumps. By now it was completely incomprehensible how anyone's vocal cords could endure the strain : according to one account, Falter screamed for at least fifteen minutes; according to another and probably more accurate one, for about five without interruption. Suddenly (while the landlord was deciding whether to break down the door with a joint effort, place a ladder outside, or call the police) the screams, having attained the ultimate limits of agony, horror, amazement, and of that other quite undefinable something, turned into a medley of moans and then stopped altogether. It grew so quiet that at first those present conversed in whispers.

Cautiously, the landlord again knocked at the door, and from behind it came sighs and unsteady footfalls. Presently one heard someone fumbling at the lock, as though he did not know how to open it. A weak, soft fist began smacking feebly from within. Then Monsieur Paon did what he could actually have done much sooner – he found another key and opened the door.

'One would like some light,' Falter said softly in the dark. Thinking for an instant that Falter had broken the lamp during his fit, the landlord automatically checked the switch, but the light obediently came on, and Falter, blinking in sickly surprise, turned his eyes from the hand that had engendered light to the newly filled glass bulb, as if seeing for the first time how it was done.

A strange, repulsive change had come over his entire exterior: he looked as if his skeleton had been removed. His sweaty and now somehow flabby face, with its hanging lip and pink eyes, expressed not only a dull fatigue, but also relief, an animal relief as after the pangs of monster-bearing. Naked to the waist, wearing only his pajama bottoms, he stood with lowered face, rubbing the back of one hand with the palm of the other. To the natural questions of Monsieur Paon and the hotel guests he gave no answer; he merely puffed out his cheeks, pushed aside those who had surrounded him, came out on the landing and began urinating copiously right on the stairs. Then he went back, lay down on his bed and fell asleep.

In the morning the hotel keeper called up Mrs L., Falter's sister, to warn her that her brother had gone mad, and he was bundled off home, listless and half-asleep. The family doctor suggested it was just a slight stroke and prescribed the correspondent treatment. But Falter did not get better. After a time, it is true, he began walking about freely, and even whistling at times, and uttering loud insults, and grabbing food the doctor had forbidden. However, the change remained. He was like a man who had lost everything: respect for life, all interest in money and business, all customary and traditional feelings, everyday habits, manners, absolutely everything. It was unsafe to let him go anywhere alone, for, with a curiosity quite superficial and quickly forgotten but offensive to others, he would address chance passersby, to discuss the origin of a scar on someone's face or a statement, not addressed to him, that he had overheard in a conversation between strangers. He would take an orange from a fruit-stand as he passed, and eat it unpeeled, responding with an indifferent half-smile to the jabber of the fruit-woman who had run after him. When he grew tired or bored he would squat on the sidewalk Turkish fashion and, for something to do, try to catch girls' heels in his fist like flies. Once he appropriated several hats, five felts and two panamas, which he had painstakingly collected in various cafés, and there were difficulties with the police.

His case attracted the attention of a well-known Italian psychiatrist, who happened to have a patient at Falter's hotel. This Dr Bonomini, a youngish man, was studying, as he himself would willingly explain, 'the dynamics of the psyche', and sought to demonstrate in his works, whose popularity was not confined to learned circles, that all psychic disorders could be explained by subliminal memories of calamities that befell the patient's forbears, and that if, for example, the subject were afflicted by megalomania, to cure him completely it sufficed to determine which of his great-grandfathers was a power-hungry failure, and explain to the great-grandson that the ancestor being dead had found eternal peace, although in complex cases it was actually necessary to resort to theatrical representation, in costumes of the period, depicting the specific demise of the ancestor whose role was assigned to the patient. These *tableaux vivants* grew so fashionable that Bonomini was obliged to explain to the public in print the dangers of staging them without his direct control.

Having questioned Falter's sister, Bonomini established that the Falters did not know much about their forebears; true, Ilya Falter had been addicted to drink; but since, according to Bonomini's theory, 'the patient's illness reflects only the distant past,' as, for instance, a folk epic 'sublimates' only remote occurrences, the details about Falter *père* were useless to him. Nevertheless he offered to try to help the patient, hoping by means of clever questioning to make Falter himself produce the explanation for his condition, after which the necessary ancestors could become deducible of their own accord; that an explanation did exist was confirmed by the fact that when Falter's intimates succeeded in penetrating his silence he would succinctly and dismissively allude to something quite out of the ordinary that he had experienced on that enigmatic night.

One day Bonomini closeted himself with Falter in the latter's room, and, like the knower of human hearts he was, with his horn-rimmed glasses and that hankie in his breast pocket, managed apparently to get out of him an exhaustive reply about the cause of his nocturnal howls. Hypnotism probably played its part in the business, for at the subsequent inquest Falter insisted that he had blabbed against his will, and that it rankled. He added, however, that never mind, sooner or later he would have made the experiment anyway, but that now he would definitely never repeat it. Be that as it may, the poor author of *The Heroics of Insanity* became the prey of Falter's Medusa. Since the intimate encounter between doctor and patient seemed to be lasting abnormally long, Eleonora L., Falter's sister, who had been knitting a gray shawl on the terrace, and for a long time already had not heard the psychiatrist's release-inducing, high-spirited, or falsely cajoling little tenor, which at first had been more or less audible through the half-open French window, entered her brother's room, and found him examining with dull curiosity the alpine sanatoriums in a brochure that had probably been brought by the doctor, while the doctor himself sprawled half on a chair and half on the carpet, with a gap of linen showing between waistcoat and trousers, his short legs spread wide and his pale café-au-lait face thrown back, felled, as was later determined, by heart failure. To the questions of the officiously meddling police Falter replied absently and tersely; but, when he finally grew tired of this pestering, he pointed out that, having accidentally solved 'the riddle of the universe', he had yielded to artful exhortation and shared that solution with his inquisitive interlocutor, whereupon the latter had died of astonishment. The local newspapers caught up the story, embellished it properly, and the person of Falter, in the guise of a Tibetan sage, for several days nourished the not over-particular news columns.

But, as you know, during those days I did not read the papers: you were dying then. Now, however, having heard the story of Falter in detail, I experienced a certain very strong and perhaps slightly shamefaced desire.

You understand, of course. In the condition I was in, people without imagination – i.e., deprived of its support and inquiry – turn to the advertisements of wonder-workers; to chiromancers in comedy turbans, who combine the magic business with a trade in rat poison or rubber sheaths; to fat, swarthy women fortune-tellers; but particularly to spiritualists, who fake a still unidentified force by giving it the milky features of phantoms and getting them to manifest themselves in silly physical ways. But I have my share of imagination, and therefore two possibilities existed: the first was my work, my art, the consolation of my art; the second consisted of taking the plunge and believing that a person like Falter, rather average when you come down to it, despite a shrewd mind's parlor games, and even a little vulgar, had actually and conclusively learned that at which no seer, no sorcerer had ever arrived.

My art? You remember him, don't you, that strange Swede or Dane – or Icelander, for all I know – anyway, that lanky, orange-tanned blond fellow with the eyelashes of an old horse, who introduced himself to me as 'a well-known writer', and, for a price that gladdened you (you were already confined to your bed and unable to speak, but would write me funny trifles with colored chalk on a slate – for instance, that the things you liked most in life were 'verse, wildflowers and foreign currency'), commissioned me to make a series of illustrations for the epic poem 'Ultima Thule', which he had just composed in his language. Of course there could be no question of my acquainting myself thoroughly with his manuscript, since French, in which we agonizingly communicated, was known to him mostly by hearsay, and he was unable to translate his imagery for me. I managed to understand only that his hero was some Northern king, unhappy and unsociable; that his kingdom, amid the sea mists, on a melancholy and remote island, was plagued by political intrigues of some kind, assassinations, insurrections, and that a white horse which had lost its rider was flying along the misty heath . . . He was pleased with my first *blanc et noir* sample, and we decided on the subjects of the other drawings. As he did not turn up in a week as he had promised, I called his hotel, and learned that he had left for America.

I concealed my employer's disappearance from you, but did not go on with the drawings; then again, you were already so ill that I did not feel like thinking about my golden pen and traceries in India ink. But when you died, when the early mornings and late evenings became especially unbearable, then, with a pitiful, feverish eagerness, the awareness of which would bring tears to my own eyes, I would continue the work for which I knew no one would come, and for that very reason that task seemed to me appropriate – its spectral, intangible nature, the lack of aim or reward would lead me away to a realm akin to the one in which, for me, you exist, my ghostly goal, my darling, such a darling earthly creation, for which no one will ever come anywhere; and since everything kept distracting me, fobbing upon me the paint of temporality instead of the graphic design of eternity, tormenting me with your tracks on the beach, with the stones on the beach, with your blue shadow on the loathsome bright beach, I decided to return to our lodging in Paris and settle down to work seriously. 'Ultima Thule', that island born in the desolate, gray sea of my heartache for you, now attracted me as the home of my least expressible thoughts.

However, before leaving the Riviera, I absolutely had to see Falter. This was the second solace I had invented for myself. I managed to convince myself that he was not simply a lunatic after all, that not only did he believe in the discovery he had made, but that this very discovery was the source of his madness, and not vice versa. I learned that he had moved to an apartment next to my *pension*. I also learned that his health was flagging; that when the flame of life had gone out in him it had left his body without supervision and without incentive; that he would probably die soon. I learned, finally, and this was especially important to me, that lately, in spite of his failing strength, he had grown unusually talkative and for days on end would treat his visitors (and alas, a different kind of curiosity-seeker than I got through to him) to speeches in which he caviled at the mechanics of human thought, oddly meandering speeches, exposing nothing, but almost Socratic in rhythm and sting. I offered to visit him, but his brother-in-law replied that the poor fellow enjoyed any diversion, and had the strength to reach my house.

And so they arrived – that is, the brother-in-law in his inevitable shabby black suit, his wife Eleonora (a tall, taciturn woman, whose clear-cut sturdiness recalled the former frame of her brother, and now served as a kind of living lesson to him, an adjacent moralistic picture) and Falter himself, whose appearance shocked me, even though I was prepared to see him changed. How can I express it? Mr L. had said that he looked as if his bones had been removed; I, on the other hand, had the impression that his soul had been extracted but his mind intensified tenfold in recompense. By this I mean that one look at Falter was sufficient to understand that one need not expect from him any of the human feelings common in everyday life, that Falter had utterly lost the knack of loving anyone, of feeling pity, if only for himself, of experiencing kindness and, on occasion, compassion for the soul of another, of habitually serving, as best he could, the cause of good, if only that of his own standard, just as he had lost the knack of shaking hands or using his handkerchief. And yet he did not strike one as a madman – oh no, quite the contrary! In his oddly bloated features, in his unpleasant, satiated gaze, even in his flat feet, shod no longer in fashionable Oxfords but in cheap *espadrilles*, one could sense some concentrated power, and this power was not in the least interested in the flabbiness and inevitable decay of the flesh that it squeamishly controlled.

His attitude toward me now was not that of our last brief encounter, but that which I remembered from the days of our youth, when he would come to coach me. No doubt he was perfectly aware that, chronologically, a quarter of a century had passed since those days, and yet as though along with his soul he had lost his sense of time (without which the *soul* cannot live), he obviously regarded me – a matter not so much of words, but of his whole manner – as if it had all been yesterday; yet he had no sympathy, no warmth whatever for me – nothing, not even a speck of it.

They seated him in an armchair, and he spread his limbs strangely, as a chimpanzee might do when his keeper makes him parody a sybarite in a recumbent position. His sister settled down to her knitting, and during the whole course of the conversation did not once raise her short-haired gray head. Her husband took two newspapers – a local one, and one from Marseilles – out of his pocket, and was also silent. Only when Falter, noticing a large photograph of you that happened to be standing right in his line of sight, asked where were you hiding, did Mr L. say, in the loud, artificial voice people use to address the deaf, and without looking up from his newspaper:

'Come, you know perfectly well she is dead.'

'Ah, yes,' remarked Falter with inhuman unconcern, and, addressing me, added, 'Oh well, may the kingdom of heaven be hers – isn't that what one is supposed to say in society?'

Then the following conversation began between us; total recall, rather than short-hand notes, now allows me to transcribe it exactly.

'I wanted to see you, Falter,' I said (actually addressing him by first name and patronymic, but, in narration, his timeless image does not tolerate any conjunction of the man with a definite country and a genetic past), 'I wanted to see you in order to have a frank talk with you. I wonder if you would consider it possible to ask your relatives to leave us alone.'

'They do not count,' abruptly observed Falter.

'When I say "frank",' I went on, 'I presuppose the reciprocal possibility of asking no matter what questions, and the readiness to answer them. But since it is I who shall ask the questions, and expect answers from you, everything depends upon your consent to be straightforward; you do not need that assurance from me.'

'To a straightforward question I shall give a straightforward answer,' said Falter.

'In that case allow me to come right to the point. We shall ask Mr and Mrs L. to step outside for a moment, and you will tell me verbatim what you told the Italian doctor.'

'Well, I'll be damned,' said Falter.

'You cannot refuse me this. In the first place, the information won't kill me – this I guarantee you; I may look tired and seedy but don't you worry, I still have enough strength left. In the second place, I promise to keep your secret to myself, and

156

even to shoot myself, if you like, immediately after learning it. You see, I allow that my loquacity may bother you even more than my death. Well, do you agree?'

'I refuse absolutely,' replied Falter, and swept away a book from the table next to him to make room for his elbow.

'For the sake of somehow starting our talk, I shall temporarily accept your refusal. Let us proceed *ab ovo*. Now then, Falter, I understand that the essence of things has been revealed to you.'

'Yes, period,' said Falter.

'Agreed – you will not tell me about it; nevertheless, I draw two important deductions: things do have an essence, and this essence *can* be revealed to the mind.'

Falter smiled. 'Only do not call them deductions, mister. They are but flag stops. Logical reasoning may be a most convenient means of mental communication for covering short distances, but the curvature of the earth, alas, is reflected even in logic: an ideally rational progression of thought will finally bring you back to the point of departure where you return aware of the simplicity of genius, with a delightful sensation that you have embraced truth, while actually you have merely embraced your own self. Why set out on that journey, then? Be content with the formula: the essence of things has been revealed – wherein, incidentally, a blunder of yours is already present; I cannot explain it to you, since the least hint at an explanation would be a lethal glimpse. As long as the proposition remains static, one does not notice the blunder. But anything you might term a deduction already exposes the flaw: logical development inexorably becomes an envelopment.'

'All right, for the present I shall be content with that much. Now allow me a question. When a hypothesis enters a scientist's mind, he checks it by calculation and experiment, that is, by the mimicry and the pantomime of truth. Its plausibility infects others, and the hypothesis is accepted as the true explanation for the given phenomenon, until someone finds its faults. I believe the whole of science consists of such exiled or retired ideas: and yet at one time each of them boasted high rank; now only a name or a pension is left. But in your case, Falter, I suspect that you have found some different method of discovery and test. May I call it "revelation" in the theological sense?'

'You may not,' said Falter.

'Wait a minute. Right now I am interested not so much in the method of discovery as in your conviction that the result is true. In other words, either you have a method of checking the result, or the awareness of its truth is inherent in it.'

'You see,' answered Falter, 'in Indo-China, at the lottery drawings, the numbers are extracted by a monkey. I happen to be that monkey. Another metaphor: in a country of honest men a yawl was moored at the shore, and it did not belong to anyone; but no one knew that it did not belong to anyone; and its assumed appurtenance to someone rendered it invisible to all. I happened to get into it. But perhaps it would be simplest of all if I said that in a moment of playfulness, not mathematical playfulness, necessarily – mathematics, I warn you, is but a perpetual game of leapfrog over its own shoulders as it keeps breeding – I kept combining various ideas, and finally found the right combination and exploded, like Berthold Schwartz. Somehow I survived; perhaps another in my place might have survived, too. However, after the incident with my charming doctor I do not have the least desire to be bothered by the police again.'

'You're warming up, Falter. But let's get back to the point: what exactly makes you certain that it is the truth? That monkey is not really a party to the cast lots.'

'Truths, and shadows of truths,' said Falter, 'in the sense of species, of course, not specimens, are so rare in the world, and available ones are either so trivial or tainted, that – how shall I put it? – that the *recoil* upon perceiving Truth, the instant reaction of one's whole being, remains an unfamiliar, little-studied phenomenon. Oh, well, sometimes in children – when a boy wakes up or regains his senses after a bout with scarlet fever and there is an electric discharge of reality, relative reality, no doubt, for you, humans, possess no other. Take any truism, that is, the corpse of a relative truth. Now analyze the physical sensation evoked in you by the words "black is darker than brown", or "ice is cold". Your thought is too lazy even to make a polite pretense of raising its rump from its bench, as if the same teacher were to enter your classroom a hundred times in the course of one lesson in old Russia. But, in my childhood, one day of great frost, I licked the shiny lock of a wicket. Let us dismiss the physical pain, or the pride of discovery, if it is a pleasant one – all that is not the real reaction to truth. You see, its impact is so little known that one cannot even find an exact word for it. All your nerves simultaneously answer "yes!" – something like that. Let us also set aside a kind of astonishment, which is merely the unaccustomed assimilation of the *thingness* of truth, not of Truth itself. If you tell me that so-and-so is a thief, then I combine at once in my mind a number of suddenly illuminated trifles that I had myself observed, yet I have time to marvel that a man who had seemed so upright turned out to be a crook, but unconsciously I have already absorbed the truth, so that my astonishment itself promptly assumes an inverted form (how could one have ever thought honest such an obvious crook?); in other words, the sensitive point of truth lies exactly halfway between the first surprise and the second.'

'Right. This is all fairly clear.'

'On the other hand, surprise carried to stunning, unimaginable dimensions,' Falter went on, 'can have extremely painful effects, and it is still nothing compared to the shock of Truth itself. And *that* can no longer be "absorbed". It was by chance that it did not kill me, just as it was by chance that it struck me. I doubt one could think of checking a sensation of such intensity. A check can, however, be made ex post facto, though I personally have no need for the complexities of the verification. Take any commonplace truth – for instance, that two angles equal to a third are equal to each other; does the postulate also include anything about ice being hot or rocks occurring in Canada? In other words, a given truthlet, to coin a diminutive, does not contain any other related truthlets and, even less, such ones that belong to different kinds or levels of knowledge or thought. What, then, would you say about a Truth with a capital T that comprises in itself the explanation and the proof of all possible mental affirmations? One can believe in the poetry of a wildflower or the power of money, but neither belief predetermines faith in homeopathy or in the necessity to exterminate antelope on the islands of Lake Victoria Nyanza; but in my case, having learned what I have – if this can be called learning – I received a key to absolutely all the doors and treasure chests in the world; only I have no need to use it, since every thought about its practical significance automatically, by its very nature, grades into the whole series of hinged lids. I may doubt my physical ability to imagine to the very end all the consequences of my discovery, and namely, to what degree I have not yet gone insane, or, inversely, how far behind I have left all that is meant by insanity; but I certainly cannot doubt that, as you put it, "essence has been revealed to me". Some water, please.'

'Here you are. But let me see, Falter – did I understand you correctly? Are you really henceforth a candidate for omniscience? Excuse me, but I don't have that impression. I can allow that you know something fundamental, but your words contain no concrete indications of absolute wisdom.'

'Saving my strength,' said Falter. 'Anyway, I never affirmed that I know everything now – Arabic, for example, or how many times in your life you have shaved, or who set the type for the newspaper which that fool over there is reading. I only say that I know everything I might want to know. Anyone could say that – couldn't he? – after having leafed through an encyclopedia; only, the encyclopedia whose exact title I have learned (there, by the way – I am giving you a more elegant definition: I know the title of things) is literally all-inclusive, and therein lies the difference between me and the most versatile scholar on earth. You see, I have learned – and here I am leading you to the very edge of the Riviera precipice, ladies don't look – I have learned one very simple thing about the world. It is by itself so obvious, so amusingly obvious, that only my wretched humanity can consider it monstrous. When in a moment I say "congruent" I shall mean something infinitely removed from all the congruencies known to you, just as the nature itself of my discovery has nothing in common with the nature of any physical or philosophical conjectures. Now the main thing in me that is congruent with the main thing in the universe could not be affected by the bodily spasm that has thus shattered me. At the same time the possible knowledge of all things, consequent to the knowledge of the fundamental one, did not dispose in me of a sufficiently solid apparatus. I am training myself by will power not to leave the vivarium, to observe the rules of your mentality as if nothing had happened; in other words, I act like a beggar, a versifier, who has received a million in foreign currency, but goes on living in his basement, for he knows that the least concession to luxury would ruin his liver.'

'But the treasure is in your possession, Falter – that's what hurts. Let us drop the discussion of your attitude toward it, and talk about the thing itself. I repeat – I have taken note of your refusal to let me peek at your Medusa, and am further willing to refrain from the most evident inferences, since, as you hint, any logical conclusion is a confinement of thought in itself. I propose to you a different method for our questions and answers: I shall not ask you about the contents of your treasure; but, after all, you will not give away its secret by telling me if, say, it lies in the East, or if there is even one topaz in it, or if even one man has ever passed in its proximity. At the same time, if you answer "yes" or "no" to a question, I not only promise to avoid choosing that particular line for a further series of related questions, but pledge to end the conversation altogether.'

'Theoretically, you are luring me into a clumsy trap,' said Falter, shaking slightly, as another might do when laughing. 'Actually, it would be a trap only if you were capable of asking me at least one such question. There is very little chance of that. Therefore, if you enjoy pointless amusement, fire away.'

I thought a moment and said, 'Falter, allow me to begin like the traditional tourist – with an inspection of an ancient church, familiar to him from pictures. Let me ask you: does God exist?'

'Cold,' said Falter.

I did not understand and repeated the question.

'Forget it,' snapped Falter. 'I said "cold", as they say in the game, when one must find a hidden object. If you are looking under a chair or under the shadow of a chair, and the object cannot be in that place, because it happens to be somewhere else, then the question of there existing a chair or its shadow has nothing whatever to do with the game. To say that perhaps the chair exists but the object is not there is the same as saying that perhaps the object is there but the chair does not exist, which means that you end up again in the circle so dear to human thought.'

'You must agree, though, Falter, that if as you say the thing sought is not anywhere near to the concept of God, and if that thing is, according to your terminology, a kind of universal "title", then the concept of God does not appear on the title page; hence, there exists no true necessity for such a concept, and since there is no need for God, no God exists.'

'Then you did not understand what I said about the relationship between a possible place and the impossibility of finding the object in it. All right, I shall put it more clearly. By the very act of your mentioning a given concept you placed your own self in the position of an enigma, as if the seeker himself were to hide. And by persisting in your question, you not only hide, but also believe that by sharing with the sought-for object the quality of "hiddenness" you bring it closer to you. How can I answer you whether God exists when the matter under discussion is perhaps sweet peas or a soccer linesman's flag? You are looking in the wrong place and in the wrong way, *cher monsieur*, that is all the answer I can give you. And if it seems to you that from this answer you can draw the least conclusion about the uselessness or necessity of God, it is just because you are looking in the wrong place and in the wrong way. Wasn't it you, though, that promised not to follow logical patterns of thought?'

'Now I too am going to trap you, Falter. Let's see how you'll manage to avoid a direct statement. One cannot, then, seek the title of the world in the hieroglyphics of deism?'

'Pardon me,' replied Falter, 'by means of ornate language and grammatical trickery Moustache-Bleue is merely disguising the expected *non* as an expected *oui*. At the moment all I do is deny. I deny the expediency of the search for Truth in the realm of common theology, and, to save your mind empty labor, I hasten to add that the epithet I have used is a dead end: do not turn into it. I shall have to terminate the discussion *for lack of an interlocutor* if you exclaim "Aha, then there is *another*, 'uncommon', truth!'" – for this would mean that you have hidden yourself so well as to have lost yourself.'

'All right. I shall believe you. Let us grant that theology muddies the issue. Is that right, Falter?'

'This is the house that Jack built,' said Falter.

'All right, we dismiss this false trail as well. Even though you could probably explain to me why it is false (for there is something queer and elusive here, something that irritates you), and then your reluctance to reply would be clear to me.'

'I could,' said Falter, 'but it would be equivalent to revealing the gist of the matter, that is, exactly what you are not going to get out of me.'

'You repeat yourself, Falter. Don't tell me you will be just as evasive if, for instance, I ask you: can one expect an after-life?'

'Does it interest you very much?'

'Just as much as it does you, Falter. Whatever you may know about death, we are both mortal.'

'In the first place,' said Falter, 'I call your attention to the following curious catch: any man is mortal; you are a man; therefore, it is also possible that *you are not mortal*. Why? Because a specified man (you or I) for that very reason ceases to be *any man*. Yet both of us are indeed mortal, but I am mortal in a different way than you.'

'Don't spite my poor logic, but give me a plain answer: is there even a glimmer of one's identity beyond the grave, or does it all end in ideal darkness?'

'*Bon*,' said Falter, as is the habit of Russian émigrés in France. 'You want to know whether Gospodin Sineusov will forever reside within the snugness of Gospodin Sineusov, otherwise Moustache-Bleue, or whether everything will abruptly vanish. There are two ideas here, aren't there? Round-the-clock lighting and the black inane. Actually, despite the difference in metaphysical color, they greatly resemble each other. And they move in parallel. They even move at considerable speed. Long live the totalizator! Hey, hey, look through your turf glasses, they're racing each other, and you would very much like to know which will arrive first at the post of truth, but in asking me to give you a "yes" or "no" for either one or the other, you want me to catch one of them at full speed by the neck – and those devils have awfully slippery necks – but even if I were to grab one of them for you, I would merely interrupt the competition, or the winner would be the other, the one I did not snatch, an utterly meaningless result inasmuch as no rivalry would any longer exist. If you ask, however, which of the two runs faster, I shall retort with another question: what runs faster, strong desire or strong fear?'

'Same pace, I suppose.'

'That's just it. For look what happens in the case of the poor little human mind. Either it has no way to express what awaits you – I mean, us – after death, and then total unconsciousness is excluded, for *that* is quite accessible to our imagination – every one of us has experienced the total darkness of dreamless sleep; or, on the contrary, death *can* be imagined, and then one's reason naturally adopts not the notion of eternal life, an unknown entity, incongruent with anything terrestrial, but precisely that which seems more probable – the familiar darkness of stupor. Indeed, how can a man who trusts in his reason admit, for instance, that someone who is dead drunk and dies while sound asleep from a chance external cause – thus losing by chance what he no longer really possessed – again acquires the ability to reason and feel thanks to the mere extension, consolidation and perfection of his unfortunate condition? Hence, if you were to ask me only one thing: do I know, in human terms, what lies beyond death – that is, if you attempted to avert the absurdity in which must peter out the competition between two opposite, but basically similar concepts – a negative reply on my part would logically make you conclude that your life cannot end in nothingness, while from an affirmative you would draw the opposite conclusion. In either case, as you see, you would remain in exactly the same situation as before, since a dry "no" would prove to you that I know no more than you about the given subject, while a moist "yes" would suggest that you accept the existence of an international heaven which your reason cannot fail to doubt.'

'You are simply evading a straightforward answer, but allow me to observe nevertheless that on the subject of death you do not give me the answer "cold".'

'There you go again,' sighed Falter. 'Didn't I just explain to you that any deduction whatsoever conforms to the curvature of thought? It is correct, as long as you remain in the sphere of earthly dimensions, but when you attempt to go beyond, your error grows in proportion to the distance you cover. And that's not all: your mind will construe any answer of mine exclusively from a utilitarian viewpoint, for you are unable to conceive death otherwise than in the image of your own grave-stone, and this in turn would distort to such an extent the sense of my answer as to turn it into a lie, *ipso facto*. So let us observe decorum even when dealing with the transcendental. I cannot express myself more clearly – and you ought to be grateful for my evasiveness. You have an inkling, I gather, that there is a little hitch in the very formulation of the question, a hitch, incidentally, that is more terrible than the fear itself of death. It's particularly strong in you, isn't it?'

'Yes, Falter. The terror I feel at the thought of my future unconsciousness is equal only to the revulsion caused in me by a mental foreview of my decomposing body.'

'Well put. Probably other symptoms of this sublunary malady are present as well? A dull pang in the heart, suddenly, in the middle of the night, like the flash of a wild creature among domestic emotions and pet thoughts: "Someday I also must die." It happens to you, doesn't it? Hatred for the world, which will very cheerfully carry on without you. A basic sensation that all things in the world are trifles and phantasmata compared to your mortal agony, and therefore to your life, for, you say to yourself, life itself is the agony before death. Yes, oh yes, I can imagine perfectly well that sickness from which you all suffer to a lesser or greater degree, and I can say one thing: I fail to understand how people can live under such conditions.'

'There, Falter, we seem to be getting somewhere. Apparently, then, if I admitted that, in moments of happiness, of rapture, when my soul is laid bare, I suddenly feel that there is no extinction beyond the grave; that in an adjacent locked room, from under whose door comes a frosty draft, there is being prepared a peacock-eyed radiance, a pyramid of delights akin to the Christmas tree of my childhood; that everything –

life, patria, April, the sound of a spring or that of a dear voice – is but a muddled preface, and that the main text still lies ahead – if I can feel that way, Falter, is it not possible to live, to live – tell me it's possible, and I'll not ask you anything more.'

'In that case,' said Falter, shaking again in soundless mirth, 'I understand you even less. Skip the preface, and it's in the bag!'

'*Un bon mouvement*, Falter – tell me your secret.'

'What are you trying to do, catch me off guard? You're crafty, I see. No, that is out of the question. In the first days – yes, in the first days I thought it might be possible to share my secret. A grown man, unless he is a bull like me, would not stand it – all right; but I wondered if one could not bring up a new generation of the *initiated*, that is, turn my attention to children. As you see, I did not immediately overcome the infection of local dialectics. In practice, however, what would happen? In the first place, one can hardly imagine pledging kiddies to a vow of priestly silence lest any of them with one dreamy word commit manslaughter. In the second place, as soon as the child grows up, the information once imparted to him, accepted on faith, and allowed to sleep in a remote corner of his consciousness may give a start and awake, with tragic consequences. Even if my secret does not always destroy a mature member of the species, it is unthinkable that it should spare a youth. For who is not familiar with that period of life when all kinds of things – the starry sky above a Caucasian spa, a book read in the toilet, one's own conjectures about the cosmos, the delicious panic of solipsism – are in themselves enough to provoke a frenzy in all the senses of an adolescent human being? There is no reason for me to become an executioner; I have no intention of annihilating enemy regiments through a megaphone; in short, there is no one for me to confide in.'

'I asked you two questions, Falter, and you have twice proved to me the impossibility of an answer. It seems to me useless to ask you about anything else – say, about the limits of the universe, or the origin of life. You would probably suggest that I be content with a speckled minute on a second-rate planet, served by a second-rate sun, or else you would again reduce everything to a riddle: is the word "heterologous" heterologous itself.'

'Probably,' agreed Falter, giving a lengthy yawn.

His brother-in-law quietly scooped his watch out of his waistcoat and glanced at his wife.

'Here's the odd thing, though, Falter. How does superhuman knowledge of the ultimate truth combine in you with the adroitness of a banal sophist who knows nothing? Admit it, all your absurd quibbling was nothing more than an elaborate sneer.'

'Oh well, that is my only defense,' said Falter, squinting at his sister, who was nimbly extracting a long gray woolen scarf from the sleeve of the overcoat already being offered to him by his brother-in-law. 'Otherwise, you know, you might have teased it out of me. However,' he added, inserting the wrong arm, and then the right one in the sleeve, and simultaneously moving away from the helping shoves of his assistants, 'however, even if I did browbeat you a little, let me console you: amid all the piffle and prate I inadvertently gave myself away – only two or three words, but in them flashed a fringe of absolute insight – luckily, though, you paid no attention.'

He was led away, and thus ended our rather diabolical dialogue. Not only had Falter told me nothing, he had not even allowed me to get close, and no doubt his last pronouncement was as much of a mockery as all the preceding ones. The following day his brother-in-law's dull voice informed me on the telephone that Falter charged 100 francs for a visit; I asked why on earth had I not been warned of this, and he promptly replied that if the interview were to be repeated, two conversations would cost me only 150. The purchase of Truth, even at a discount, did not tempt me, and, after sending him the sum of that unexpected debt, I forced myself not to think about Falter any more. Yesterday, though ... Yes, yesterday I received a note from Falter himself, from the hospital: he wrote, in a clear hand, that he would die on Tuesday, and that in parting he ventured to inform me that – here followed two lines which had been painstakingly and, it seemed, ironically, blacked out. I replied that I was grateful for his thoughtfulness and that I wished him interesting posthumous impressions and a pleasant eternity.

But all this brings me no nearer to you, my angel. Just in case, I am keeping all the windows and doors of life wide open, even though I sense that you will not condescend to the time-honored ways of apparitions. Most terrifying of all is the thought that, inasmuch as you glow henceforth within me, I must safeguard my life. My transitory bodily frame is perhaps the only guarantee of your ideal existence: when I vanish, it will vanish as well. Alas, with a pauper's passion I am doomed to use physical nature in order to finish recounting you to myself, and then to rely on my own ellipsis...

Solus Rex

As always happened, the king was awakened by the clash between the predawn watch and the mid-morning one (*morndammer wagh* and *erldag wagh*). The former, unduly punctual, would leave its post at the prescribed minute, while the latter would be late by a constant number of seconds, not because of negligence, but probably because somebody's gouty timepiece was habitually slow. Therefore those departing and those arriving always met at one and the same place – the narrow footpath directly under the king's bedroom window, between the rear wall of the palace and a tangled growth of dense but meagerly blooming honeysuckle, under which was scattered all manner of trash: chicken feathers, broken earthenware, and large, red-cheeked tin cans that had contained 'Pomona', a national brand of preserved fruit. The meeting would invariably be accompanied by the muffled sound of a brief, good-natured tussle (and it was this that awakened the king), as one of the predawn sentries, being of a roguish bent, would pretend he did not want to surrender the slate bearing the password to one of the mid-morning men, an irritable and stupid old codger, veteran of the Swirhulm Campaign. Then all would grow still again, and the only audible sound would be the businesslike, now and then accelerating, crepitation of rain, which would systematically fall for precisely three hundred six days out of three hundred sixty-five or six, so that the weather's peripeties had long since ceased to trouble anyone (here the wind addressed the honeysuckle).

The king made a right turn out of his sleep and propped a big white fist under his cheek, on which the blazon embroidered on the pillowcase had left a chessboard impression. Between the inside edges of the brown, loosely drawn curtains, in the single but broad window, there seeped a beam of soapy light, and the king at once remembered an imminent duty (his presence at the inauguration of a new bridge across the Egel) whose disagreeable image seemed inscribed with geometric inevitability into that pale trigon of day. He was not interested in bridges, canals or shipbuilding, and even though after five years – yes, exactly five years (eighteen hundred and twenty-six days) – of nebulous reign he really ought to have acquired the habit of attending diligently to a multitude of matters that filled him with loathing because of their organic sketchiness in his mind (where very different things, in no way related to his royal office, were infinitely and unquenchably perfect), he felt depressingly aggravated every time he was obliged to have contact not only with anything that demanded a false smile from his deliberate ignorance, but also with that which was nothing more than a veneer of conventional standards on a senseless or perhaps even nonexistent object. If the inauguration of the bridge, the plans for which he did not even remember though he had no doubt approved them, struck him as merely a vulgar festival, it was also because nobody ever bothered to inquire whether he was interested in that intricate fruit of technology, suspended in mid-air, and yet today he would have to ride slowly across in a lustrous convertible with a toothy grille, and this was torture; and then there was that other engineer about whom people had been telling him ever since he had happened to mention (just like that, simply to get rid of someone or something) that he would enjoy doing some climbing, if only the island had a single decent mountain (the old, long-dead coastal volcano did not count, and, furthermore, a lighthouse – which, incidentally, did not work either – had been built on its summit). This engineer, whose dubious fame thrived in the drawing rooms of court ladies and courtesans, attracted by his honey-brown complexion and insinuating speech, had proposed elevating the central part of the insular plain and transforming it into a mountain massif, by means of subterranean inflation. The inhabitants of the chosen locality would be allowed to remain in their dwellings while the soil was being puffed up. Poltroons who preferred to withdraw from the test area where their little brick houses huddled and amazed red cows mooed, sensing the change in altitude, would be punished by their having to spend much more time on their return along the newly formed escarpments than they had on their recent retreat over the doomed flatland. Slowly the meadows swelled; boulders moved their round backs; a lethargic stream tumbled out of bed and, to its own surprise, turned into an alpine waterfall; trees traveled in file cloudward and many of them (the firs, for instance) enjoyed the ride; the villagers, leaning on their porch railings, waved their handkerchiefs and admired the pneumatic development of landscape. So the mountain would grow and grow, until the engineer ordered that the monstrous pumps be stopped. The king, however, did not wait for the stoppage, but dozed off again, with barely time to regret that, constantly resisting as he did the Councilors' readiness to support the realization of every harebrained scheme (while, on the other hand, his most natural, most human rights were constricted by rigid laws), he had not given permission for the experiment, and now it was too late, the inventor had committed suicide after patenting a gallow tree for indoor use (thus, anyway, the spirit of slumber retold it to the slumberer).

The king slept on till half past seven and, at the habitual minute, his mind jolted into action and was already on its way to meet Frey when Frey entered the bedroom. That decrepit, asthmatic *konwacher* invariably emitted in motion a queer supplementary sound, as if he were in a great hurry, although haste was apparently not in his line, seeing he had not yet got around to dying. He lowered a silver basin onto a taboret with a heart design cut out in its seat, as he had already been doing for half a century, under two kings; today he was waking a third, for whose predecessors this vanilla-scented and seemingly witch-charmed water had probably served an ablutionary purpose. Now, however, it was quite superfluous; and yet every morning the basin and taboret appeared, along with a towel that had been folded five years before. Continuing to emit his special sound, the old valet admitted the daylight in its entirety. The king always wondered why Frey did not open the curtains first, instead of groping in the penumbra to move the taboret with its useless utensil toward the bed. But speaking to Frey was out of the question because of his deafness, that went so well with the snow-owl white of his hair: he was cut off from the world by the cotton wool of old age, and, as he went out with a bow to the bed, the wall clock in the bedroom began to ticktack more distinctly, as if it had been given a recharge of time.

The bedroom now came into focus, with the dragon-shaped crack traversing its ceiling and the huge clothes tree standing like an oak in the corner. An admirable ironing board stood leaning against the wall. A thing for yanking one's riding boot off by the heel, an obsolete appliance in the shape of a huge cast-iron stag beetle, lurked under the border of an armchair robed in a white furniture cover. An oak wardrobe, obese, blind and drugged by naphthaline, stood next to an ovoid wicker-work receptacle for soiled linen, set on end there by some unknown Columbus. Various objects hung at random on the bluish walls: a clock (it had already tattled about its presence), a medicine cabinet, an old barometer that indicated remembered rather than real weather, a pencil sketch of a lake with reeds and a departing duck, a myopic photograph of a leather-legginged gentleman astride a blurry-tailed horse held by a solemn groom in front of a porch, the same porch with strained-faced servants assembled on its steps, some fluffy flowers pressed under dusty glass in a circular frame ... The paucity of the furnishings and their utter irrelevance to the needs and the tenderness of whoever used this spacious bedroom (once, it seems, inhabited by the *Husmuder*, as the wife of the preceding king had been dubbed) gave it an oddly untenanted appearance, and if it were not for the intrusive basin and the iron bed, on the edge of which sat a man in a nightshirt with a frilly collar, his strong bare feet resting upon the floor, it was impossible to imagine that anyone spent his nights here. His toes groped for and found a pair of morocco slippers and, donning a dressing gown as gray as the morning, the king walked across the creaking floorboards to the felt-padded door. When he subsequently recalled that morning, it seemed to him that, upon arising, he had experienced, both in mind and in muscles, an unaccustomed heaviness, the fateful burden of the coming day, so that the awful misfortune which that day brought (and which beneath the mask of trivial boredom stood *already* on guard at the Egel bridge), absurd and unforeseeable as it was, therefore seemed to him a kind of resolvent. We are inclined to attribute to the immediate past (I just had it in my hands, I put it right there, and now it's not there) lineaments relating it to the unexpected present, which in fact is but a bounder pluming himself on a purchased escutcheon. We, the slaves of linked events, endeavor to close the gap with a spectral ring in the chain. As we look back, we feel certain that the road we see behind us is the very one that has brought us to the tomb or the fountainhead near which we find ourselves. Life's erratic leaps and lapses can be endured by the mind only when signs of resilience and quagginess are discoverable in anterior events. Such, incidentally, were the thoughts that occurred to the no longer independent artist Dmitri Nikolaevich Sineusov, and evening had come, and in vertically arranged ruby letters glowed the word RENAULT.

The king set out in search of breakfast. He never knew in which of the five possible chambers situated along the cold stone gallery, with cobwebs in the corners of its ogival windows, his coffee would be waiting. Opening the doors one by one, he kept trying to locate the little set table, and finally found it where it happened least frequently: under a large, opulently dark portrait of his predecessor. King Gafon was portrayed at the age at which he remembered him, but features, posture and bodily structure were endowed with a magnificence that had never been characteristic of that stoop-shouldered, fidgety, and sloppy old man with a peasant crone's wrinkles above his hairless and somewhat crooked upper lip. The words of the family arms, 'see and rule' (*sassed ud halsem*), used to be changed by wags, when referring to him, to 'armchair and filbert brandy' (*sasse ud hazel*). He reigned thirty-odd years, arousing neither particular love nor particular hatred in anyone, believing equally in the power of good and the power of money, docile in his acquiescence to the parliamentary majority, whose vapid humanitarian aspirations appealed to his sentimental soul, and generously rewarding from a secret treasury the activities of those deputies whose devotion to the crown assured its stability. Kingcraft had long since become for him the flywheel of a mechanical habit, and the benighted submissiveness of the country, where the *Peplerhus* (parliament) faintly shone like a bleary and crackling rushlight, appeared as a similar form of regular rotation. And if the very last years of his reign were poisoned nevertheless by bitter sedition, coming as a belch after a long and carefree dinner, not he was to blame, but the person and behavior of the crown prince. Indeed, in the heat of vexation good burghers found that the one-time scourge of the learned world, the now forgotten Professor ven Skunk, did not err much when he affirmed that childbearing was but an illness, and that every babe was an 'externalized', self-existent parental tumor, often malignant.

The present king (pre-accessionally, let us designate him as K in chess notation) was the old man's nephew, and in the beginning no one dreamed that the nephew would accede to a throne rightfully promised to King Gafon's son, Prince Adulf, whose utterly indecent folkname (based on a felicitous assonance) must, for the sake of decorum, be translated 'Prince Fig'. K grew up in a remote palace under the eye of a morose and ambitious grandee and his horsey, masculine wife, so he barely knew his cousin and started seeing him a little more often only at the age of twenty, when Adulf was near forty.

We have before us a well-fed, easy-going fellow, with a stout neck, a broad pelvis, a big-cheeked, evenly pink face, and fine, bulging eyes. His nasty little mustache, resembling a pair of blue-black feathers, somehow did not match his fat lips, which always looked greasy, as if he had just finished sucking on a chicken bone. His dark, thick, unpleasantly smelling and also greasy hair lent a foppish something, uncommon in Thule, to his large, solidly planted head. He had a penchant for showy clothes and was at the same time as unwashed as a *papugh* (seminarian). He was well versed in music, sculpture and graphics, but could spend hours in the company of dull, vulgar persons. He wept profusely while listening to the melting violin of the great Perelmon, and shed the same tears while picking up the shards of a favorite cup. He was ready to help anyone in any way, if at that moment he was not occupied with other matters; and, blissfully wheezing, poking and nibbling at life, he constantly contrived, in regard to third parties whose existence he did not bother about, to cause sorrows far exceeding in depth that of his own soul – sorrows pertaining to another, *the* other, world.

In his twentieth year K entered the University of Ultimare, situated at four hundred miles of purple heather from the capital, on the shore of the gray sea, and there learned something about the crown prince's morals, and would have heard much more if he did not avoid talks and discussions that might overburden his already none too easy anonymity. The Count his guardian, who came to visit him once a week (sometimes arriving in the sidecar of a motorcycle driven by his energetic wife), continually emphasized how nasty, disgraceful and dangerous it would be if any of the students or professors learned that this lanky, gloomy youth, who excelled as much at his studies as at *vanbol* on the two-hundred-year-old court behind the library building, was not at all a notary's son, but a king's nephew. Whether it was submission to one of those many whims, enigmatic in their stupidity, with which someone unknown and mightier than the king and the *Peplerhus* together for some reason troubled the shabby, monotonous, northern life, faithful to half-forgotten covenants, of that *'île triste et lointaine'*; or whether the peeved grandee had his own private scheme, his far-sighted calculation (the rearing of kings was supposed to be kept secret), we do not know; nor was there any reason to speculate about this, since, anyway, the unusual student was busy with other matters. Books, wallball, skiing (winters then used to be snowy), but, most of all, nights of special meditation by the hearth, and, a little later, his romance with Belinda – all sufficiently filled up his existence to leave him unconcerned with the vulgar little intrigues of metapolitics. Moreover, while diligently studying the annals of the fatherland, it never occurred to him that within him slumbered the very blood that had coursed through the veins of preceding kings; or that actual life rushing past was also 'history' – history that had issued from the tunnel of the ages into pallid sunlight. Either because his subject of concentration ended a whole century before the reign of Gafon, or because the magic involuntarily evolved by the most sober chroniclers seemed more precious to him than his own testimony, the bookman in him overcame the eyewitness, and later on, when he tried to reestablish connection with the present, he had to content himself with knocking together provisional passages, which only served to deform the familiar remoteness of legend (that bridge on the Egel, that blood-spattered bridge!).

It was, then, before the beginning of his second college year that K, having come to the capital for a brief vacation and taken modest lodgings at the so-called 'Cabinet Members' Club', met, at the very first court reception, the crown prince, a boisterous, plump, indecently young-looking *charmeur*, defying one not to recognize his charm. The meeting took place in the presence of the old king, who sat in a high-backed armchair by a stained-glass window, quickly and nimbly devouring those tiny olive-black plums that were more a delicacy than a medicine for him. Even though Adulf seemed at first not to notice his young relative and continued to address two stooge-courtiers, the prince nevertheless started on a subject carefully calculated to fascinate the newcomer, to whom he offered a three-quarter view of himself: paunch-proud, hands thrust deep into the pockets of his wrinkled check trousers, he stood rocking slightly from heels to toes.

'For instance,' he said in the triumphant voice he reserved for public occasions, 'take our entire history, and you will see, gentlemen, that the root of power has always been construed among us as having originated in magic, with obedience conceivable only when, in the mind of the obeyer, it could be identified with the infallible effect of a spell. In other words, the king was either sorcerer or himself bewitched, sometimes by the people, sometimes by the Councilors, sometimes by a political foe who would whisk the crown off his head like a hat from a hatrack. Recall the hoariest antiquity and the rule of the *mossmons* (high priests, 'bog people'), the worship of luminescent peat, that sort of thing; or take those ... those first pagan kings – Gildras and, yes, Ofodras, and that other one, I forget what he was called, anyway, the fellow who threw his goblet into the sea, after which, for three days and nights, fishermen scooped up seawater transformed into wine ... *Solg ud digh vor je sage vel, ud jem gotelm quolm osje musikel*' ('sweet and rich was the wave of the sea and lassies

178

drank it from seashells' – the prince was quoting Uperhulm's ballad). 'And the first friars, who arrived in a skiff equipped with a cross instead of a sail, and all that business of the "Fontal Rock" – for it was only because they guessed the weak spot of our people that they managed to introduce the crazy Roman creed. What is more,' continued the prince, suddenly moderating the crescendos of his voice, for a dignitary of the clergy was now standing a short distance away, 'if the so-called church never really engorged on the body of our state, and, in the last two centuries, entirely lost its political significance, it is precisely because the elementary and rather monotonous miracles that it was able to produce very soon became a bore' the cleric moved away, and the prince's voice regained its freedom, 'and could not compete with the natural sorcery, *la magie innée et naturelle* of our fatherland. Take the subsequent, unquestionably historical kings and the beginning of our dynasty. When Rogfrid the First mounted, or rather scrambled up onto the wobbly throne that he himself called a sea-tossed barrel, and the country was in the throes of such insurrection and chaos that his aspiration to kinghood seemed a childish dream, do you recall the first thing he does upon acceding to power? He immediately mints kruns, half-kruns and grosken depicting a sixdigitate hand. Why a hand? Why the six fingers? Not one historian has been able to figure it out, and it is doubtful that Rogfrid even knew himself. The fact remains, however, that this magical measure promptly pacified the country. Later, under his grandson, when the Danes attempted to impose upon us their protégé, and he landed with immense forces, what happened? Suddenly, with the utmost simplicity, the antigovernment party – I forget what it was called, anyway, the traitors, without whom the whole plot would not have come into existence – sent a messenger to the invader with a polite announcement that they were henceforth unable to support him; because, you see, "the ling"' that is, the heather of the plain across which the turncoat army was to pass to join with the foreign forces ' "had entwined the stirrups and shins of treachery, thus preventing further advance", which apparently is to be taken literally, and not interpreted in the spirit of those stale allegories on which schoolboys are nourished. Then again

– ah, yes, a splendid example – Queen Ilda, we must not omit Queen Ilda of the white breast and the abundant amours, who would resolve all state problems by means of incantations, and so successfully that any individual who did not meet her approval would lose his reason; you know yourselves that to this day insane asylums are known among the populace as *ildehams*. And when that populace begins to take part in legislative and administrative matters, it is absurdly clear that magic is on the people's side. I assure you, for instance, that if poor King Edaric found himself unable to take his seat at the reception for the elected officers, it was certainly not a question of piles. And so on and so forth –' (the prince was beginning to have enough of the topic he had selected) '– the life of our country, like some amphibian, keeps its head up amid simple nordic reality, while submerging its belly in fable, in rich, vivifying sorcery. It's not for nothing that every one of our mossy stones, every old tree has participated at least once in some magical occurrence or other. Here's a young student, he is reading History, I am sure he will confirm my opinion.'

As he listened seriously and trustingly to Adulf's reasoning, K was astounded to what extent it coincided with his own views. True, the textbook selection of examples adduced by the talkative crown prince seemed to K a bit crude; did not the whole point lie not in the striking manifestations of witchcraft but in the delicate shadings of a fantastic something, which profoundly, and at the same time mistily, colored the Island's history? He was, however, unconditionally in agreement with the basic premise, and that was the answer he gave, lowering his head and nodding to himself. Only much later did he realize that the coincidence of ideas which had so astonished him had been the consequence of an almost unconscious cunning on the part of their promulgator, who undeniably had a special kind of instinct that allowed him to guess the most effective bait for any fresh listener.

When the king had finished his plums he beckoned to his nephew and, having no idea what to talk to him about, asked how many students there were at the university. K lost countenance – he did not know the number, and was not alert enough to name one at random. 'Five hundred? One thousand?' persisted the king, with a note of juvenile eagerness in his voice. 'I'm sure there must be more,' he added in a conciliatory tone, not having received an intelligible answer; then, after a reflective pause, he went on to inquire whether his nephew enjoyed riding. Here the crown prince butted in with his usual luscious unconstraint, inviting his cousin for an outing together the following Thursday.

'Astonishing, how much he has come to resemble my poor sister,' said the king with a mechanical sigh, taking off his glasses and returning them to the breast pocket of his brown frogged jacket. 'I am too poor to give you a horse,' he continued, 'but I have a fine little riding whip. Gotsen' (addressing the Lord Chamberlain), 'where is that fine little riding whip with the doggie's head? Look for it afterwards and give it to him ... an interesting little object, historical value and all that. Well, I'm delighted to give it to you, but a horse is beyond my means – all I have is a pair of nags and I'm keeping them for my hearse. Don't be vexed – I'm not rich.' ('*Il ment*,' said the crown prince under his breath and walked off, humming.)

On the day of the outing the weather was cold and restless, a nacreous sky skimmed overhead, the sallow bushes curtseyed in the ravines, the horsehooves plapped as they scattered the slush of thick puddles in chocolate ruts, crows croaked; and then, beyond the bridge, the riders left the road and set off at a trot across the dark heather, above which a slim, already yellowing birch rose here and there. The crown prince proved to be an excellent horseman, although he had evidently never attended a riding school, for his seat was indifferent. His heavy, broad, corduroy-and-chamois-encased bottom, bouncing up and down in the saddle, and his rounded, sloping shoulders aroused in his companion an odd, vague kind of pity, which vanished completely whenever K glanced at the prince's rosy face, radiating health and sufficiency, and heard his urgeful speech.

The riding whip had come the previous day but had not been taken: the prince (who, by the way, had set the fashion of using bad French at court) had called it with scorn '*ce machin ridicule*' and contended that it belonged to the groom's little boy, who must have forgotten it on the king's porch. '*Et mon *bonhomme de père, tu sais, a une vraie passion pour les objets trouvés.'*

'I've been thinking how much truth there is in what you were saying. Books say nothing about it at all.'

'About what?' asked the prince, laboriously trying to reconstruct which stray theory he had been expounding lately in front of his cousin.

'Oh, you remember! The magical origin of power, and the fact –'

'Yes, I do, I do,' hastily interrupted the prince and forthwith found the best way to have done with the faded topic: 'I didn't finish then because there were too many ears around. You see, our whole misfortune lies today in the government's strange ennui, in national inertia, in the dreary bickering of *Peplerhus* members. All this is so because the very force of the spells, both popular and royal, has somehow evaporated, and our ancestral sorcery has been reduced to mere hocus-pocus. But let's not discuss these depressing matters now, let's turn to more cheerful ones. Say, you must have heard a good deal about me at college? I can imagine! Tell me, what did they talk about? Why are you silent? They called me a libertine, didn't they?'

'I kept away from malicious chatter,' said K, 'but there was indeed some gossip to that effect.'

'Well, hearsay is the poetry of truth. You are still a boy – quite a pretty boy to boot – so there are many things you won't understand right now. I shall offer you only this observation: all people are basically naughty, but when it is done under the rose, when, for instance, you hasten to gorge yourself on jam in a dark corner, or send your imagination on God knows what errands, all that doesn't count; nobody considers it a crime. Yet when a person frankly and assiduously satisfies the appetites inflicted upon him by his imperious body, then, oh then, people begin to denounce intemperance! And another consideration: if, in my case, that legitimate satisfaction were limited simply to one and the same unvarying method, popular opinion would become resigned, or at most would reproach me for changing my mistresses too often. But God, what a ruckus they raise because I do not stick to the code of debauchery but gather my honey wherever I find it! And mark, I am fond of everything – whether a tulip or a plain little grass stalk – because you see,' concluded the prince, smiling and slitting his eyes, 'I really seek only the fractions of beauty, leaving the integers to the good burghers, and those fractions can be found in a ballet girl as well as in a docker, in a middle-aged Venus as well as in a young horseman.'

'Yes,' said K, 'I understand. You are an artist, a sculptor, you worship form . . .'

The prince reined in his horse and guffawed.

'Oh, well, it isn't exactly a matter of sculpture – *à moins que tu ne confondes la galanterie avec la Galatée* – which, however, is pardonable at your age. No, no – it's all much less complicated. Only don't be so bashful with me, I won't bite you, I simply can't stand lads *qui se tiennent toujours sur leurs gardes*. If you don't have anything more interesting in view, we can return via Grenlog and dine on the lakeside, and then we'll think up something.'

'No, I'm afraid I – well – I have something to take care of – It so happens that tonight I –'

'Oh, well, I'm not forcing you,' the prince said affably, and a little farther, by the mill, they said good-bye.

As many very shy people would have done in his place, K, when forcing himself to face that ride, foresaw an especially trying ordeal for the very reason of Adulf's passing for a jovial talker: with a mild, minor-mode person it would have been easier to establish the tone of the outing beforehand. As he prepared himself for it, K tried to imagine all the awkward moments that might result from the necessity of raising his normal mood to Adulf's sparkling level. Moreover he felt obligated by their first meeting, by the fact that he had imprudently concurred with the opinions of someone who therefore could rightfully expect that both men would get along just as nicely on subsequent occasions. In making a detailed inventory of his potential blunders and, above all, in fancying with the utmost clarity the tension, the leaden load in his jaws, the desperate boredom he would feel (because of his innate capacity, on all occasions, for watching askance his projected self) – in tabulating all this, including futile efforts to merge with his other self and find interesting such things as were supposed to be interesting, K also pursued a secondary, practical aim: to disarm the future, whose only force is surprise. In this he nearly succeeded. Fate, constrained by its own evil choice, was apparently content with the innocuous items he had left beyond the field of prevision: the pale sky, the heath-country wind, a creaking saddle, an impatiently responsive horse, the unflagging monologue of his self-complacent companion, all fused into a fairly endurable sensation, particularly since K had mentally set a certain time limit for the ride. It was only a matter of seeing it through. But when the prince, with a novel proposal, threatened to extend this limit into the unknown, all of whose possibilities had once again to be agonizingly appraised (and here 'something interesting' was again being forced upon K, requiring an expression of happy anticipation), this additional period of time – superfluous! unforeseen! – was intolerable; and so, at the risk of seeming impolite, he had used the pretext of a non-existent impediment. True, as soon as he turned his horse, he regretted this discourtesy just as acutely as, a moment ago, he had been concerned for his freedom. Consequently, all the nastiness expected from the future deteriorated into a doubtful echo of the past. He thought for a moment if he should not overtake the prince and consolidate the foundation of friendship through a belated, but hence doubly precious, acquiescence to a new ordeal. But his fastidious apprehension of offending a kind, cheerful man did not outweigh his fear of obviously being unable to match that kindness and cheerfulness. Thus it happened that fate outwitted him after all, and, by means of a last furtive pin-prick, rendered valueless that which he was prepared to consider a victory.

A few days later he received another invitation from the prince, asking that he 'drop in' any evening of the following week. K could not refuse. Moreover, a sense of relief that the other was not offended treacherously smoothed the way.

He was ushered into a large yellow room, as hot as a greenhouse, where a score of people, fairly evenly divided by sex, sat on divans, hassocks and a deep rug. For a fraction of a second the host seemed vaguely perplexed by his cousin's arrival, as if he had forgotten that he had invited him, or thought he had asked him for a different day. However, this momentary expression immediately gave way to a grin of welcome, after which the prince ignored his cousin, and neither, for that matter, was any attention paid to K by the other guests, evidently close friends of the prince: extraordinarily thin, smooth-haired young women, half-a-dozen middle-aged gentlemen with clean-shaven, bronzed faces, and several young men in the open-necked silk shirts that were fashionable at the time. Among them K suddenly recognized the famous young acrobat, Ondrik Guldving, a sullen blond boy, with a bizarre gentleness of gesture and gait, as if the expressiveness of his body, so remarkable in the arena, were muffled by clothes. To K this acrobat served as a key to the entire constellation of the gathering; and, even if the observer was ridiculously inexperienced and chaste, he immediately sensed that those gauze-dim, delectably elongated girls, their limbs folded with varied abandon, who were making not conversation but mirages of conversation (consisting of slow half-smiles and 'h'ms' of interrogation or response through the smoke of cigarettes inserted in precious holders), belonged to that essentially deaf-and-dumb world that in former days had been known as 'demi-monde' (all curtains drawn, no *other* world known). The fact that, interspersed among them, were ladies one saw at court balls did not change things in the least. The male group was likewise somehow homogeneous, despite its comprising representatives of the nobility, artists with dirty fingernails and roughs of the stevedore type. And precisely because the observer was inexperienced and chaste, he immediately had doubts about his initial, involuntary impression and accused himself of common prejudice, of trusting slavishly the trite talk of the town. He decided that everything was in order, i.e., that his world was in no way disrupted by the inclusion of this new province, and that everything about it was simple and comprehensible: a fun-loving, independent person had freely selected his friends.

The quietly carefree and even somehow childish rhythm of this gathering was particularly reassuring to K. The mechanical smoking, the various dainties on gold-veined little plates, the comradely cycles of motion (somebody found some sheet music for somebody; a girl tried on another girl's necklace),

185

the simplicity, the serenity, all of it denoted in its own way that kindliness which K, who himself did not possess it, recognized in all of life's phenomena, be it the smile of a bonbon in its goffered bonnet, or the echo of an old friendship divined in another's small talk. With a frown of concentration, occasionally releasing a series of agitated groans, which would end in a grunt of vexation, the prince was busy trying to drive six tiny balls into the center of a pocket-size maze of glass. A redhead in a green dress and sandals on her bare feet kept repeating, with comic mournfulness, that he would never succeed; but he persisted for a long time, juggling the recalcitrant gimmick, stamping his foot, and starting all over again. Finally he tossed it on a sofa, where some of the others promptly started on it. Then a man with handsome features, distorted by a tic, sat down at the piano, struck the keys with disorderly vigor in parody of somebody's way of playing, and right away rose again, whereupon he and the prince began arguing about the talent of a third party, probably the author of the truncated melody, and the redhead, scratching a graceful thigh through her dress, started explaining to the prince the injured party's position in a complicated musical feud. Abruptly the prince consulted his watch and turned to the blond young acrobat who was drinking orangeade in a corner: 'Ondrik,' he said with a worried air 'I think it is time.' Ondrik somberly licked his lips, put down his glass and came over. With fat fingers, the prince undid Ondrik's fly, extracted the entire pink mass of his private parts, selected the chief one and started to rub regularly its glossy shaft.

'At first,' related K, 'I thought that I had lost my mind, that I was hallucinating.' Most of all he was shocked by the natural quality of the procedure. Nausea welled within him, and he left. Once in the street, he even ran for a while.

The only person with whom he felt able to share his indignation was his guardian. Although he had no affection for the not very attractive Count, he resolved to consult him as the sole familiar he had. He asked the Count in despair how could it be that a man of Adulf's morals, a man, moreover, no longer young, and therefore unlikely to change, would become the ruler of the country. By the light in which he had suddenly seen the crown prince, he also perceived that besides hideous ribaldry, and despite a taste for the arts, Adulf was really a savage, a self-taught oaf, lacking real culture, who had appropriated a handful of its beads, had learned how to flaunt the glitter of his adaptive mind, and of course did not worry in the least about the problems of his impending reign. K kept asking was it not crazy nonsense, the delirium of dreams, to imagine such a person king; but in setting those questions he hardly expected matter-of-fact replies: it was the rhetoric of young disenchantment. Nevertheless, as he went on expressing his perplexity, in abrupt brittle phrases (he was not born eloquent), K overtook reality and had a glimpse of its face. Admittedly, he at once fell back again, but that glimpse imprinted itself in his soul, revealing to him in a flash what perils awaited a state doomed to become the plaything of a prurient ruffian.

The Count heard him out attentively, now and then turning on him the gaze of his lashless vulturine eyes: they reflected a strange satisfaction. A calculating and cool mentor, he replied most cautiously, as if not quite agreeing with K, calming him down by saying that what he had happened to catch sight of was acting upon his judgement with undue force; that the only purpose of the hygiene established by the prince was not to allow a young friend to waste his strength on wenching; and that Adulf had qualities which might show themselves upon his ascension. At the end of the interview the Count offered to have K meet a certain wise person, the well-known economist Gumm. Here the Count pursued a double purpose: on one hand, he freed himself of all responsibility for what might follow, and remained aloof, which would do very nicely in case of some mishap; and on the other hand, he was passing K over to an experienced conspirator, thus beginning the realization of a plan that the evil and wily Count had been nursing, it seems, for quite a time.

Meet Gumm, meet economist Gumm, a round-tummied little old man in a woolen waistcoat, with blue spectacles pushed up high on his pink forehead, bouncy, trim, giggly Gumm. Their meetings increased in frequency, and at the end of his second year at college, K even sojourned for about a week in Gumm's house. By that time K had discovered enough things about the crown prince's behavior not to regret that first explosion of indignation. Not so much from Gumm himself, who seemed always to be rolling somewhither, as from his relatives and entourage, K learnt about the measures which had already been tried to subdue the prince. At first, people had attempted to inform the old king about his son's frolics, so as to obtain parental restraint. Indeed, when this or that person, after gaining, through the thorns of protocol, access to the king's *kabinet*, depicted frankly those stunts to His Majesty, the old man, flushing purple and nervously pulling together the skirts of his dressing gown, displayed greater wrath than one might have hoped for. He shouted that he would put an end to it, that the cup of endurance (wherein his morning coffee stormily splashed) was overflowing, that he was happy to hear a candid report, that he would banish the lecherous cur for six months to a *suyphellhus* (monastery ship, floating hermitage), that he would – And when the audience had come to a close, and the pleased official was about to bow his way out, the old king, still puffing, but already pacified, would take him aside, with a business-like confidential air (though actually they were alone in the study), and say, 'Yes, yes, I understand all that, all that is so, but listen – quite between us – tell me, if we look at it reasonably – after all my Adulf is a bachelor, a gay dog, he's fond of a little sport – is it necessary to get all worked up? Remember, we also were boys once.' That last consideration sounded rather silly, for the king's distant youth had flowed with milky tranquillity, and afterwards, the late queen, his wife, treated him with unusual severity till he was sixty. She was, incidentally, a remarkably obstinate, stupid and petty-minded woman with a constant propensity for innocent but extremely absurd fantasies; and very possibly it was owing to her that the habitus of the court and, to a certain extent, of the state acquired those peculiar, difficult-to-define features, oddly blending stagnation and caprice, improvidence and the primness of non-violent insanity, that so much tormented the present king.

The second, chronologically speaking, form of opposition was considerably deeper: it consisted of rallying and fortifying public resources. One could scarcely rely on the conscious participation of the plebeian class: among the insular plow-men, weavers, bakers, carpenters, cornmongers, fisherfolk and so forth, the transformation of any crown prince into any king was accepted as meekly as a change in the weather: the rustic gazed at the auroral gleam amid the cumulated clouds, shook his head and that was all; in his dark lichenian brain a tradition-al place was always reserved for traditional disaster, national or natural. The meagerness and sluggishness of economics, the frozen level of prices, which had long since lost vital sen-sitivity (through which there is formed all at once a connec-tion between an empty head and an empty stomach), the grim constancy of inconsiderable but just sufficient harvests, the secret pact between greens and grain, which had agreed, it seemed, to supplement each other and thus hold agronomy in equipoise – all this, according to Gumm (see *The Basis and Anabasis of Economics*) kept the people in languid submission; and if some sort of sorcery prevailed here, then so much the worse for the victims of its viscous spells. Furthermore – and the enlightened found therein a source of especial sadness – Prince Fig enjoyed a kind of smutty popularity among the lower classes and the petty bourgeoisie (between whom the distinction was so wobbly that one could regularly observe such puzzling phenomena as the return of a shop-keeper's prosper-ous son to the humble manual trade of his grandfather). The hearty laughter invariably accompanying talk about Fig's pranks prevented them from being condemned: the mask of mirth stuck to one's mouth, and that mimicry of approval could no longer be distinguished from the real thing. The more lewdly Fig romped, the louder folks guffawed, the mightier and merrier red fists thumped on the deal tables of pubs. A characteristic detail: one day when the prince, passing on horseback, a cigar between his teeth, through a backwoodsy hamlet, noticed a comely little girl to whom he offered a ride, and notwithstanding her parents' horror (which respect barely helped to restrain), swept her away, while her old granddad kept running along the road until he toppled into a ditch, the whole village, as agents reported, expressed their admiration by roars of laughter, congratulated the family, reveled in surmise and did not stint in mischievous inquiries when the child returned after an hour's absence, holding a hundred-krun note in one hand, and, in the other, a fledgling that had fallen out of its nest in a desolate grove where she had picked it up on her way back to the village.

In military circles displeasure with the prince was based not so much on considerations of general morals and national prestige as on direct resentment suscitated by his attitude toward flaming punch and booming guns. King Gafon himself, in contrast to his pugnacious predecessor, was a 'deeply civilian' old party; nonetheless the army put up with it, his complete non-comprehension of military matters being redeemed by the timorous esteem in which he held them; per contra, the Guard could not forgive his son's open sneer. War games, parades, puffy-cheeked music, regimental banquets with the observation of colorful customs, and various other conscientious recreations on the part of the small insular army produced nothing but scornful ennui in Adulf's eminently artistic soul. Yet the army's unrest did not go further than desultory murmurs, plus, maybe, the making of midnight oaths (to the gleam of tapers, goblets and swords) – to be forgotten next morning. Thus the initiative belonged to the enlightened minds of the public, which sad to say were not numerous; the anti-adulfian opposition included, however, certain statesmen, newspaper editors, and jurists – all respectable, tough-sinewed old fellows, wielding plenty of secret or manifest influence. In other words, public opinion rose to the occasion, and the ambition to curb the crown prince as his iniquity progressed became considered a sign of decency and intelligence. It only remained to find a weapon. Alas, this precisely was lacking. There existed the press, there existed a parliament, but by the code of the constitution the least disrespectful poke at a member of the royal family must result in the newspaper's being banned or the chamber's dissolved. A single attempt to stir up the nation failed. We are referring to the celebrated trial of Dr Onze.

That trial presented something unparalleled even in the unparalleled annals of Thulean justice. A man renowned for his virtue, a lecturer and writer on civic and philosophical questions, a personality so highly regarded, endowed with such strictness of views and principles, in a word, such a dazzlingly unstained character that, in comparison, the reputation of anyone else appeared spotty, was accused of various crimes against morals, defended himself with the clumsiness of despair, and finally acknowledged his guilt. So far there was nothing very unusual about it: goodness knows into what furuncles the mamillae of merit may turn under scrutiny! The unusual and subtle part of the matter lay in the fact that the indictment and the evidence formed practically a replica of all that could be imputed to the crown prince. One could not help being amazed by the precision of details obtained in order to insert a full-length portrait in the prepared frame without touching up or omitting anything. Much of it was so new, and individualized so precisely the commonplaces of long-coarsened rumor, that at first the masses did not realize *who* had sat for the picture. Very soon, however, the daily reports in the papers began to stir up quite exceptional interest among such readers as had caught on, and people who used to pay up to twenty kruns to attend the trial now did not spare five hundred or more.

The initial idea had been generated in the womb of the *prokuratura* (magistracy). The oldest judge in the capital took a fancy to it. All one needed was to find a person sufficiently upright not to be confused with the prototype of the affair, sufficiently clever not to act as a clown or a cretin before the tribunal, and, in particular, sufficiently dedicated to the cause to sacrifice everything to it, endure a monstrous mud bath, and exchange his career for hard labor. Candidates for that rôle were not available: the conspirators, most of them well-to-do family men, liked every part except the one without which the play could not be staged. The situation already looked hopeless – when one day, at a meeting of the plotters, appeared Dr Onze dressed entirely in black and, without sitting down, declared that he put himself completely at their disposal. A natural impatience to grasp the occasion hardly allowed them time to marvel; for at first blush it surely must have been difficult to understand how the rarefied life of a thinker could be compatible with the willingness to be pilloried for the sake of a political intrigue. Actually, his was not such an uncommon case. Being constantly occupied with spiritual problems, and constantly adapting the laws of the most rigid principles to the most fragile abstractions, Dr Onze did not find it possible to refuse a personal application of the same method when presented with the opportunity of performing a deed that was disinterested and probably senseless (and therefore still abstract, owing to the utmost purity of its nature). Furthermore, one should remember that Dr Onze was giving up his chair, the mollitude of his book-lined study, the continuation of his latest opus – in brief, everything that a philosopher has the right to treasure. Let us mention that he was in indifferent health; let us emphasize the fact that before submitting the case to a close examination he had been obliged to devote three nights to delving in rather special works dealing with problems of which an ascetic could know little; and let us add that not long before he took his decision, he had become engaged to a senescent virgin after years of unexpressed love, during which time her fiancé of long standing fought phtisis in distant Switzerland until he expired, hence freeing her of her pact with compassion.

The case started by that truly heroic female's suing Dr Onze for allegedly luring her to his secret *garçonnière*, 'a den of luxury and libertinism'. A similar claim (the only difference being that the apartment surreptitiously taken and fitted by the conspirators was not the one which the prince used to rent at one time for special pleasures but faced it on the opposite side of the street – which immediately established the mirror-image idea characteristic of the entire trial) had been filed against Fig by a not over-bright maiden, who did not happen to know that her seducer was the heir to the throne, i.e. a person who in no circumstances could be arraigned. There followed the testimony of numerous witnesses (some of them altruistic adherents, others paid agents: there had not been quite enough of the first); their declarations had been brilliantly composed by a committee of experts, among whom one noted a distinguished historian, two major literati, and several experienced jurists. In these declarations the activity of the crown prince developed gradually, in the correct chronological order, but with some calendric abridgment compared to the time it had taken the prince to exasperate the public so badly. Group fornication, ultra-urningism, abduction of youngsters and many other amusements were described to the accused in the form of detailed questions to which he replied much more briefly. Having studied the whole affair with the methodical diligence peculiar to his mentality, Dr Onze, who had never considered theatrical art (in fact, he did not go to the theater), now, by means of a savant's approach, unconsciously achieved a splendid impersonation of the kind of criminal whose denial of the charge (an attitude which in the present case was meant to let the prosecution get into its stride) finds nourishment in contradictory statements and assistance in bewildered stubbornness.

Everything proceeded as planned; alas, it soon became clear that the conspirators had no idea what really to hope for. For the eyes of the people to open? But the people knew all along Fig's nominal value. For moral revulsion to turn into civic revolt? But nothing indicated the way to such a metamorphosis. Or maybe the whole scheme was to be but a link in a long chain of progressively more efficient disclosures? But then the boldness and bite of the affair, by the very fact of their lending it an unrepeatable character of exclusiveness, could not help breaking, between the first link and the next, a chain that demanded above all some gradual form of malleation.

The publication of all the details of the case only helped to enrich the papers: their circulation grew to such an extent that in the resulting lush shade certain alert people (as for example Sien) managed to create new organs which pursued this or that object, but whose success was guaranteed because of their reports on the trial. The honestly indignant citizens were vastly outnumbered by the lip-smackers and the curious. Plain folks read and laughed. In those public proceedings they saw a marvelously entertaining gag thought up by rascals. The crown prince's image acquired in their minds the aspect of a punchinello whose varnished pate gets, perhaps, thumped by the stick of a mangy devil, but who remains the pet of the gapers, the star of the show-box. On the other hand, the personality of sublime Dr Onze not only failed to be recognized as such but provoked happy hoots of malice (echoed disgracefully by the yellow press), the populace having mistaken his position for a wretched readiness to please on the part of a bribed high-brow.

In a word, the pornographic popularity which had always surrounded the prince was only augmented, and even the most ironic conjectures as to how he must feel reading about his own escapades bore the mark of that good nature with which we involuntarily encourage another chap's showy recklessness.

The nobility, the councilors, the court and 'courtierist' members of the *Peplerhus* were caught napping. They tamely decided to lie in wait and thus lost invaluable political tempo. True, a few days before the verdict, members of the royalist party succeeded, by intricate or merely crooked means, in getting a law passed forbidding the newspapers to report on 'divorce cases or other hearings apt to contain scandalous items'; but as, constitutionally, no law could be enforced until forty days had elapsed since its acceptance (a period termed 'parturiency of Themis'), the papers had ample time to cover the trial to the very end.

Prince Adulf himself regarded the business with complete indifference, which, moreover, was so naturally expressed that one wondered if he understood about whom they really were talking. Since every scrap of the affair must have been familiar to him, one is forced to conclude that either he had suffered an amnesic shock or that his self-control was superb. Once only his intimates thought they saw a shadow of vexation flit across his large face: 'What a pity,' he cried, 'why didn't that *polisson* invite me to his parties? *Que de plaisirs perdus!*' As to the king, he also looked unconcerned, but to judge by the way he cleared his throat while filing away the newspaper in a drawer and removing his reading glasses, and also by the frequency of his secret sessions with this or that councilor summoned at an unseasonable hour, one gathered that he was strongly perturbed. It was said that during the days of the trial he offered several times, with feigned casualness, to lend his son the royal yacht so that Adulf might undertake 'a little round-the-world voyage', but Adulf only laughed and kissed him on his bald spot. 'Really, my dear boy,' insisted the old king, 'it's so delightful being at sea! You might take musicians with you, a barrel of wine!' '*Hélas!*' answered the prince, 'a see-sawing sea line compromises my solar plexus.'

The trial entered its final stage. The defense alluded to the accused's 'youth', to his 'hot blood', to the 'temptations' attending a bachelor's life – all of which was a rather coarse parody of the king's overindulgence. The prosecutor made a speech of savage force – and overshot the mark by demanding the death penalty. The defendant's last word introduced an utterly unexpected note. Exhausted by lengthy tension, harrowed by having been forced to wallow in another's filth and involuntarily staggered by the prosecutor's blast, the luckless scholar lost his nerve and, after a few incoherent mumblings, suddenly started, in a new, hysterically clear voice, to tell how one night in his youth, having drunk his first glass of hazel brandy, he accepted to go with a classmate to a brothel, and how he did not get there only because he fainted in the street. This unforeseen avowal convulsed the public with long laughter, while the prosecutor, losing his head, attempted to stop the defendant's mouth by physical means. Then the jury retired for a silent smoke to the room allotted to them, and presently came back to announce the verdict. It was suggested that Dr Onze be sentenced to eleven years' hard labor.

The sentence was wordily approved by the press. At secret visits his friends shook hands with the martyr, as they took farewell of him ... But here, good old Gafon, for the first time in his life, unexpectedly for everybody including, maybe, his own self, acted rather wittily: he took advantage of an incontestable prerogative and granted Onze a full pardon.

Thus both the first and second modes of pressure upon the prince practically came to nothing. There remained a third, a most decisive and certain, way. All the talks in Gumm's entourage tended exclusively toward the realization of that third measure, though its actual name, apparently, nobody pronounced: Death enjoys a sufficient number of euphemisms. K, upon getting involved in the tangled circumstances of a plot, did not quite make out what was happening, and the reason of that blindness lay not solely in youthful inexperience; it depended upon his considering himself, instinctively, though quite erroneously, to be the main instigator (whereas, of course, he was no more than an honorary walk-on actor – or an honorary hostage) and therefore refusing to believe that the enterprise he had initiated could end in bloodshed; indeed, no enterprise really existed, since he vaguely felt that by the very act of surmounting his disgust in studying his cousin's life he was accomplishing something sufficiently important and needful; and when with the passing of time he got a little bored with that study and with constant talks about the same thing, he still kept participating in them, dutifully stuck to the tedious topic, and continued to think he was performing his duty by collaborating with some kind of force that remained obscure to him but that finally would transform, by a stroke of its wand, an impossible prince into an acceptable heir apparent. Even if it occurred to him to welcome the possibility of simply forcing Adulf to forego his claim to the throne (and the vagaries of figurative speech used by the plotters might have chanced to imply such an interpretation), he, strangely enough, never brought that thought to the end, i.e. to himself as the next in line. For almost two years, in the margin of college work, he constantly associated with rotund Gumm and his friends, and imperceptibly found himself caught in a very dense and delicate web; and perhaps the enforced boredom he felt more and more keenly should not be reduced to the mere incapacity – otherwise characteristic of his nature – to keep concerned with things that gradually grew the integument of habit (through which he no longer distinguished the radiance of their passionate revival); but perhaps it was the deliberately changed voice of a subliminal warning. Meanwhile the business that had been commenced long before his participation in it neared its gory denouement.

On a cold summer evening he was invited to a secret assembly; he went, for the invitation hinted at nothing unusual. Later he recalled, it is true, how unwillingly, with what a burdensome sense of compulsion, he set out for the meeting; but with similar feelings he had gone to meetings before. In a large room, unheated, and, as it were, fictitiously furnished (wallpaper, fireplace, sideboard with dusty drinking horn on one shelf – all looked like stage properties), there sat a score of men, more than half of whom K did not know. Here for the first time he saw Dr Onze: that marble-white calvity depressed along its middle, those thick blond eyelashes, the little freckles above the brows, the rufous shade on the cheekbones, the tightly compressed lips, the frock coat of a fanatic and the eyes of a fish. A frozen expression of meek, lambent melancholy did not embellish his unfortunate features. He was addressed with pointed respect. Everyone knew that after the trial his fiancée had broken with him, explaining that she irrationally went on seeing on the wretched man's face the traces of soily vice to which he had confessed in assuming another's character. She retired to a distant village, where she became wholly absorbed in teaching; and Dr Onze himself, soon after the event prefaced by that assembly, sought reclusion in a smallish monastery.

Among those present, K also noted the celebrated jurist Schliss, several *frad* (liberal) members of the *Peplerhus*, the son of the minister of public education ... And on an uncomfortable leathern divan sat three lanky and somber army officers.

He found a cane-seated free chair next to the window on whose ledge sat a small man who kept apart from the others. He had a plebeian type of face and fiddled with the postal department cap in his hands. K was close enough to observe his coarse-shod huge feet, which did not go at all with his puny figure, so that one obtained something like a photograph taken at point-blank range. Only later did K learn that this man was Sien.

At first it seemed to K that the people collected in the room were engaged in the kind of talk which had long grown familiar to him. Something within him (again that innermost friend!) even *longed*, with a sort of childish eagerness, that this meeting would not differ from all previous ones. But Gumm's strange, somehow sickening gesture when in passing he put his hand on K's shoulder and nodded mysteriously – this, as well as the slow, guarded sound of voices, and the expression of those three officers' eyes, caused K to prick up his ears. Hardly two minutes passed before he knew that what they were coldly working out here, in this bogus room, was the already decided assassination of the crown prince.

He felt the breath of fate near his temples and the same, almost physical, nausea he had once experienced after that soirée at his cousin's. By the look which the silent pygmy in the embrasure gave him (a look of curiosity mixed with sarcasm),

K realized that his confusion had not passed unnoticed. He got up, and then everyone turned toward him, and the bristly-haired, heavy man who was speaking at that minute (K had long ceased to hear the words) stopped short. K went up to Gumm, whose triangular eyebrows rose expectantly. 'I must be going,' said K, 'I'm not feeling well, I think, I had better go.' He bowed; a few persons politely stood up; the man on the window-ledge lit his pipe, smiling. As K advanced toward the exit, he had the nightmare sensation that, maybe, the door was a still-life painting, that its handle was *en trompe-l'oeil,* and could not be turned. But all at once the door became real, and, escorted by a youth, who had softly come out of some other room in his bedslippers with a bundle of keys, K proceeded to go down a long and dark staircase.

The Potato Elf

This is the first faithful translation of 'Kartofel'nyy el'f', written in 1929 in Berlin, published there in the émigré daily *Rul* (15, 17, 18 and 19 December 1929) and included in *Vozvrashchenie Chorba*, Slovo, Berlin, 1930, a collection of my stories. A very different English version (by Serge Bertenson and Irene Kosinska), full of mistakes and omissions, appeared in *Esquire,* December 1939, and has been reprinted in an anthology (*The Single Voice*, Collier, London, 1969).

Although I never intended the story to suggest a screenplay or to fire a script writer's fancy, its structure and recurrent pictorial details do have a cinematic slant. Its deliberate introduction results in certain conventional rhythms – or in a pastiche of such rhythms. I do not believe, however, that my little man can move even the most lachrymose human-interest fiend, and this redeems the matter.

Another aspect separating 'The Potato Elf' from the rest of my short stories is its British setting. One cannot rule out thematic automatism in such cases, yet on the other hand this curious exoticism (as being different from the more familiar Berlin background of my other stories) gives the thing an artificial brightness which is none too displeasing; but all in all it is not my favorite piece, and if I include it in this collection it is only because the act of retranslating it properly is a precious personal victory that seldom falls to a betrayed author's lot.

1

Actually his name was Frederic Dobson. To his friend the conjuror, he talked about himself thus:

'There was no one in Bristol who didn't know Dobson the tailor for children's clothes. I am his son – and am proud of it out of sheer stubbornness. You should know that he drank like an old whale. Some time around 1900, a few months before I was born, my gin-soaked dad rigged up one of those wax-work cherubs, you know – sailor suit, with a lad's first long trousers – and put it in my mother's bed. It's a wonder the poor thing did not have a miscarriage. As you can well understand, I know all this only by hearsay – yet, if my kind informers were not liars, this is, apparently, the secret reason I am –'

And Fred Dobson, in a sad and good-natured gesture, would spread out his little hands. The conjuror, with his usual dreamy smile, would bend down, pick up Fred like a baby, and, sighing, place him on the top of a wardrobe, where the Potato Elf would meekly roll up and start to sneeze softly and whimper.

He was twenty, and weighed less than fifty pounds, being only a couple of inches taller than the famous Swiss dwarf, Zimmermann (dubbed 'Prince Balthazar'). Like friend Zimmermann, Fred was extremely well built, and had there not been those wrinkles on his round forehead and at the corners of his narrowed eyes, as well as a rather eerie air of tension (as if he were resisting growth), our dwarf would have easily passed for a gentle eight-year-old boy. His hair, the hue of damp straw, was sleeked down and evenly parted by a line which ran up the exact middle of his head to conclude a cunning agreement with its crown. Fred walked lightly, had an easy demeanor and danced rather well, but his very first manager deemed it wise to weight the notion of 'elf' with a comic epithet upon noticing the fat nose inherited by the dwarf from his plethoric and naughty father.

The Potato Elf, by his sole aspect, aroused a storm of applause and laughter throughout England, and then in the main cities of the Continent. He differed from most dwarfs in being of a mild and friendly nature. He became greatly attached to the miniature pony Snowdrop on which he trotted diligently around the arena of a Dutch circus; and, in Vienna, he conquered the heart of a stupid and glum giant hailing from Omsk by stretching up to him the first time he saw him and pleading like an infant to be taken up in Nurse's arms.

He usually performed not alone. In Vienna, for example, he appeared with the Russian giant and minced around him, neatly attired in striped trousers and a smart jacket, with a voluminous roll of music under his arm. He brought the giant's guitar. The giant stood like a tremendous statue and took the instrument with the motions of an automaton. A long frock coat that looked carved out of ebony, elevated heels and a top hat with a sheen of columnar reflections increased the height of the stately three-hundred-and-fifty-pound Siberian. Thrusting out his powerful jaw, he beat the strings with one finger. Backstage, in womanish tones, he complained of giddiness. Fred grew very fond of him and even shed a few tears at the moment of separation, for he rapidly became accustomed to people. His life, like a circus horse's, went round and round with smooth monotony. One day in the dark of the wings he tripped over a bucket of house paint and mellowly plopped into it – an occurrence he kept recalling for quite a long while as something out of the ordinary.

In this way the dwarf traveled around most of Europe, and saved money, and sang with a *castrato*-like silvery voice, and in German variety theaters the audience ate thick sandwiches and candied nuts on sticks, and in Spanish ones, sugared violets and also nuts on sticks. The world was invisible to him. There remained in his memory the same faceless abyss laughing at him, and afterwards, when the performance was over, the soft, dreamy echo of a cool night that seems of such a deep blue when you leave the theater.

Upon returning to London he found a new partner in the

person of Shock, the conjuror. Shock had a tuneful delivery, slender, pale, virtually ethereal hands, and a lick of chestnut brown hair that came down on one eyebrow. He resembled a poet more than a stage magician, and demonstrated his skill with a sort of tender and graceful melancholy, without the fussy patter characteristic of his profession. The Potato Elf assisted him amusingly, and, at the end of the act, would turn up in the gallery with a cooing exclamation of joy, although a minute before everyone had seen Shock lock him up in a black box right in the middle of the stage.

All this happened in one of those London theaters where there are acrobats soaring in the tinkle and shiver of the trapezes, and a foreign tenor (a failure in his own country) singing barcaroles, and a ventriloquist in naval uniform, and bicyclists, and the inevitable clown-eccentric shuffling about in a minuscule hat and a waistcoat coming down to his knees.

2

Latterly Fred had been growing gloomy, and sneezing a lot, soundlessly and sadly, like a little Japanese spaniel. While not experiencing for months any hankering after a woman, the virginal dwarf would be beset now and then by sharp pangs of lone amorous anguish which went as suddenly as they came, and again, for a while, he would ignore the bare shoulders showing white beyond the velvet boundary of loges, as well as the little girl acrobats, or the Spanish dancer whose sleek thighs were revealed for a moment when the orange-red curly fluff of her nether flounces would whip up in the course of a rapid swirl.

'What you need is a female dwarf,' said pensively Shock, producing with a familiar flick of finger and thumb a silver coin from the ear of the dwarf whose little arm went up in a brushing-away curve as if chasing a fly.

That same night, as Fred, after his number, snuffling and grumbling, in bowler and tiny topcoat, was toddling along a dim backstage passage, a door came ajar with a sudden splash of gay light and two voices called him in. It was Zita and Arabella, sister acrobats, both half-undressed, suntanned, black-haired, with elongated blue eyes. A shimmer of theatrical disorder and the fragrance of lotions filled the room. The dressing table was littered with powder puffs, combs, cut-glass atomizers, hairpins in an ex-chocolate box and rouge sticks.

The two girls instantly deafened Fred with their chatter. They tickled and squeezed the dwarf, who, glowering, and empurpled with lust, rolled like a ball in the embrace of the bare-armed teases. Finally, when frolicsome Arabella drew him to her and fell backward upon the couch, Fred lost his head and began to wriggle against her, snorting and clasping her neck. In attempting to push him away, she raised her arm and, slipping under it, he lunged and glued his lips to the hot pricklish hollow of her shaven axilla. The other girl, weak with laughter, tried in vain to drag him off by his legs. At that moment the door banged open, and the French partner of the two aerialists came into the room wearing marble-white tights. Silently, without any resentment, he grabbed the dwarf by the scruff of the neck (all you heard was the snap of Fred's wing collar as one side broke loose from the stud), lifted him in the air and threw him out like a monkey. The door slammed. Shock, who happened to be wandering past, managed to catch a glimpse of the marble-bright arm and of a black little figure with feet retracted in flight.

Fred hurt himself in falling and now lay motionless in the corridor. He was not really stunned, but had gone all limp with eyes fixed on one point, and fast chattering teeth.

'Bad luck, old boy,' sighed the conjuror, picking him up from the floor. He palpated with translucent fingers the dwarf's round forehead and added, 'I told you not to butt in. Now you got it. A dwarf woman is what you need.'

Fred, his eyes bulging, said nothing.

'You'll sleep at my place tonight,' decided Shock and carried the Potato Elf toward the exit.

3

There existed also a Mrs Shock.

She was a lady of uncertain age, with dark eyes which had a yellowish tinge around the iris. Her skinny frame, parchment complexion, lifeless black hair, a habit of strongly exhaling tobacco smoke through her nostrils, the studied untidiness of her attire and hairdo – all this could hardly attract many men, but, no doubt, was to Mr Shock's liking, though actually he never seemed to notice his wife, as he was always engaged in imagining secret devices for his show, always appeared unreal and shifty, thinking of something else when talking about trivialities, but keenly observing everything around him when immersed in astral fancies. Nora had to be constantly on the lookout since he never missed the occasion to contrive some small, inutile, yet subtly artful deception. There had been, for instance, that time when he amazed her by his unusual gluttony: he smacked his lips juicily, sucked chicken bones clean, again and again heaped up food on his plate; then he departed after giving his wife a sorrowful glance; and a little later the maid, giggling into her apron, informed Nora that Mr Shock had not touched one scrap of his dinner, and had left all of it in three brand-new pans under the table.

She was the daughter of a respectable artist who painted only horses, spotty hounds and huntsmen in pink coats. She had lived in Chelsea before her marriage, had admired the hazy Thames sunsets, taken drawing lessons, gone to ridiculous meetings attended by the local Bohemian crowd – and it was there that the ghost-gray eyes of a quiet slim man had singled her out. He talked little about himself, and was still unknown. Some people believed him to be a composer of lyrical poems. She fell headlong in love with him. The poet absentmindedly became engaged to her, and on the very first day of matrimony explained, with a sad smile, that he did not know how to write poetry, and there and then, in the middle of the conversation, he transformed an old alarm-clock into a nickel-plated chronometer, and the chronometer into a miniature gold watch, which Nora had worn ever since on her wrist. She understood that nevertheless conjuror Shock was, in his own way, a poet; only she could not get used to his demonstrating his art every minute, in all circumstances. It is hard to be happy when one's husband is a mirage, a peripatetic legerdemain of a man, a deception of all five senses.

4

She was idly tapping a fingernail against the glass of a bowl in which several goldfish that looked cut out of orange peel breathed and fin-flashed when the door opened noiselessly, and Shock appeared (silk hat askew, strand of brown hair on his brow) with a little creature all screwed up in his arms.

'Brought him,' said the conjuror with a sigh.

Nora thought fleetingly: child. Lost. Found. Her dark eyes grew moist.

'Must be adopted,' softly added Shock, lingering in the doorway.

The small thing suddenly came alive, mumbled something and started to scrabble shyly against the conjuror's starched shirtfront. Nora glanced at the tiny boots in chamois spats, at the little bowler.

'I'm not so easy to fool,' she sneered.

The conjuror looked at her reproachfully. Then he laid Fred on a plush couch and covered him with a lap-robe.

'Blondinet roughed him up,' explained Shock, and could not help adding, 'Bashed him with a dumbbell. Right in the tummy.'

And Nora, kind-hearted as childless women frequently are, felt such an especial pity that she almost broke into tears. She proceeded to mother the dwarf, she fed him, gave him a glass of port, rubbed his forehead with eau-de-cologne, moistened with it his temples and the infantine hollows behind his ears.

Next morning Fred woke up early, inspected the unfamiliar room, talked to the goldfish, and after a quiet sneeze or two, settled on the ledge of the bay-window like a little boy.

A melting, enchanting mist washed London's gray roofs. Somewhere in the distance an attic window was thrown open, and its pane caught a glint of sunshine. The horn of an automobile sang out in the freshness and tenderness of dawn.

Fred's thoughts dwelt on the previous day. The laughing accents of the girl tumblers got oddly mixed up with the touch of Mrs Shock's cold fragrant hands. At first he had been ill-treated, then he had been caressed; and, mind you, he was a very affectionate, very ardent dwarf. He dwelt in fancy on the possibility of his rescuing Nora some day from a strong, brutal man resembling that Frenchman in white tights. Incongruously, there floated up the memory of a fifteen-year-old female dwarf with whom he appeared together at one time. She was a bad-tempered, sick, sharp-nosed little thing. The two were presented to the spectators as an engaged couple, and, shivering with disgust, he had to dance an intimate tango with her.

Again a lone klaxon sang out and swept by. Sunlight was beginning to infuse the mist over London's soft wilderness.

Around half past seven the flat came to life. With an abstract smile Mr Shock left for an unknown destination. From the dining room came the delicious smell of bacon and eggs. With her hair done anyhow, wearing a kimono embroidered with sunflowers, appeared Mrs Shock.

After breakfast she offered Fred a perfumed cigarette with a red-petaled tip and half-closing her eyes had him tell her about his existence. At such narrative moments Fred's little voice deepened slightly: he spoke slowly, choosing his words, and, strange to say, that unforeseen dignity of diction became him. Bent-headed, solemn and elastically tense, he sat sideways at Nora's feet. She reclined on the plush divan, her arms thrown back, revealing her sharp bare elbows. The dwarf, having finished his tale, lapsed into silence but still kept turning this way and that the palm of his tiny hand, as if softly continuing to speak. His black jacket, inclined face, fleshy little nose, tawny hair, and that middle parting reaching the back of his head vaguely moved Nora's heart. As she looked at him through her lashes she tried to imagine that it was not an adult dwarf sitting there, but her non-existing little son in the act of telling her how his schoolmates bullied him. Nora stretched her hand

and stroked his head lightly – and, at that moment, by an enigmatic association of thought, she called forth something else, a curious, vindictive vision.

Upon feeling those light fingers in his hair, Fred at first sat motionless, then began to lick his lips in feverish silence. His eyes, turned askance, could not detach their gaze from the green pompon on Mrs Shock's slipper. And all at once, in some absurd and intoxicating way, everything came into motion.

5

On that smoke-blue day, in the August sun, London was particularly lovely. The tender and festive sky was reflected in the smooth spread of the asphalt, the glossy pillar boxes glowed crimson at the street corners, through the Gobelin green of the Park cars flashed and rolled with a low hum – the entire city shimmered and breathed in the mellow warmth, and only underground, on the platforms of the Tube, could one find a region of coolness.

Every separate day in the year is a gift presented to only one man – the happiest one; all other people use his day, to enjoy the sunshine or berate the rain, never knowing, however, to whom that day really belongs; and its fortunate owner is pleased and amused by their ignorance. A person cannot foreknow which day exactly will fall to his lot, what trifle he will remember forever: the ripple of reflected sunlight on a wall bordering water or the revolving fall of a maple leaf; and it often happens that he recognizes *his* day only in retrospection, long after he has plucked, and crumpled, and chucked under his desk the calendar leaf with the forgotten figure.

Providence granted Fred Dobson, a dwarf in mouse-gray spats, the merry August day in 1920 which began with the melodious hoot of a motor horn and the flash of a casement swung open in the distance. Children coming back from a walk told their parents, with gasps of wonder, that they had met a dwarf in a bowler hat and striped trousers, with a cane in one hand and a pair of tan gloves in the other.

After ardently kissing Nora good-bye (she was expecting visitors), the Potato Elf came out on the broad smooth street, flooded with sunlight, and instantly knew that the whole city had been created for him and only for him. A cheerful taxi driver turned down with a resounding blow the iron flag of his meter; the street started to flow past, and Fred kept slipping off the leathern seat, while chuckling and cooing under his breath.

He got out at the Hyde Park entrance, and without noticing the looks of curiosity, minced along, by the green folding chairs, by the pond, by the great rhododendron bushes, darkling under the shelter of elms and lindens, above a turf as bright and bland as billiard cloth. Riders sped past, lightly going up and down on their saddles, the yellow leather of their leggings creaking, the slender faces of their steeds springing up, their bits clinking; and expensive black motor cars, with a dazzling glitter of wheel spokes, progressed sedately over the ample lacework of violet shade.

The dwarf walked, inhaling the warm whiffs of benzine, the smell of foliage that seemed to rot with the over-abundance of green sap, and twirled his cane, and pursed his lips as if about to whistle, so great was the sense of liberation and lightness overwhelming him. His mistress had seen him off with such hurried tenderness, had laughed so nervously, that he realized how much she feared that her old father, who always came to lunch, would begin to suspect something if he found a strange gentleman in the house.

That day he was seen everywhere: in the park where a rosy nurse in a starched bonnet offered him for some reason a ride in the pram she was pushing; and in the halls of a great museum; and on the escalator that slowly crept out of rumbling depths where electric winds blew among brilliant posters; and in an elegant shop where only men's handkerchiefs were sold; and on the crest of a bus where he was hoisted by someone's kind hands.

And after a while he became tired – all that motion and glitter dazed him, the laughing eyes staring at him got on his nerves, and he felt he must ponder carefully the ample sensation of freedom, pride and happiness which kept accompanying him.

When finally a hungry Fred entered the familiar restaurant where all kinds of performers gathered and where his presence could not surprise anyone, and when he looked around at those people, at the old dull clown who was already drunk, at the Frenchman, a former enemy, who now gave him a friendly nod, Mr Dobson realized with perfect clarity that never again would he appear on the stage.

The place was darkish, with not enough lamps lit inside and not enough outside day filtering in. The dull clown resembling a ruined banker, and the acrobat who looked oddly uncouth in mufti, were playing a silent game of dominoes. The Spanish dancing girl, wearing a cartwheel hat that cast a blue shadow on her eyes, sat with crossed legs all alone at a corner table. There were half-a-dozen people whom Fred did not know; he examined their features which years of make-up had bleached; meanwhile the waiter brought a cushion to prop him up, changed the tablecloth, nimbly laid the cover.

All at once, in the dim depths of the restaurant, Fred distinguished the delicate profile of the conjuror, who was talking in undertone to an obese old man of an American type. Fred had not expected to run here into Shock – who never frequented taverns – and in point of fact had totally forgotten about his existence. He now felt so sorry for the poor magician that, at first, he decided to conceal everything; but then it occurred to him that Nora could not cheat anyway and would probably tell her husband that very evening ('I've fallen in love with Mr Dobson ... I'm leaving you') – and that she should be spared a difficult, disagreeable confession, for was he not her knight, did he not feel proud of her love, should he not, therefore, be justified in causing her husband pain, no matter the pity?

The waiter brought him a piece of kidney pie and a bottle of ginger beer. He also switched on more light. Here and there, above the dusty plush, crystal flowers glowed forth, and the dwarf saw from afar a golden gleam bring out the conjuror's chestnut forelock and the light and shade shuttle over his tender transparent fingers. His interlocutor rose, clawing at the belt of his pants and obsequiously grinning, and Shock accompanied him to the cloakroom. The fat American donned a wide-brimmed hat, shook Shock's ethereal hand, and, still hitching up his pants, made for the exit. Momentarily one discerned a chink of lingering daylight, while the restaurant lamps glowed yellower. The door closed with a thud.

'Shock!' called the Potato Elf, wiggling his short feet under the table.

Shock came over. On his way, he pensively took a lighted cigar out of his breast pocket, inhaled, let out a puff of smoke and put the cigar back. Nobody knew how he did it.

'Shock,' said the dwarf, whose nose had reddened from the ginger beer, 'I must speak to you. It is most important.'

The conjuror sat down at Fred's table and leaned his elbow upon it.

'How's your head – doesn't hurt?' he inquired indifferently.

Fred wiped his lips with the napkin; he did not know how to start, still fearing to cause his friend too much anguish.

'By the way,' said Shock, 'tonight I appear together with you for the last time. That chap is taking me to America. Things look pretty good.'

'I say, Shock –' and the dwarf, crumbling bread, groped for adequate words. 'The fact is ... Be brave, Shock. I love your wife. This morning, after you left, she and I, we two, I mean, she –'

'Only I'm a bad sailor,' mused the conjuror, 'and it's a week to Boston. I once sailed to India. Afterwards I felt as a leg does when it goes to sleep.'

Fred, flushing purple, rubbed the tablecloth with his tiny fist. The conjuror chuckled softly at his own thoughts, and then asked, 'You were about to tell me something, my little friend?'

The dwarf looked into his ghostly eyes and shook his head in confusion.

'No no, nothing ... One can't talk to you.'

Shock's hand stretched out – no doubt he intended to snip out a coin from Fred's ear – but for the first time in years of masterly magic, the coin, not grasped by the palm muscles firmly enough, fell out the wrong way. He caught it up and rose.

'I'm not going to eat here,' said he, examining curiously the crown of the dwarf's head. 'I don't care for this place.'

Sulky and silent, Fred was eating a baked apple.

The conjuror quietly left. The restaurant emptied. The languorous Spanish dancer in the large hat was led off by a shy, exquisitely dressed young man with blue eyes.

'Well, if he doesn't want to listen, that settles it,' reflected the dwarf; he sighed with relief and decided that after all Nora would explain things better. Then he asked for notepaper and proceeded to write her a letter. It closed as follows:

Now you understand why I cannot continue to live as before. What feelings would you experience knowing that every evening the common herd rocks with laughter at the sight of your chosen one? I am breaking my contract, and tomorrow I shall be leaving. You will receive another letter from me as soon as I find a peaceful nook where after your divorce we shall be able to love one another, my Nora.

Thus ended the swift day given to a dwarf in mouse-colored spats.

6

London was cautiously darkening. Street sounds blended in a soft hollow note, as if someone had stopped playing but still kept his foot on the piano pedal. The black leaves of the limes in the park were patterned against the transparent sky like aces of spades. At this or that turning, or between the funereal silhouettes of twin towers, a burning sunset was revealed like a vision.

It was Shock's custom to go home for dinner and change into professional tails so as to drive afterwards straight to the theater. That evening Nora awaited him most impatiently, quivering with evil glee. How glad she was to have now her own private secret! The image of the dwarf himself she dismissed. The dwarf was a nasty little worm.

She heard the lock of the entrance door emit its delicate click. As so often happens when one has betrayed a person, Shock's face struck her as new, as almost that of a stranger. He gave her a nod, and shamefully, sadly lowered his longlashed eyes. He took his place opposite her at the table without a word. Nora considered his light gray suit that made him seem still more slender, still more elusive. Her eyes lit up with warm triumph; one corner of her mouth twitched malevolently.

'How's your dwarf?' she inquired, relishing the casualness of her question. 'I thought you'd bring him along.'

'Haven't seen him today,' answered Shock, beginning to eat. All at once he thought better of it – took out a vial, uncorked it with a careful squeak and tipped it over a glassful of wine.

Nora expected with irritation that the wine would turn a bright blue, or become as translucent as water, but the claret did not change its hue. Shock caught his wife's glance and smiled dimly.

'For the digestion – just drops,' he murmured. A shadow rippled across his face.

'Lying as usual,' said Nora. 'You've got an excellent stomach.'

The conjuror laughed softly. Then he cleared his throat in a businesslike way, and drained his glass in one gulp.

'Get on with your food,' said Nora. 'It will be cold.'

With grim pleasure she thought, 'Ah, if you only knew. You'll never find out. That's my power!'

The conjuror ate in silence. Suddenly he made a grimace, pushed his plate away and started to speak. As usual, he kept looking not directly at her, but a little above her, and his voice was melodious and soft. He described his day, telling her he had visited the King at Windsor where he had been invited to amuse the little dukes who wore velvet jackets and lace collars. He related all this with light vivid touches, mimicking the people he had seen, twinkling, cocking his head slightly.

'I produced a whole flock of white doves from my gibus,' said Shock.

'And the dwarf's little palms were clammy, and you're making it all up,' reflected Nora in brackets.

'Those pigeons, you know, went flying around the Queen. She shoo-flied them but kept smiling out of politeness.'

Shock got up, swayed, lightly leaned on the table edge with two fingers and said, as if completing his story:

'I'm not feeling well, Nora. That was poison I drank. You shouldn't have been unfaithful to me.'

His throat swelled convulsively, and, pressing a handkerchief to his lips, he left the dining room. Nora sprang up; the amber beads of her long necklace caught at the fruit knife upon her plate and brushed it off.

'It's all an act,' she thought bitterly. 'Wants to scare me, to torment me. No, my good man, it's no use. You shall see!'

How vexing that Shock had somehow discovered her secret! But at least she would now have the opportunity to reveal all her feelings to him, to shout that she hated him, that she despised him furiously, that he was not a person, but a phantom of rubber, that she could not bear to live with him any longer, that –

The conjuror sat on the bed, all huddled up and gritting his teeth in anguish, but he managed a faint smile when Nora stormed into the bedroom.

'So you thought I'd believe you,' she said, gasping. 'Oh no, that's the end! I, too, know how to cheat. You repel me, oh, you're a laughingstock with your unsuccessful tricks –'

Shock, still smiling helplessly, attempted to get off the bed. His foot scraped against the carpet. Nora paused in an effort to think what else she could yell in the way of insult.

'Don't,' uttered Shock with difficulty. 'If there was something that I ... please, forgive ...'

The vein in his forehead was tensed. He hunched up still more, his throat rattled, the moist lock on his brow shook and the handkerchief at his mouth got all soaked with bile and blood.

'Stop playing the fool!' cried Nora and stamped her foot. He managed to straighten up. His face was wax pale. He threw the balled rag into a corner.

'Wait, Nora ... You don't understand ... This is my very last trick ... I won't do any other ...'

Again a spasm distorted his terrible, shiny face. He staggered, fell on the bed, threw back his head on the pillow.

She came near, she looked, knitting her brows. Shock lay with closed eyes and his clenched teeth creaked. When she bent over him, his eyelids quivered, he glanced at her vaguely, not recognizing his wife, but suddenly he did recognize her and his eyes flickered with a humid light of tenderness and pain.

At that instant Nora knew that she loved him more than anything in the world. Horror and pity overwhelmed her. She whirled about the room, poured out some water, left the glass on the washstand, dashed back to her husband, who had raised his head and was pressing the edge of the sheet to his lips, his whole body shuddering as he retched heavily, staring with unseeing eyes which Death had already veiled. Then Nora with a wild gesture dashed into the next room, where there was a telephone, and there, for a long time, she joggled the holder, repeated the wrong number, rang again, sobbing for breath and hammering the telephone table with her fist; and finally when the doctor's voice responded, Nora cried that her husband had poisoned himself, that he was dying; upon which she flooded the receiver with a storm of tears, and cradling it crookedly, ran back into the bedroom.

The conjuror, bright-faced and sleek, in white waistcoat and impeccably pressed black trousers, stood before the pier glass and, elbows parted, was meticulously working upon his tie. He saw Nora in the mirror, and without turning gave her an absentminded twinkle while whistling softly and continuing to knead with transparent fingertips the black ends of his silk bow.

7

Drowse, a tiny town in the north of England, looked, indeed, so somnolent that one suspected it might have been somehow mislaid among those misty, gentle-sloped fields where it had fallen asleep forever. It had a post office, a bicycle shop, two or three tobacconists with red and blue signs, an ancient gray church surrounded by tombstones over which stretched sleepily the shade of an enormous chestnut tree. The main street was lined with hedges, small gardens and brick cottages diagonally girt with ivy, One of these had been rented to a certain F. R. Dobson whom nobody knew except his housekeeper and the local doctor, and he was no gossiper. Mr Dobson, apparently, never went out. The housekeeper, a large stern woman, who had formerly been employed in an insane asylum, would answer the casual questions of neighbors by explaining that Mr Dobson was an aged paralytic, doomed to vegetate in curtained silence. No wonder the inhabitants forgot him the same year that he arrived in Drowse: he became an unnoticeable presence whom people took for granted as they did the unknown bishop whose stone effigy had been standing so long in its niche above the church portal. The mysterious old man was thought to have a grandchild – a quiet fair-haired little boy who sometimes, at dusk, used to come out of the Dobson cottage with small, timid steps. This happened, however, so seldom that nobody could say for sure that it was always the same child, and, of course, twilight at Drowse was particularly blurry and blue, softening every outline. Thus the uncurious and sluggish Drowsians missed the fact that the supposed grandson of the supposed paralytic did not grow as the years went by and that his flaxen hair was nothing but an admirably made wig; for the Potato Elf started to go bald at the very beginning of his new existence, and his head was soon so smooth and glossy that Ann, his housekeeper, thought at times what fun it would be to fit one's palm over that globe. Otherwise, he had not much changed: his tummy, perhaps, had grown plumper, and purple veins showed through on his dingier, fleshier nose which he powdered when dressed up as a little boy. Furthermore, Ann and his doctor knew that the heart attacks besetting the dwarf would come to no good.

He lived peacefully and inconspicuously in his three rooms, subscribed to a circulating library at the rate of three or four books (mostly novels) per week, acquired a black yellow-eyed cat because he mortally feared mice (which bumped about somewhere behind the wardrobe as if rolling minute balls of wood), ate a lot, especially sweetmeats (sometimes jumping up in the middle of the night and pattering along the chilly floor, eerily small and shivery in his long nightshirt, to get, like a little boy, at the chocolate-coated biscuits in the pantry), and recalled less and less frequently his love affair and the first dreadful days he had spent in Drowse.

Nevertheless, in his desk, among wispy, neatly folded playbills, he still preserved a sheet of peach-colored notepaper with a dragon-shaped watermark, scribbled over in an angular, barely legible hand. Here is what it said:

Dear Mr Dobson

I received your first letter, as well as your second one, in which you ask me to come to D. All this, I am afraid, is an awful misunderstanding. Please try to forget and forgive me. Tomorrow my husband and I are leaving for the States and shall probably not be back for quite some time. I simply do not know what more I can write you, my poor Fred.

It was then that the first attack of angina pectoris occurred. A meek look of astonishment remained since then in his eyes. And during a number of days afterwards he would walk from room to room, swallowing his tears and gesturing in front of his face with one trembling tiny hand.

Presently, though, Fred began to forget. He grew fond of the coziness he had never known before – of the blue film of flame over the coals in the fireplace, of the dusty small vases on their own rounded small shelves, of the print between two casements: a St Bernard dog, complete with barrelet, reviving a mountaineer on his bleak rock. Rarely did he recollect his past life. Only in dream did he sometimes see a starry sky come alive with the tremor of many trapezes while he was being clapped into a black trunk: through its walls he distinguished Shock's bland singsong voice but could not find the trap in the floor of the stage and suffocated in sticky darkness, while the conjuror's voice grew sadder and more remote and melted away, and Fred would wake up with a groan on his spacious bed, in his snug, dark room, with its faint fragrance of lavender, and would stare for a long time, gasping for breath and pressing his child's fist to his stumbling heart, at the pale blur of the window blind.

As the years passed, the yearning for a woman's love sighed in him fainter and fainter, as if Nora had drained him of all the ardor that had tormented him once. True, there were certain times, certain vague spring evenings, when the dwarf, having shyly put on short pants and the blond wig, left the house to plunge into crepuscular dimness, and there, stealing along some path in the fields, would suddenly stop as he looked with anguish at a dim pair of lovers locked in each other's arms near a hedge, under the protection of brambles in blossom. Presently that too passed, and he ceased seeing the world altogether. Only once in a while the doctor, a white-haired man with piercing black eyes, would come for a game of chess and, across the board, would consider with scientific delight those tiny soft hands, that little bulldoggish face, whose prominent brow would wrinkle as the dwarf pondered a move.

8

Eight years elapsed. It was Sunday morning. A jug of cocoa under a cozy in the guise of a parrot's head was awaiting Fred on the breakfast table. The sunny greenery of apple trees streamed through the window. Stout Ann was in the act of dusting the little pianola on which the dwarf occasionally played wobbly waltzes. Flies settled on the jar of orange marmalade and rubbed their front feet.

Fred came in, slightly sleep-rumpled, wearing carpet slippers and a little black dressing gown with yellow frogs. He sat down slitting his eyes and stroking his bald head. Ann left for church. Fred pulled open the illustrated section of a Sunday paper and, alternately drawing in and pouting his lips, examined at length prize pups, a Russian ballerina folding up in a swan's languishing agony, the top hat and mug of a financier who had bamboozled everyone ... Under the table the cat, curving her back, rubbed herself against his bare ankle. He finished his breakfast; rose, yawning: he had had a very bad night, never yet had his heart caused him such pain, and now he felt too lazy to dress, although his feet were freezing. He transferred himself to the window-nook armchair and curled up in it. He sat there without a thought in his head, and near him the black cat stretched, opening tiny pink jaws.

The doorbell tinkled.

'Doctor Knight,' reflected Fred indifferently, and remembering that Ann was out, went to open the door himself.

Sunlight poured in. A tall lady all in black stood on the

threshold. Fred recoiled, muttering and fumbling at his dressing gown. He dashed back into the inner rooms, losing one slipper on the way but ignoring it, his only concern being that whoever had come must not notice he was a dwarf. He stopped, panting, in the middle of the parlor. Oh, why hadn't he simply slammed shut the entrance door! And who on earth could be calling on him? A mistake, no doubt.

And then he heard distinctly the sound of approaching steps. He retreated to the bedroom; wanted to lock himself up, but there was no key. The second slipper remained on the rug in the parlor.

'This is dreadful,' said Fred under his breath and listened.

The steps had entered the parlor. The dwarf emitted a little moan and made for the wardrobe, looking for a hiding place.

A voice that he certainly knew pronounced his name, and the door of the room opened:

'Fred, why are you afraid of me?'

The dwarf, bare-footed, black-robed, his pate beaded with sweat, stood by the wardrobe, still holding on to the ring of its lock. He recalled with the utmost clarity the orange-gold fish in their glass bowl.

She had aged unhealthily. There were olive-brown shadows under her eyes. The little dark hairs above her upper lip had become more distinct than before; and from her black hat, from the severe folds of her black dress, there wafted something dusty and woeful.

'I never expected –' Fred slowly began, looking up at her warily.

Nora took him by the shoulders, turned him to the light, and with eager, sad eyes examined his features. The embarrassed dwarf blinked, deploring his wiglessness and marveling at Nora's excitement. He had ceased thinking of her so long ago that now he felt nothing except sadness and surprise. Nora, still holding him, shut her eyes, and then, lightly pushing the dwarf away, turned toward the window.

Fred cleared his throat and said:

'I lost sight of you entirely. Tell me, how's Shock?'

'Still performing his tricks,' replied Nora absently. 'We returned to England only a short while ago.'

Without removing her hat she sat down near the window and kept staring at him with odd intensity.

'It means that Shock –' hastily resumed the dwarf, feeling uneasy under her gaze.

'– Is the same as ever,' said Nora, and, still not taking her glistening eyes from the dwarf, quickly peeled off and crumpled her glossy black gloves which were white inside.

'Can it be that she again –?' abruptly wondered the dwarf. There rushed through his mind the fish bowl, the smell of eau de cologne, the green pompons on her slippers.

Nora got up. The black balls of her gloves rolled on the floor.

'It's not a big garden but it has apple trees,' said Fred, and continued to wonder inwardly: had there really been a moment when I –? Her skin is quite sallow. She has a mustache. And why is she so silent?

'I seldom go out, though,' said he, rocking slightly back and forth in his seat and massaging his knees.

'Fred, do you know why I'm here?' asked Nora.

She rose and came up to him quite close. Fred with an apologetic grin tried to escape by slipping off his chair.

It was then that she told him in a very soft voice:

'The fact is I had a son from you.'

The dwarf froze, his gaze fixing a minuscule casement burning on the side of a dark blue cup. A timid smile of amazement flashed at the corners of his lips, then it spread, and lit up his cheeks with a purplish flush.

'My ... son ...'

And all at once he understood everything, all the meaning of life, of his long anguish, of the little bright window upon the cup.

He slowly raised his eyes. Nora sat sideways on a chair and was shaking with violent sobs. The glass head of her hat-pin glittered like a teardrop. The cat, purring tenderly, rubbed itself against her legs.

He dashed up to her, he remembered a novel read a short while ago: 'You have no cause,' said Mr Dobson, 'no cause whatever for fearing that I may take him away from you. I am so happy!'

She glanced at him through a mist of tears. She was about to explain something, but gulped – saw the tender and joyful radiance with which the dwarf's countenance breathed – and explained nothing.

She hastened to pick up her crumpled gloves.

'Well, now you know. Nothing more is necessary. I must be going.'

A sudden thought stabbed Fred. Acute shame joined the quivering joy. He inquired, fingering the tassel of his dressing gown.

'And . . . and what is he like? He is not –'

'Oh, on the contrary,' replied Nora rapidly. 'A big boy, like all boys.' And again she burst into tears.

Fred lowered his eyes.

'I would like to see him.'

Joyously he corrected himself:

'Oh, I understand! He must not know that I am like this. But perhaps you might arrange –'

'Yes, by all means,' said Nora, hurriedly, and almost sharply, as she stepped through the hall. 'Yes, we'll arrange something. I must be on my way. It's a twenty-minute walk to the railway station.'

She turned her head in the doorway and for the last time, avidly and mournfully, she examined Fred's features. Sunlight trembled on his bald head, his ears were of a translucent pink. He understood nothing in his amazement and bliss. And after she had gone, Fred remained standing for a long time in the hallway, as if afraid to spill his full heart with an imprudent movement. He kept trying to imagine his son, and all he could do was to imagine his own self dressed as a schoolboy and wearing a little blond wig. And by the act of transferring his own aspect onto his boy, he ceased to feel that he was a dwarf.

He saw himself entering a house, a hotel, a restaurant, to meet his son. In fancy, he stroked the boy's fair hair with poignant parental pride . . . And then, with his son and Nora (silly goose – to fear he would snatch him away!), he saw himself walking down a street, and there –

Fred clapped his thighs. He had forgotten to ask Nora where and how he could reach her!

Here commenced a crazy, absurd sort of phase. He rushed to his bedroom, began to dress in a wild hurry. He put on the best things he had, an expensive starched shirt, practically new, striped trousers, a jacket made by Resartre of Paris years ago – and as he dressed, he kept chuckling, and breaking his finger-nails in the chinks of tight commode drawers, and had to sit down once or twice to let his swelling and knocking heart rest; and again he went skipping about the room looking for the bowler he had not worn for years, and at last, on consulting a mirror in passing, he glimpsed the image of a stately elderly gentleman, in smart formal dress, and ran down the steps of the porch, dazzled by a new idea: to travel back with Nora – whom he would certainly manage to overtake – and to see his son that very evening!

A broad dusty road led straight to the station. It was more or less deserted on Sundays – but unexpectedly a boy with a cricket bat appeared at a corner. He was the first to notice the dwarf. In gleeful surprise he slapped himself on the top of his bright-colored cap as he watched Fred's receding back and the flicking of his mouse-gray spats.

And instantly, from God knows where, more boys appeared, and with gaping stealthiness started to follow the dwarf. He walked faster and faster, now and then looking at his watch, and chuckling excitedly. The sun made him feel a little queasy. Meanwhile, the number of boys increased, and chance passers-by stopped to look in wonder. Somewhere afar church chimes rang forth: the drowsy town was coming to life – and all of a sudden it burst into uncontrollable, long-restrained laughter.

The Potato Elf, unable to master his eagerness, switched to a jog. One of the lads darted in front of him to have a look at his face; another yelled something in a rude hoarse voice. Fred, grimacing because of the dust, ran on, and abruptly it seemed to him that all those boys crowding in his wake were his sons, merry, rosy, well-built sons – and he smiled a bewildered smile as he trotted along, puffing and trying to forget the heart breaking his chest with a burning ram.

A cyclist, riding beside the dwarf on glittering wheels, pressed his fist to his mouth like a megaphone and urged the sprinter along as they do at a race. Women came out on their

222

porches and, shading their eyes and laughing loudly, pointed out the running dwarf to one another. All the dogs of the town woke up. The parishioners in the stuffy church could not help listening to the barking, to the inciting halloos. And the crowd that kept up with the dwarf continued to grow around him. People thought it was all a capital stunt, circus publicity or the shooting of a picture.

Fred was beginning to stumble, there was a singing in his ears, the front stud of his collar dug into his throat, he could not breathe. Moans of mirth, shouts, the tramping of feet deafened him. Then through the fog of sweat he saw at last her black dress. She was slowly walking along a brick wall in a torrent of sun. She looked back, she stopped. The dwarf reached her and clutched at the folds of her skirt.

With a smile of happiness he glanced up at her, attempted to speak, but instead raised his eyebrows in surprise and collapsed in slow motion on the sidewalk. All around people noisily swarmed. Someone, realizing that this was no joke, bent over the dwarf, then whistled softly and bared his head. Nora looked listlessly at Fred's tiny body resembling a crumpled black glove. She was jostled. A hand grasped her elbow.

'Leave me alone,' said Nora in a toneless voice. 'I don't know anything. My son died a few days ago.'

The Circle

By the middle of 1936, not long before leaving Berlin forever and finishing *Dar* (*The Gift*) in France, I must have completed at least four-fifths of its last chapter when at some point a small satellite separated itself from the main body of the novel and started to revolve around it. Psychologically, the separation may have been sparked either by the mention of Tanya's baby in her brother's letter or by his recalling the village schoolmaster in a doomful dream. Technically, the circle which the present corollary describes (its last sentence existing implicitly before its first one) belongs to the same serpent-biting-its-tail type as the circular structure of the fourth chapter in *Dar* (or, for that matter, *Finnegans Wake*, which it preceded). A knowledge of the novel is not required for the enjoyment of the corollary which has its own orbit and colored fire, but some practical help may be derived from the reader's knowing that the action of *The Gift* starts on 1 April 1926, and ends on 29 June 1929 (spanning three years in the life of Fyodor Godunov-Cherdyntsev, a young émigré in Berlin); that his sister's marriage takes place in Paris at the end of 1926; and that her daughter is born three years later, and is only seven in June 1936, and not 'around ten', as Innokentiy, the schoolmaster's son, is permitted to assume (behind the author's back) when he visits Paris in 'The Circle'. It may be added that the story will produce upon readers who are familiar with the novel a delightful effect of oblique recognition, of shifting shades enriched with new sense, owing to the world's being seen not through the eyes of Fyodor, but through those of an outsider less close to him than to old Russia's idealistic radicals (who, let it be said in passing, were to loathe Bolshevist tyranny as much as liberal aristocrats did).

'Krug' was published in 1936, in Paris, but the exact date and periodical (presumably, *Posledniya Novosti*) has not yet been established in bibliographic retrospect. It was reprinted twenty years later in the collection of my short stories *Vesna v Fialte*, Chekhov Publishing House, New York, 1956.

In the second place, because he was possessed by a sudden mad hankering after Russia. In the third place, finally, because he regretted those years of youth and everything associated with it – the fierce resentment, the uncouthness, the ardency and the dazzlingly green mornings when the coppice deafened you with its golden orioles. As he sat in the café and kept diluting with syphoned soda the paling sweetness of his cassis, he recalled the past with a constriction of the heart, with melancholy – what kind of melancholy? – well, a kind not yet sufficiently investigated. All that distant past rose with his breast, raised by a sigh, and slowly his father ascended from the grave, squaring his shoulders: Ilya Ilyich Bychkov, *le maître d'école chez nous au village*, in flowing black tie, picturesquely knotted, and pongee jacket, whose buttons began, in the old fashion, high on the breastbone but stopped also at a high point, letting the diverging coat flaps reveal the watch-chain across the waistcoat; his complexion was reddish, his head bald yet covered with a tender down resembling the velvet of a deer's vernal antlers; there were lots of little folds along his cheeks, and a fleshy wart next to the nose producing the effect of an additional volute described by the fat nostril. In his high-school and college days, Innokentiy used to travel from town on holidays to visit his father at Leshino. Diving still deeper, he could remember the demolition of the old school at the end of the village, the clearing of the ground for its successor, the foundation-stone ceremony, the religious service in the wind, Count Konstantin Godunov-Cherdyntsev throwing the traditional gold coin, the coin sticking edgewise in the clay. The new building was of a grainy granitic gray on its outside; its inside, for several years and then for another long spell (that is, when it joined the staff of memory) sunnily smelled of glue;

227

the classes were graced with glossy educational appliances such as enlarged portraits of insects injurious to field or forest; but Innokentiy found even more irritating the stuffed birds provided by Godunov-Cherdyntsev. Flirting with the common people! Yes, he saw himself as a stern plebeian: hatred (or so it seemed) suffocated him when as a youth he used to look across the river at the great manorial park, heavy with ancient privileges and imperial grants, casting the reflection of its black amassments onto the green water (with the creamy blur of a racemosa blooming here and there among the fir trees).

The new school was built on the threshold of this century, at a time when Godunov-Cherdyntsev had returned from his fifth expedition to central Asia and was spending the summer at Leshino, his estate in the Government of St Petersburg, with his young wife (at forty he was twice as old as she). To what a depth one has plunged, good God! In a melting crystalline mist, as if it were all taking place under water, Innokentiy saw himself as a boy of three or four entering the manor house and floating through marvelous rooms, with his father moving on tiptoe, a damp nosegay of lilies of the valley bunched in his fist so tight that they squeaked – and everything around seemed moist too, a luminous, squeaking, quivering haze, which was all one could distinguish – but in later years it turned into a shameful recollection, his father's flowers, tiptoeing progress and sweating temples darkly symbolizing grateful servility, especially after Innokentiy was told by an old peasant that Ilya Ilyich had been disentangled by 'our good master' from a trivial but tacky political affair, for which he would have been banished to the backwoods of the empire had the Count not interceded.

Tanya used to say that they had relatives not only in the animal kingdom but also among plants and minerals. And, indeed, Russian and foreign naturalists had described under the specific name of 'godunovi' a new pheasant, a new antelope, a new rhododendron, and there was even a whole Godunov Range (he himself described only insects). Those discoveries of his, his outstanding contributions to zoology, and a thousand perils, for disregarding which he was famous, could not, however, make people indulgent to his high descent and great wealth. Furthermore, let us not forget that certain sections of our intelligentsia had always held non-applied scientific research in contempt, and therefore Godunov was rebuked for showing more interest in 'Sinkiang bugs' than in the plight of the Russian peasant. Young Innokentiy readily believed the tales (actually idiotic) told about the Count's traveling concubines, his Chinese-style inhumanity and the secret errands he discharged for the Tsar – to spite the English. The reality of his image remained dim: an ungloved hand throwing a gold piece (and, in the still earlier recollection, that visit to the manor house, the lord of which got confused by the child with a Kalmuck, dressed in sky blue, met on the way through a reception hall). Then Godunov departed again, to Samarkand or to Vernyi (towns from which he usually started his fabulous strolls), and was gone a long time. Meanwhile his family summered in the south, apparently preferring their Crimean country place to their Petropolitan one. Their winters were spent in the capital. There, on the Quay, stood their house, a two-floor private residence, painted an olive hue. Innokentiy sometimes happened to walk by; his memory retained the feminine forms of a statue showing its dimpled sugar-white buttock through the patterned gauze on a whole-glassed window. Olive-brown atlantes with strangely arched ribs supported a balcony: the strain of their stone muscles and their agonizingly twisted mouths struck our hot-headed uppergrader as an allegory of the enslaved proletariat. Once or twice, on that Quay, in the beginning of the gusty Neva spring, he glimpsed the little Godunov girl with her fox terrier and governess; they positively whirled by, yet were so vividly outlined: Tanya wore boots laced up to the knee and a short navy blue coat with knobbed brass buttons, and as she marched rapidly past, she slapped the pleats of her short navy blue skirt – with what? I think with the dog leash she carried – and the Ladoga wind tossed the ribbons of her sailor cap, and a little behind her sped her governess, karakul-jacketed, her waist flexed, one arm thrown out, the hand encased in a muff of tight-curled black fur.

He lodged at his aunt's, a seamstress, in an Okhta tenement. He was morose, unsociable, applied ponderous groaning efforts to his studies while limiting his ambition to a passing mark, but to everybody's astonishment finished school brilliantly and at the age of eighteen entered St Petersburg University as a medical student – at which point his father's worship of Godunov-Cherdyntsev mysteriously increased. He spent one summer as a private tutor with a family in Tver. By May of the following year, 1914, he was back in the village of Leshino – and discovered not without dismay that the manor across the river had come alive.

More about that river, about its steep bank, about its old bath house. This was a wooden structure standing on piles; a stepped path, with a toad on every other step, led down to it, and not everyone could have found the beginning of that clayey descent in the alder thicket at the back of the church. His constant companion in riparian pastimes was Vasiliy, the blacksmith's son, a youth of indeterminable age (he could not say himself whether he was fifteen or a full twenty), sturdily built, ungainly, in skimpy patched trousers, with huge bare feet dirty carrot in color, and as gloomy in temper as was Innokentiy at the time. The pinewood piles cast concertina-shaped reflections that wound and unwound on the water. Gurgling and smacking sounds came from under the rotten planks of the bath house. In a round, earth-soiled tin box depicting a horn of plenty – it had once contained cheap fruit drops – worms wriggled listlessly. Vasiliy, taking care that the point of the hook would not stick through, pulled a plump segment of worm over it, leaving the rest to hang free; then seasoned the rascal with sacramental spittle and proceeded to lower the lead-weighted line over the outer railing of the bath house. Evening had come. Something resembling a broad fan of violet-pink plumes or an aerial mountain range with lateral spurs spanned the sky, and the bats were already flitting, with the overstressed soundlessness and evil speed of membraned beings. The fish had begun to bite, and scorning the use of a rod, simply holding the tensing and jerking line between finger and thumb, Vasiliy tugged at it ever so slightly to test the solidity of the underwater spasms – and suddenly landed a roach or a gudgeon. Casually, and even with a kind of devil-may-care crackling snap, he would wrench the hook out of the toothless round little mouth and place the frenzied creature (rosy blood oozing from a torn gill) in a glass jar where already a chevin was swimming, its lower lip stuck out. Angling was especially good in warm overcast weather when rain, invisible in the air, covered the water with mutually intersecting widening circles, among which appeared here and there a circle of different origin, with a sudden center: the jump of a fish that vanished at once or the fall of a leaf that immediately sailed away with the current. And how delicious it was to go bathing beneath that tepid drizzle, on the blending line of two homogeneous but differently shaped elements – the thick river water and the slender celestial one! Innokentiy took his dip intelligently and indulged afterwards in a long rub-down with a towel. The peasant boys, per contra, kept floundering till complete exhaustion; finally, shivering, with chattering teeth and a turbid snot trail from nostril to lip, they would hop on one foot to pull their pants up to their wet thighs.

That summer Innokentiy was gloomier than ever and scarcely spoke to his father, limiting himself to mumbles and 'h'ms'. Ilya Ilyich, on his part, experienced an odd embarrassment in his son's presence – mainly because he assumed, with terror and tenderness, that Innokentiy lived wholeheartedly in the pure world of the underground as he had himself at that age. Schoolmaster Bychkov's room: motes of dust in a slanting sunbeam; lit by that beam, a small table he had made with his own hands, varnishing the top and adorning it with a pyrographic design; on the table, a photograph of his wife in a velvet frame – so young, in such a nice dress, with a little pelerine and a corset-belt, charmingly oval-faced (that ovality coincided with the idea of feminine beauty in the eighteen-nineties); next to the photograph a crystal paperweight with a mother-of-pearl Crimean view inside, and a cockerel of cloth for wiping pens; and on the wall above, between two casement windows, a portrait of Leo Tolstoy, entirely composed of the text of one of his stories printed in microscopic type. Innokentiy slept on a leathern couch in an adjacent smaller chamber. After a long day in the open air he slept soundly; sometimes, however, a dream image would take an erotic turn, the force of its thrill would carry him out of the sleep circle, and for several moments he would remain lying as he was, squeamishness preventing him from moving.

In the morning he would go to the woods, a medical manual under his arm and both hands thrust under the tasseled cord girting his white Russian blouse. His university cap, worn askew in conformance to left-wing custom, allowed locks of brown hair to fall on his bumpy forehead. His eyebrows were knitted in a permanent frown. He might have been quite good-looking had his lips been less blubbery. Once in the forest, he seated himself on a thick birch bole which had been felled not long before by a thunderstorm (and still quivered with all its leaves from the shock), and smoked, and obstructed with his book the trickle of hurrying ants or lost himself in dark meditation. A lonely, impressionable, and touchy youth, he felt over-keenly the social side of things. He loathed the entire surroundings of the Godunovs' country life, such as their menials – 'menials', he repeated, wrinkling his nose in voluptuous disgust. In their number he included the plump chauffeur, with his freckles, corduroy livery, orange-brown leggings and starched collar propping a fold of his russet neck that used to flush purple when, in the carriage shed, he cranked up the no less revolting convertible upholstered in glossy red leather; and the senile flunkey with gray side whiskers who was employed to bite off the tails of new-born fox terriers; and the English tutor who could be seen striding across the village, hatless, raincoated, white-trouser – which had the village boys allude wittily to underpants and bare-headed religious processions; and the peasant girls, hired to weed the avenues of the park morning after morning under the supervision of one of the gardeners, a deaf little hunchback in a pink shirt, who in conclusion would sweep the sand near the porch with particular zest and ancient devotion. Innokentiy with the book still under his arm – which hindered his crossing his arms, something he would have liked to do – stood leaning against a tree in the park and considered sullenly various items, such as the shiny roof of the white manor which was not yet astir.

The first time he saw them that summer was in late May (Old Style) from the top of a hill. A cavalcade appeared on the road curving around its base: Tanya in front, astraddle, boy-like, on a bright bay; next Count Godunov-Cherdyntsev himself, an insignificant-looking person riding an oddly small mouse-gray pacer; behind them the breeched Englishman; then some cousin or other; and coming last, Tanya's brother, a boy of thirteen or so, who suddenly spurred his mount, overtook everybody, and dashed up the steep bit to the village, working his elbows jockey-fashion.

After that there followed several other chance encounters and finally – all right, here we go. Ready? On a hot day in mid-June –

On a hot day in mid-June the mowers went swinging along on both sides of the path leading to the manor, and each mower's shirt stuck in alternate rhythm now to the right shoulderblade, now to the left. 'May God assist you!' said Ilya Ilyich in a passerby's traditional salute to men at work. He wore his best hat, a panama, and carried a bouquet of mauve bog orchids. Innokentiy walked alongside in silence, his mouth in circular motion (he was cracking sunflower seeds between his teeth and munching at the same time). They were nearing the manor park. At one end of the tennis court the deaf pink dwarf gardener, now wearing a workman's apron, soaked a brush in a pail and, bent in two, walked backward as he traced a thick creamy line on the ground. 'May God assist you,' said Ilya Ilyich in passing.

The table was laid in the main avenue; Russian dappled sunlight played on the tablecloth. The housekeeper, wearing a gorget, her steely hair smoothly combed back, was already in the act of ladling out chocolate which the footmen were serving in dark-blue cups. At close range the Count looked his age: there were ashy streaks in his yellowish beard, and wrinkles fanned out from eye to temple; he had placed his foot on the edge of a garden bench and was making a fox terrier jump: the dog jumped not only very high, trying to hap the already wet ball he was holding, but actually contrived, while hanging in mid-air, to jerk itself still higher by an additional twist of its entire body. Countess Elizaveta Godunov, a tall rosy woman in a big wavery hat, was coming up from the garden with another lady to whom she was vivaciously talking, and making the Russian two-hand splash gesture of uncertain dismay. Ilya

Ilyich stood with his bouquet and bowed. In this varicolored haze (as perceived by Innokentiy, who despite having briefly rehearsed on the eve an attitude of democratic scorn was overcome by the greatest embarrassment) there flickered young people, running children, somebody's black shawl embroidered with gaudy poppies, a second fox terrier, and above all, above all, those eyes gliding through shine and shade, those features still indistinct but already threatening him with fatal fascination, the face of Tanya whose birthday was being fêted.

Everybody was now seated. He found himself at the shade end of the long table, at which end convives did not indulge so much in mutual conversation as keep looking, all their heads turned in the same direction, at the brighter end where there was loud talk, and laughter, and a magnificent pink cake with a satiny glaze and sixteen candles, and the exclamations of children, and the barking of both dogs that had all but jumped onto the table – while here at this end the garlands of linden shade linked up people of the meanest rank: Ilya Ilyich, smiling in a sort of daze; an ethereal but ugly damsel whose shyness expressed itself in onion sweat; a decrepit French governess with nasty eyes who held in her lap under the table a tiny invisible creature that now and then emitted a tinkle; and so forth. Innokentiy's direct neighbor happened to be the estate steward's brother, a blockhead, a bore and a stutterer; Innokentiy talked to him only because silence would have been worse, so that despite the paralyzing nature of the conversation, he desperately tried to keep it up; later, however, when he became a frequent visitor, and chanced to run into the poor fellow, Innokentiy never spoke to him, shunning him as a kind of snare or shameful memory.

Rotating in slow descent, the winged fruit of a linden lit on the table cloth.

At the nobility's end Godunov-Cherdyntsev raised his voice, speaking across the table to a very old lady in a lacy gown, and as he spoke encircled with one arm the graceful waist of his daughter who stood near and kept tossing up a rubber ball on her palm. For quite a time Innokentiy tussled with a luscious morsel of cake that had come to rest beyond the edge of his plate. Finally, following an awkward poke, the damned raspberry stuff rolled and tumbled under the table (where we shall leave it). His father either smiled vacantly or licked his mustache. Somebody asked him to pass the biscuits; he burst into happy laughter and passed them. All at once, right above Innokentiy's ear, there came a rapid gasping voice: unsmilingly, and still holding that ball, Tanya was asking him to join her and her cousins; all hot and confused, he struggled to rise from table, pushing against his neighbor in the process of disengaging his right leg from under the shared garden bench.

When speaking of her, people exclaimed, 'What a pretty girl!' She had light-gray eyes, velvet-black eyebrows, a largish, pale, tender mouth, sharp incisors, and – when she was unwell or out of humor – one could distinguish the dark little hairs above her lip. She was inordinately fond of all summer games, tennis, badminton, croquet, doing everything deftly, with a kind of charming concentration – and, of course, that was the end of the artless afternoons of fishing with Vasiliy, who was greatly perplexed by the change and would pop up in the vicinity of the school towards evening, beckoning Innokentiy with a hesitating grin and holding up at face level a canful of worms. At such moments Innokentiy shuddered inwardly as he sensed his betrayal of the people's cause. Meanwhile he derived not much joy from the company of his new friends. It so happened that he was not really admitted to the center of their existence, being kept on its green periphery, taking part in open-air amusements, but never being invited into the house. This infuriated him; he longed to be asked for lunch or dinner just to have the pleasure of haughtily refusing; and, in general, he remained constantly on the alert, sullen, sun-tanned and shaggy, the muscles of his clenched jaws twitching – and feeling that every word Tanya said to her playmates cast an insulting little shadow in his direction, and, good God, how he hated them all, her boy cousins, her girl friends, the frolicsome dogs. Abruptly, everything dimmed in noiseless disorder and vanished, and there he was, in the deep blackness of an August night, sitting on a bench at the bottom of the park and waiting, his breast prickly because of his having stuffed between shirt and skin the note which, as in an old novel, a barefooted little girl had brought him from the manor. The laconic style of the assignation led him to suspect a humiliating practical joke, yet he succumbed to the summons – and rightly so: a light crunch of footfalls detached itself from the even rustle of the night. Her arrival, her incoherent speech, her nearness struck him as miraculous; the sudden intimate touch of her cold nimble fingers amazed his chastity. A huge, rapidly ascending moon burned through the trees. Shedding torrents of tears and blindly nuzzling him with salt-tasting lips, Tanya told him that on the following day her mother was taking her to the Crimea, that everything was finished, and – oh, how could he have been so obtuse! 'Don't go anywhere, Tanya!' he pleaded, but a gust of wind drowned his words, and she sobbed even more violently. When she had hurried away he remained on the bench without moving, listening to the hum in his ears, and presently walked back in the direction of the bridge along the country road that seemed to stir in the dark, and then came the war years – ambulance work, his father's death – and after that, a general disintegration of things, but gradually life picked up again, and by 1920 he was already the assistant of Professor Behr at a spa in Bohemia, and three or four years later worked, under the same lung specialist, in Savoy, where one day, somewhere near Chamonix, Innokentiy happened to meet a young Soviet geologist; they got into conversation, and the latter mentioned that it was here, half a century ago, that Fedchenko, the great explorer of Fergana, had died the death of an ordinary tourist; how strange (the geologist added) that it should always turn out that way: death gets so used to pursuing fearless men in wild mountains and deserts that it also keeps coming at them in jest, without any special intent to harm, in all other circumstances, and to its own surprise catches them napping. Thus perished Fedchenko, and Severtsev and Godunov-Cherdyntsev, as well as many foreigners of classic fame – Speke, Dumont d'Urville. And after several years more spent in medical research, far from the cares and concerns of political expatriation, Innokentiy happened to be in Paris for a few hours for a business interview with a colleague, and was already running downstairs, gloving one hand, when, on one of the landings, a tall stoop-shouldered lady emerged from the lift – and he at once recognized Countess

Elizaveta Godunov-Cherdyntsev; 'Of course I remember you, how could I not remember?' she said, gazing not at his face but over his shoulder as if somebody were standing behind him (she had a slight squint). 'Well, come in, my dear,' she continued, recovering from a momentary trance, and with the point of her shoe turned back a corner of the thick door mat, replete with dust, to get the key. Innokentiy entered after her, tormented by the fact that he could not recall what he had been told exactly about the how and the when of her husband's death.

And a few moments later Tanya came home, all her features fixed more clearly now by the etching needle of years, with a smaller face and kinder eyes; she immediately lit a cigarette, laughing, and without the least embarrassment recalling that distant summer, while he kept marveling that neither Tanya nor her mother mentioned the dead explorer and spoke so simply about the past, instead of bursting into the awful sobs that he, a stranger, kept fighting back – or were those two displaying, perhaps, the selfcontrol peculiar to their class? They were soon joined by a pale dark-haired little girl about ten years of age: 'This is my daughter, come here, darling,' said Tanya, putting her cigarette butt, now stained with lipstick, into a sea shell that served as an ashtray. Then her husband, Ivan Ivanovich Kutaysov, came home, and the Countess, meeting him in the next room, was heard to identify their visitor, in her domestic French brought over from Russia, as *'le fils du maître d'école chez nous au village'*, which reminded Innokentiy of Tanya saying once in his presence to a girl friend of hers whom she wanted to notice his very shapely hands: *'Regarde ses mains'*; and now, listening to the melodious, beautifully idiomatic Russian in which the child replied to Tanya's questions, he caught himself thinking, malevolently and quite absurdly, 'Aha, there is no longer the money to teach kids foreign languages!' – for it did not occur to him at that moment that in those émigré times, in the case of a Paris-born child going to a French school, this Russian language represented *the* idlest and best luxury.

The Leshino topic was falling apart; Tanya, getting it all wrong, insisted that he used to teach her the pre-Revolution songs of radical students, such as the one about 'The despot who feasts in his rich palace hall while destiny's hand has already begun to trace the dread words on the wall.' 'In other words, our first *stengazeta* (Soviet wall gazette),' remarked Kutaysov, a great wit. Tanya's brother was mentioned: he lived in Berlin, and the Countess started to talk about him. Suddenly Innokentiy grasped a wonderful fact: nothing is lost, nothing whatever; memory accumulates treasures, stored-up secrets grow in darkness and dust, and one day a transient visitor at a lending library wants a book that has not once been asked for in twenty-two years. He got up from his seat, made his adieus, was not detained over-effusively. How strange that his knees should be trembling. That was really a shattering experience. He crossed the square, entered a café, ordered a drink, briefly rose to remove his own squashed hat from under him. What a dreadful feeling of uneasiness. He felt that way for several reasons. In the first place, because Tanya had remained as enchanting and as invulnerable as she had been in the past.

More about Penguins
and Pelicans

Penguinews, which appears every month, contains details of all the new books issued by Penguins as they are published. From time to time it is supplemented by *Penguins in Print*, which is a complete list of all titles available. (There are some five thousand of these.)

A specimen copy of *Penguinews* will be sent to you free on request. For a year's issues (including the complete lists) please send 50p if you live in the British Isles, or 75p if you live elsewhere. Just write to Dept EP, Penguin Books Ltd, Harmondsworth, Middlesex, enclosing a cheque or postal order, and and your name will be added to the mailing list.

In the U.S.A.: For a complete list of books available from Penguin in the United States write to Dept CS, Penguin Books Inc., 7110 Ambassador Road, Baltimore, Maryland 21207.

In Canada: For a complete list of books available from Penguin in Canada write to Penguin Books Canada Ltd, 41 Steelcase Road West, Markham, Ontario